Dear Dr. Siegel

It with great pleasure that I send you this book.

Eugen Schwarzpd

D1507702

# My Reconstructed Life

# My Reconstructed Life

## Eugen Schoenfeld

Kennesaw State UNIVERSITY
Kennesaw State University Press

Kennesaw State University Press
Kennesaw State University
Bldg.27, Ste. 220 MB# 2701
1000 Chastain Road
Kennesaw, GA 30144

Betty L. Siegel, President of the University
Lendley Black, Vice President for Academic Affairs
Laura Dabundo, Director of the Press
Shirley Parker-Cordell, Administrative Assistant
Michelle Hinson, Manuscript Editor
Margo Lakin-Lepage, Editorial Assistant
Carole Maugé-Lewis, Designer

The photographs are from the author's personal collection.

Library of Congress Cataloging-in-Publication Data

Schoenfeld, Eugen, 1925-
 My reconstructed life / Eugen Schoenfeld.
    p. cm.
 ISBN-13: 978-1-933483-00-9
1. Schoenfeld, Eugen, 1925- 2. Jews--Ukraine--Mukacheve--
Biography. 3. Mukacheve (Ukraine)--Biography. 4. Holocaust
survivors--Georgia--Biography. 5. Jewish sociologists--
Georgia--Biography. I. Title.
  DS135.U43.S357 2005
  940.53'18'092--dc22

                                             2005018067

Printed in the United States of America

10 9 8 7 6 5 4 3 2 1

# CONTENTS

vi

# FOREWORD

There was a time when historians deprecated the value of memoirs. Only written documents, they argued, could be relied upon for serious research purposes. Only documents, they contended, told the true story. Today we know that this is not the case. Memoirs expose the reader to a textured, nuanced, and personal history of an event or era. While memory can be capricious and two individuals can remember the same moment differently, historians have learned to use memoirs to gain a better understanding of what a particular moment was like. This is all the more true in the case of persecution. Generally, the victims do not have the opportunity to amass a cache of official documents which provide the details of their experience. In this situation, of course, the documents we do have are a reflection of events through the prism of the persecutor. This obviously skews our knowledge and perspectives of the situation.

This is particularly the case in relation to the Holocaust. Memoirs, diaries, and letters written by Jews both during and after the Holocaust expose us to an aspect of this history which documents cannot. As Elie Wiesel has observed, "What survivors can say, nobody else can . . . They have a knowledge of what happened, of who died and of who bears responsibility." We cannot write a history based on memoirs alone, but now we know that we cannot write a history without them.

In My Reconstructed Life, Eugen Schoenfeld tells the improbable story of his life. He was born in a small shtetl in the Carpathian Mountains and ended up a professor of Sociology at Georgia State University. The fact that a small boy from this background would become a professor is noteworthy in and of itself. What makes it remarkable, however, is that between one axis of his life – his youth in a small Jewish community in Hungary's mountain – and the other – his distinguished career at a state university – he endured and survived the Holocaust. Though each life is uniquely valuable, the course of Schoenfeld's life reminds us of the tremendous intellectual and professional losses perpetrated by the Holocaust.

Professor Schoenfeld has wisely chosen to include more than just the details of those terribly traumatic years. He places his experience during the Holocaust within the context of his life before and after. He explains that he felt compelled to write this book because he wanted to "seek those inner forces" which helped him reestablish his life "after the devastation." This part of the story, though far more ordinary, is as compelling as what happened to him during the Holocaust. No matter how many survivors I meet, I continue to be amazed at their resiliency and ability, not only to reconstruct their lives, but to add new and compelling chapters to it.

Professor Schoenfeld stresses, as do virtually all other survivors, that survival was "a matter of luck." Many victims who had a compelling desire to survive did not. But what happened to the survivors afterwards was not simply a matter of luck. In order for them to reconstruct their lives, they had to draw upon wellsprings of inner strength and healing. In this memoir, Professor Schoenfeld shares with readers not only his descent into the abyss but his ability to rise up from it and build a new and vibrant life.

Over the many years that I have taught courses about the Holocaust, I have learned that the most compelling moment comes when survivors speak in the first person singular, when they say: "This is my story. This is what happened to me." Soon those voices will be gone. The tyranny of the clock mandates that it will be so. That is why it is so important that Professor Schoenfeld and increasing numbers of other survivors give us the gift of their personal recollections.

We are grateful for these memoirs and their portrayal of life before, during, and after the Holocaust.

Deborah E. Lipstadt, Ph.D.
Professor, Modern Jewish and Holocaust Studies
Emory University
Atlanta, GA.

# PREFACE

Akavya, the son of M'halel, suggests that if one contemplates the following three factors one will not sin: Know from where you come, to where you are going, and before whom you are destined to give an accounting. I would like to paraphrase Akavya's statement to read: Contemplate where you came from and where you are going, and then you will understand yourself. I have attempted indeed to contemplate on my past and how my experiences have influenced my decisions in regards to my future. I began this task many years ago because I wished to tell my children and future generations something about myself so that it may help them understand their own existence that I hope will be rooted in our common heritage.

I have often asked students who were enrolled in my class on the sociology of ethnicity to tell me of their ethnic and cultural background. Very few knew from where their parents and grandparents came. So many of them, the students informed me, wished to have known something about their parents' and great grandparents' origins. They felt that there was something essential missing that kept them from truly rooting themselves in a past. They felt that both their ontological and existential selves would have been more complete should they have been knowledgeable about their roots. I hope that this book will provide my family of the present and future with this knowledge.

However, there is an even greater and universally more profound reason for this book. I am a person who not only experienced the devastation of the Holocaust but who also, like other survivors of this tragedy, had to rebuild my life. I hope to share some of my insights on how I did resurrect myself as a person both physically and emotionally from the cataclysm.

My life's journey began in the culture of a shtetl; then I went through the darkness of a conflagration and became a social scientist in academia. My life and experience hence existed in two worlds: the religious world of a distant past and the secular world of the present. Shtetl life, even though it physically existed in the twentieth century, philosophically and theologically was closer to the medieval world than to modernity. I am still rooted simultaneously in these two worlds. In this sense this book depicts the dialectic nature of my struggles to find a path between two disparate worlds.

I want to express my thanks to those who made the task of writing this book easier. I am indebted to Mel Hecker for his encouragement and to Laura Dabundo for her editorial help and encouragement. I dedicate this book to my wife Jean for fifty-five years of happiness, to my children, grandchildren, and great grandson who represent my triumph over Hitler, and to the memory of those whose lives were taken in the Holocaust, my mother Yocheved, my brother Benjamin, and my sister Esther.

1st Adar (one) 5765
February 10, 2005

My parents, Yolanda and Henryk Schonfeld, 1924

(From left to right) My mother Yolanda
(in Hebrew Yocheved), my younger brother
Benjamin, me, and my father Henryk, 1931.

My brother Benjamin, sister Esther,
and me. Picture taken in front
of my grandparents home, 1938.

My fraternal grandmother, an infant
cousin, and my cousin Flora, visiting
from the U.S., 1938.

A river view of my hometown, Munkacs

Horthy Square near the City Hall.
Both main synagogues were on this street.

Rakoczi street. The first Schonfeld store, unrelated to us,
was a bicycle store. Next to it, beyond the archway,
was my father's book and stationery store.

The Court House.

The fort in Munkacs. Its original sections are approximately 700 years old. The hill was used to grow grapes.

Two students in a religious school
(Yeshivoh Bachurim) studying the Talmud.

A bench in the synagogue courtyard where three young
students are memorizing passages from the Talmud.

Jewish villagers at rest and at work.

Kossuth street. In the distance is the Lutheran Church.
The majority of people in the Munkacs were Jews, followed by
Russian Orthodox, Catholic, and Lutheran.

The Catholic Church.

Russian Orthodox Church. The church, about four hundred
years old, was totally constructed of wood shingles.

The Russian Orthodox monastery on the banks of the Latorca
River. Each summer, processions of faithful from various
villages would make their pilgrimage to this monastery.

Bridge over the Latorca River.

Ruthenians in their traditional costumes.
In the distance are the Carpathian Mountains.

Ruthenian women in their traditional costumes. These blouses and scarves were worn on Sundays and holidays.

The Carpathian Mountains, just outside of Munkacs.

The Carpathian Mountains. Home of my maternal grandparents where I spent many summers during my youth.

Me, after arriving in the United States, 1948.

# PROLOGUE

As usual, while my wife was shopping in one of the stores in one of America's modern marketplaces called shopping malls, I was perusing the stalls of the bookstore. Among the newly arrived photography books, I discovered Roman Vishniac's *A Vanished World*. Randomly I opened the book and one glimpse of the page brought tears to my eyes. I became agitated as one usually does when confronting a long-lost memory. For on that page was the picture of my *Cheder*, the series of one room schools that resembled miniature townhouses. In my mind's eye, I was immediately transported back, as though I was in a time machine, to early 1930 when I was brought to this place at the age of five and turned over to the rabbi, the teacher who ruled his domain with a Bismarkian iron fist. His task was twofold: He was charged with indoctrinating me with the discipline of study and instruction in the holy language, Biblical Hebrew, so that I could fulfill the obligation of Jewish males to read the prayers and study the Torah. The rabbi's second task was to teach us the difficult path of being an observant Jew. We had to learn the ritual laws that guided a person's existence from the time one rose in the morning till one went to sleep. Later in our pre-teens, we were instructed from the book *Shulchan Aruch,* the authoritative guide to ritual performance.

I was shaken by the Vishniac book for the pictures in it brought back memories of my hometown, Munkacs. This was my shtetl, my Jewish community and its people. There they were in the pages of the book: the rich and the paupers, the upright citizens and the city's fools. There was Meyer Tziz, whom I taunted, together with other merciless young people, by shouting at him "Kukuriku." I do not know why he reacted to this stimulus, but he did so violently. There was also Hershele Kakash, a mildly disposed dwarf with an extremely generous nature. Walking with his cane and his pocket stuffed full of paper, he was always ready to write a draft on the Jewish Bank for a million Czech kroner for anyone who asked him.

Looking at these pages I confronted my vanished world. This was my world, my shtetl, my culture, my life that no longer exists -- it is indeed a vanished world. It is not that the city disappeared. It still exists, now a part of Ukraine. What has vanished is its Jewish life. As I looked through the book I wished to resurrect it – to bring it back to life. I left Munkacs right after my return to it following liberation from internment in the German concentration camps, and I have never returned. Munkacs and my life there are associated with good memories that I do not wish to alter by revisiting. I wish to remember it as it was and not as it is today, a city devoid of Jews.

In my forty years of teaching sociology, I have often talked to students about a peculiar relationship between immigrant parents and their children. It seems that second generation Americans often wish to discard their parents' culture and their way of life. In fact many children of immigrants have expressed disdain for their parents' way of life, which they considered to be unAmerican. Their children in turn, that is, the third and fourth generation of Americans, do seek their roots and wish to know something about their past. Many students have declared to me, "I wish that my grandparents would have talked to me about their past." Indeed, my children in their youth were not very interested in my ancestral past or my experiences. Now in their middle ages, they seem to be more receptive to my stories. I am writing this account of my life for them and for my grandchildren, hoping that by knowing their roots they may establish greater stability in their lives.

For a long time I have neither spoken nor written about my life, especially about my Holocaust experiences. My silence was not due so much to my children's lack of desire to listen as to my own emotions. Ever since my arrival in the United States people have been asking me to tell them about my experiences in the concentration camps. For 30 years I have been reluctant to talk about this experience. Perhaps it was the memory and the associated pain of having lost my family that kept me from relating my Holocaust experiences. But it is also quite possible that the reason for my hesitancy to speak is due to my sense of guilt for surviving. I was also reluctant to become a member of any survivors group or for that matter to be introduced, or better, displayed as a survivor. On one occasion, 30 years after having settled in the United States, I was introduced at some public function as a survivor. Not only did I feel embarrassed by this introduction, but I also felt angry. I felt then, and I still do now, that being a survivor of the Holocaust is not an accomplishment. I survived mostly because I was lucky. I was embarrassed because I feel that I do not deserve, nor does any other survivor, to be singled out for any honor simply for having survived the ordeal of the Holocaust. Honors, I believed then as I do now, should be bestowed only upon those persons whose work and achievement have contributed to the well-being of the world.

But as I became older, I started to realize that the ordeal which I shared with so many others has socially significant meaning, and as such it is important that I share these experiences with others.

In the last 15 years I have lectured about the Holocaust in public schools, colleges, and churches and at public forums. I am not relating my experiences and talking about the causes of the Holocaust in order to gain sympathy either for myself or for the Jewish people. And above all, I am not seeking to achieve honor for having survived the ordeal of the Holocaust. Rather, my aim is to make readers aware that, given certain conditions, holocausts under various guises and names can and will occur, even in the United States. My desire and hope are to share my limited knowledge with the audience and make them aware of the conditions that often precipitate hatred and persecution of minorities. For in the final analysis, only the people themselves can negate the power of governments who seek to implement any form of genocide.

The story of the Holocaust has many aspects. Many personal accounts have been written and movies have been made. But as I see it, these stories, books, and films have one common denominator -- they all follow a Hollywood-like scenario. The story usually starts with the German occupation of whatever country in which the protagonist lives. This is followed by how Jews were gathered into ghettos from which they were transported by the infamous trains to various camps. The tales then proceed to describe various difficulties and troubles the protagonist experiences, such as separation and loss of family, illness, harsh labor, and so on. Finally, the tale comes to a happy ending, namely the liberation.

The true and lasting consequences of the Holocaust for those who survived the ordeal start with liberation. It is only after liberation that the survivors become aware of the enormity of their losses. It is only after liberation that we become aware that we are alone without family, home, country, and, of course, income and work. We faced the enormous task of healing ourselves from the psychological devastation that we experienced, to reconstruct our lives and gain some semblance of normalcy. This is my story. I am quite aware that, for the reader to understand fully the Holocaust and with it the murder not only of millions of people but also a culture, I need to start by describing life in the pre-Holocaust years. No American could understand the scale of changes that we had to make unless I first make the reader aware of our lives in the Eastern European shtetl. Only after this will I relate very briefly my life in the camps and then tell the story of my life after the camps and my attempt to reconstruct my life.

On May 2, 1945, I was reborn. On that date I was liberated from Muhldorf Wald Lager, one of the many German concentration camps. I was freed by Lt. Schwartz, who appeared at the camp gate with a tank and a squad of U.S. soldiers. My fellow inmates and I, the survivors of years of internment, were jubilant. Hours before, the U.S. forces had arrived; the SS guards had gone, and we were able to move freely, although most of us were too weak to do so. However, a few days after our liberation, the initial feeling of joy that we had experienced abated. Instead, I began to experience a sense of anxiety. Most of us who survived, including my father and my other relatives, became fearful of what we would find when we returned to our hometowns. We talked about what we would do, where we would go. Above all else we wondered with anxiety, of course, who among our immediate family had survived. The general mood that prevailed in the camp was fear and anxiety. What haunted us was the uncertainty of our future, the answer to the simple, yet difficult question: What now?

The day after liberation we, the survivors, were taken to a military hospital for treatment and recuperation. While all of us suffered at least from malnutrition, others had far more serious illnesses. There were those among the liberated whose condition had so deteriorated that they could not be saved. The rest of us, after gaining some weight and strength, were being repatriated, a euphemism for sending us back to the country of our origin. Not all of the survivors went back to their pre-Holocaust homes. Having experienced the hostile attitudes of their non-Jewish neighbors, most of those who survived decided to seek entrance to other countries.

However, a month after liberation, I returned to my hometown, Munkacs, in the Carpathian region, formerly both

Czechoslovakia and Hungary. Coming back to my hometown, once a thriving Jewish community, I found it mostly empty of Jews. The city I knew, and in which I grew up, a city I considered my hometown, seemed dead to me. The streets and buildings were the same, they hadn't changed, but the city itself was devoid of that which made it my hometown. My home, the house where I was born and spent my youth, was at my return, occupied by strangers. My family and friends were all gone and so were the almost 18,000 Jews who once called Munkacs home. The day after my arrival I was also informed that Munkacs was now part of the U.S.S.R. Were I to remain in the city, I would have to learn a new language, be a part of a new culture, and above all live in a political system that I didn't like and among people and a regime that were hostile to Jews. I didn't want to be a part of a country that had a long history of antisemitism, one that supported pogroms, a semiofficial and sanctioned killing of Jews.

All these thoughts added to my sense of confusion, estrangement, and foreboding. I was in a state of shock, experiencing a condition that sociologists call anomy. I felt as though my life had lost its meaning, values, moral perspectives, and direction.

Although I returned to my birthplace, to the town of my youth, in my mind I was sure that this place held no future for me. I became quite aware that in little over a year I was not only cut off from my past but also from the future that I had dreamed about. I had to pose this very difficult question: What shall I do now? My past, and with it my plans for my future that my parents and I had dreamed about, seemed not only unattainable but also meaningless. I knew that I had to reconstruct my life. I had to have new plans and a new direction.

I am sure that most of those who survived, like me, shared similar problems: the loss of family, wealth, home, future expectations, but, above all else, the customs and traditions that in the last two millennia gave our life a sense of direction and meaning. Most survivors, including me, had to reconstruct our lives and perspectives. Not only did we need new plans for our future, we also needed a new world to live in and a new worldview by which we could interpret and make sense of our Holocaust experiences.

Most survivors, I suppose, were able to integrate their experiences into a new meaning system and find the motivation and strength to face life anew. How was that accomplished?

The story of the Holocaust and its survivors is not complete without examining and describing the spirit that helped them to reestablish a facsimile of a normal life. It is this facet of my life experiences that I wish to examine and record; to tell how I rebuilt my ego, my psyche, and my life. However, for the reader to understand the changes in my life and in me, I must begin with describing my life in a small town in the Carpathian Mountains. Paraphrasing the teaching of Akavya, the son of Mehalel, I must examine my past, the roots from where I hail, and only then will I understand and know where I am going. My present existence, my worldviews, and my beliefs are the result of a combination of my life in Munkacs, my imprisonment in the concentration camps, and my post-Holocaust experiences. It is my pre-Holocaust past that helped me to rebuild my life after my liberation. Without examining my roots neither I nor the reader will understand my views of life. Let me now turn to Munkacs, the cradle of my existence.

Note: Yiddish terms are defined where they appear in the text as well as in a glossary at the end of the book.

## Chapter One
## Jewish Life in
## the Carpathian
## Mountains

My life for the first 18 years was spent in Munkacs, a small shtetl in the foothills of the Carpathian Mountains. It was a Jewish town. I call it that because two thirds of its 27,000 residents were Jewish. By the time of my birth, on November 8, 1925, shtetl life and its culture were on the wane. Were it not for the Nazi atrocities, shtetl life as it existed in the nineteenth century would have responded to the laws of evolution and would have, most likely, disappeared by the twenty-first century. It would have died a natural death. Culture – and by that I mean the social institutions as well as lifestyles, values, beliefs, customs, and worldviews – changes with time. It changes in response to many conditions. Cultures respond to changes in technology, to advances of knowledge and communication and, of course, to the evolutionary changes in the productive system.

Shtetl life, that is, a life reflecting a unique Yiddish culture that existed in the latter part of the eighteenth, nineteenth, and twentieth centuries, until the Holocaust, was located primarily in the villages and small towns in Eastern Europe: Poland, Russia, Austria-Hungary, and Romania. Shtetl culture was a part of life among the Chassidic Jews that developed as a response to poverty and the harsh life that they had to endure. A *shtetl*, for those unacquainted with the term, is the diminutive of *shtud*, the Yiddish word for a town. A shtetl is a small, East European town with a large Jewish population and a particular form of religious culture.

Munkacs, my city of birth, was a shtetl. Munkacs was a part of Austria-Hungary until 1918 when it became part of the newly created Czechoslovakia. However, by 1938, as a part of the British and French attempt to appease Hitler at the Vienna Conference, Munkacs and most of the region known as Carpathia was returned to Hungary. The majority of the city's inhabitants were Jews.

It was a Jewish town, which was evident in many ways. It was evident on the Sabbath. On that day business halted, and instead of the weekday throngs of customers frequenting the stores and the coffeehouse, the streets were much quieter. On the Sabbath one saw mostly Jews in their Chassidic garb, consisting of a long silk caftan (*bekeshe*), black slippers, and fur-covered hat (*straymel*), hurrying to their respective synagogues. This town, now a part of the Ukraine, no longer exists as a shtetl. Most of the Jews were killed, and those who survived immigrated either to Israel or to the United States. Munkacs, at least as I knew it, no longer exists. Today it is a Ukrainian city with a population of over 100,000, but its most distinctive change is that it is now a city sans Jews.

I was the oldest son of Henryk and Yolanda Schönfeld (their Hungarian names). My father followed his grandfather Naftuli's occupation as an author, publisher, and a merchant in religious books. Early in his life my father apprenticed as a printer, but after World War I he changed his occupation, and with money that was saved by my grandmother, he bought an existing book and stationery store. This money for starting the store had been earned by my grandfather, Lezer Yaakov, who had spent a few years in New York City working as a cigar roller. Like so many immigrants, my grandfather left his family and came to the United States to make his fortune and then return to his homeland. He lived frugally and sent most of his money back to his wife, Hudje. She guarded the money that had been earmarked to buy a store and thereby leave the ghetto where they lived in poverty. As a printer my father developed an interest in and a love of learning and reading, which he sought to transmit to me.

My mother Yolanda was the oldest daughter of Avruhom and Feige Neuman. They lived about 60 kilometers north of Munkacs in the Carpathian Mountains, just a stone's throw from the pre--1938 Polish-Czech border. My grandfather Avruhom was a Vizsnitzer Chassid, that is, he accepted the Vizsnitzer Rebbe as his charismatic mentor.

I think the reader will gain a better understanding of my life if I were to describe the nature of the shtetl, at least my experience of shtetl life. Of course the shtetl in its heyday was quite different from life in Munkacs during the 1930s. I was born when shtetl life was at its nadir. Most of the readers who are familiar with the shtetl think of its depiction in the writings of Mendele Mocher S'farim, Y.L. Perez, and, of course, Shalom Aleichem, who told of Motel in the play *Fiddler on the Roof.* All of these works presented an idealized version of the shtetl. But let me tell you about Munkacs, a city that was often described as a "city and mother in Israel."

My life in Munkacs, like those of all observant Jews, who constituted perhaps more than 85 percent of the Jews in the city, was governed by Jewish customs and Jewish religious laws. To a great extent, for most Jews in my city, and I may say among all who lived in Carpathia, customs, religion, and superstition were so greatly intertwined that they became one and the same. For instance, it was customary that when one trimmed his finger- or toenails, one worked by alternating nails. Of course, this practice was not a part of religious law per se; it was, I suppose, a response to a long-forgotten fear of black magic. Nonetheless, this custom was observed as closely as were clearly stated religious laws.

The rhythm of life in Munkacs was determined by the Jewish holidays. Jewish holidays exerted perhaps the most significant influence on life, and in some ways they may have been even more significant in one's life than one's work. Life, in some aspects, was not only a linear progression marked by various life stages. Life was also a cyclical movement of annual and weekly rituals. It consisted of repetitive acts of preparations for the various religious holidays. As one holiday ended another one loomed on the horizon. The end of one holiday was marked by the anticipation for the next one.

Jewish holidays are historical remembrances clothed in religiously sacred garments. The holidays are the sanctification of the collective experiences. From a sociological perspective, holidays are essential for the individual's and the community's maintenance of identity. Even more important is that the observance of holidays as a collective act elevates the spirit and gives the participant a sense of well-being that he or she might otherwise fail to experience. For the believer, the holidays are to be observed not because they have certain specific social functions and psychological consequences; they are to be kept because they were decreed by God. And even holidays, such as Chanukah or Purim, which were rabbinical decrees, are still considered by the faithful to have the same significance as God-given laws written in the Pentateuch.

The observance of holidays has both intended and unintended consequences. On the one hand, Jews observed holidays because they are commandments, they are God- ordained *mitzvoth,* and the violation thereof will deprive the deviant from salvation, that is, from life in the world to come, and will surely lead also to punishment after death. However, the observance of the laws, in general, and the holidays, in particular, had other latent social functions.

The observance of most Jewish holidays and their rituals are decreed in the Torah, the Pentateuch. Later on, the observance of other historical events, both feast and fast days, were rabbinical decrees according to the Talmud, to Biblical writings, and to the Apocrypha. However, with time and depending upon place of residence, Jews have added to and or modified the forms of the decreed observances. Yet the observance of the holidays brings with it important and unexpected consequences such as identity maintenance. For instance, in ancient Israel before the dispersion of Jews throughout the world, there were many who lived "outside of the land" (*meechutz l'aretz*), outside of Israel. These Jews, whether in Babylon or Egypt, did not easily assimilate into the social milieu of their host land, because they thought of themselves as members of a community both ethnic and religious.

Jews, even after the destruction of their homeland and their dispersion, have always identified themselves as a nationality, a people who temporarily are without a homeland. Never in the two millennia have they wavered from the belief that they will return to the land that was promised to them by God. Meanwhile, the community served them in lieu of a homeland. For this reason, I believe, Jews have always placed greater importance on the community and its needs than on the individual. It is not that the individual is unimportant. After all, the Talmud tells us that he who saves one life saves the whole world. Yet, the ancient sages also realized that to remain a Jew one must be a part of a Jewish collective. Thus, the observance of Jewish holidays ties the individual to his collective and to its social institutions. Jews are tied to their Jewish community's schools. Jewish law mandates that all communities that have at least ten children must provide for their Jewish education. Educating the children is one of the fundamental requirements of being Jewish. Jews are also tied to economic institutions. After all, Jews have needs that are not provided for by the larger community. They need to have kosher food and special clothing that is *shatnez* free; that is, the cloth is not made from a mixture of wool and linen. Jews also maintain their own courts where cases are judged by *dayanim*, judges whose judgments are rendered on the basis of Talmudic laws. These institutions, as well as the synagogues, constituted the infrastructure of the individual's existence. The value systems by which we make judgments and decisions are not individual products but are transmitted to us by the community. It is the community that is the foundation of one's collective consciousness.

For Jews, the word *echod* (one) is the essence of belief. As God is one so are the Jews. This emphasis on oneness and unity is the product of our religious belief, of our ethnicity, and of our history. This sense of the unity of the Jewish community led to the rabbinic declaration "All Israel is responsible for one another." It was best expressed by one Talmudic sage in the following organismic analogy: Jewish people, he said, can be equated to a hand. If one finger hurts does not the whole hand suffer? This view is also expressed in another saying: All Jews are responsible for each other. Self-help has been and continues to be an essential aspect of Jewish life. The holidays, including the Sabbath, became a central mechanism in the exercise of collective welfare. *Tzedokoh*, the Hebrew word for charity, is a derivative of *tzedek*, the Hebrew word for justice. Hence, to fulfill one's obligation for charity is actually an act of justice, namely an act by which one can insure that all people in the community have access to life's chances. This is accomplished by giving to charitable organizations, the function of which is to assure that all Jews have the minimal requirements for life and for the observance of the holidays. The requirement for the giving to collective welfare institutions does not necessarily exempt one from personal giving, individual charitable acts. Before all holidays the poor Jews made their rounds to their benefactors expecting and receiving alms that would enable them and their families to properly observe the holiday rituals. An example of this tradition is, for instance, the "eating days." Many financially poor students who came to the city from impoverished villages to study in the *yeshivoth* (rabbinic schools) were assigned by a community committee to a household where they took their meals on specified days.

Holidays also served as a means for tension reduction. The synagogue in Mukacs was not only a place for services; that is, a place where God is worshiped. It was not only a place to glorify God, but also a place for collective petitions for health, income, and, most importantly, where the community beseeched God for protection from antisemitism in its various forms. It was also where individual and collective problems could be discussed with friends. Weekdays were devoted to work, but on the Sabbath, particularly as one walked with friends and neighbors to the synagogue, one could discuss fears and concerns. For the youth, holidays also provided structured means for rebellion. Such traditional forms of rebellion against authority were central in the synagogue services during the Fast of the Ninth Day of Av (*Tishah B'Av*), the day when the Jews commemorate the destruction of both ancient Temples. While adults were engaged in the recitation of Jeremiah's Lamentation (*Eychoh*), children beginning from preteen to their middle teen years came to the service with pockets full of cockleburs, which they threw with great precision at the beards of older congregants. These burrs, when entangled with hair, were as difficult to remove as chewing gum. Of course, the older men threatened the perpetrators with informing their parents, but no one took these threats seriously. This was an established tradition which allowed the teenagers to take revenge on their elders.

The most frequent holiday of all is the Sabbath. One may think that, because of their collective name, the High Holy Days of *Rosh Hashanah* (New Year) and *Yom Kippur* (the Day of Atonement) would be the most important holidays of all. The ancient rabbis disagreed with this assumption and considered the Sabbath to be the holiest day of all. According to tradition, it is the day that has been sanctified and set aside by God to commemorate the creation of the world. "And God blessed the seventh day, and hallowed it; because that in it He rested from all his work which God in creating had made."

Preparation for the Sabbath began on Wednesday. On that day my mother (like most Jewish wives) went to the market to buy the live chickens that would provide the main meal for the Sabbath feasts. The buying of the chickens was a long process. First, the chickens had to be examined. Mother blew on the feathers to reveal the color of the chicken's skin. Only those that displayed a beautiful golden-yellow skin would be accepted. Once she determined that the quality was good, then the bargaining began that often lasted at least ten minutes. A brace of chickens was brought home to be taken next day to the *shochet*, the ritual slaughterer. Thursdays, the *schnorers* (beggars) came to ask for donations so that they could purchase the groceries for their Sabbath. Each schnorer had in effect assigned households to visit and so when they came, it was almost like a personal visit. They knew how much money they would receive and hence what they could expect in total to spend for the Sabbath. Friday morning, grandfather, whose synagogue was near the fish market, bought the live carp after morning service for my mother and also grandmother. My mother, with the help

of our maid, then prepared the gefilte-fish. Since no one wanted
to handle live fish, it became my task to kill the fish by hitting
it with a piece of wood.

On Friday, the special bread called *challah* was baked.
Just before mother began  braiding the strips of dough to form
the challah, she  tore a piece of the dough which she then threw
into the fire in the stove.  This act was the taking of challah,
which symbolized the compulsory donation of food to the
Temple priests in ancient times.  Friday afternoon was allocated for bathing.  The more devout went to the ritual bath for
the weekly baptism, an act which consisted of total immersion
in the *mikvah*, the ritual pool of live waters.  It was also on
Friday that the  men who professed an Orthodox belief but who
refrained from letting their beard grow shaved for the honor of
the Sabbath. The Biblical statement,  "And you will not shave
the corners of your beards,"  was taken as a clear inhibition
against the use of a razor.  In order that they would not violate
the law, Orthodox men who removed their beards did not use
a razor; instead they used depilatory substance.  The depilatory substance came as a powder known as "razor," which was
mixed with water, which then was smeared on the face, and
after a certain number of minutes was scraped off with a wooden
spatula.  The mixture had a terrible odor, and most Fridays,
weather permitting, the shaving was done outdoors so that one
would not disturb the peace of the Sabbath with the vile odor of
the razor.

Once all ablutions were completed, Sabbath clothes
were donned.  For most modern Orthodox persons,  that meant
a business suit, but  the Chassidic Jews had special garb  consisting of the  *straymel*  (a soft black hat edged with fur); and
*bekeshe* (a long, usually  black, silk caftan);  a white shirt often
with little strings  instead of buttons;  white silk  socks; patent-
leather slippers; and the *chagorah* (a silk sash girding the waist).

The unmarried men wore black suits and   beaver hats or black cloth hats with wide brims.

On most Friday afternoons, it was my task to take the sholent or kugel to the bakery. The *sholen*t was a bean casserole with meat, and the *kugel* was made from grated potatoes and meat. Both of these dishes were taken to the bakery in the afternoon so that when the commercial baking was finished, they could be placed in the oven and cooked slowly overnight. Each pot with its owner's name glued onto it was placed in the oven to be claimed the next day after services. In this manner we could have hot meals without violating the religious injunction against making fires in our homes on the Sabbath.

Weekdays, different from the Sabbath, were days of haste. Each weekday morning we arose around six and after hastily brushing our teeth and washing our faces, my father and I hurried to the synagogue for morning prayers. By seven we returned for breakfast. The rollman with his large basket filled with various breakfast rolls was waiting for us to choose the croissant we wished to have that morning. Then, I had to hurry to be in class on time. My siblings and I had to be at school by eight, and the trip usually took us, if we hurried, not fewer than fifteen minutes.

But on the Sabbath morning we enjoyed our leisure. Although, from habit, we awoke at six; however, because our school and also father's store were closed on the Sabbath, there was no need to hurry. While services began at eight, people came and left as they wished. For instance, we left for services at nine and stayed till they ended, usually at eleven thirty. This was the Sabbath leisure. We could linger in our beds, but most of the time we children preferred to spend the morning hours with our parents. As soon as we awoke, we rushed to climb into their beds. I always lay down next to my father, and my younger brother and sister were most often with our mother. On Sabbath mornings, I related to my father my weekly experiences in school, and above all my after-school studies with the rabbi. He in turn talked about his own dreams for the future, especially my future. In the early part of our lives, we believed in our dreams and were secure that we had futures.

Sabbath was characterized by leisure. One never hurried on that day, with the exception of being late for services. In the summer time, after the midday meal, the family customarily took a stroll in the park, where we met our friends, and generally spent good quality time together. Still, on this day, perhaps even more so than on weekdays, we could not forget our obligations to others. In each synagogue it was the sexton's task to see that people who visited the city and had to stay over on the Sabbath were assigned to Jewish homes where they would be welcomed for the Sabbath meals. It was also the day to remember those hospitalized. Jewish women, members of the *Bikur Cholim* organization  (those  who took on the task to visit the sick), visited many homes where they collected traditional foods to bring to those who were in the hospital and, because of poverty or distance from friends and family, did not have sources of traditional Sabbath food.

The right of leisure on the Sabbath was ingrained in me. I never felt guilty for not studying that day. Quite often, especially in the winter, I took guiltless afternoon naps. But in the winter nightfall came early and so did the end of the Sabbath. Early evenings after the *havdalah* services (a ritual designed to separate the holy Sabbath from the profane weekday), my sense of justified leisure was over, and once again I felt the pressure to study, to do homework for the next day's classes.

In addition to the Sabbath, life also revolved around the yearly holidays, of which there were many. The annual cycle of holidays began with the New Year and the Day of Atonement. One began to prepare ritually and emotionally for these holidays a month before Rosh Hashanah (the New Year).

There are ten days between the New Year and the Day of Atonement. These days are known as the Days of Penance. It was important that we develop a proper attitude and that we prepare ourselves emotionally and spiritually to stand before our maker, who on these ten days sits in judgment not only of us Jews but of the whole human race. Tradition holds that on Rosh Hashanah we are judged. God in heaven examines our actions of the prior year, and a trial ensues. The *Saneygor*, the accusing angel, recites our sins and misdeeds and asks God to punish us harshly. We are, however, defended by the *Kateygor*, the defending angel, who always seeks to provide mitigating reasons for our sins. God on his throne sits as the judge. We remind God that in his wisdom He has decreed that in rendering a judgment it must be mitigated by mercy. Still, on these holy days we must face justice. One can expect that the ideas of being judged and being sentenced will generate fear and trepidation among the believers. After all, can anyone be immune from fear and concern when judgment may include illness, poverty, and even death? And so, the prayers in the synagogue are more intense, somewhat louder than on other holidays.

Ten days after Rosh Hashanah comes the Day of Atonement. The day before, all of our family participated in a ritual which was in essence more like magic, the ritual of *kaparoth*, the atonement service, which is designed to transfer human sins onto a chicken. Holding a chicken over one's head, the participant recites the magic formula: "This fowl is my exchange; this is my ransom; and this is my atonement. This fowl shall meet death, but I shall find a long and pleasant life of peace." The ritual of kaparoth was instituted after the destruction of the Temple in Jerusalem and was considered to be a substitute for the ceremony of the scapegoat. In that ritual, the High Priest transferred the sins of all the Jews onto a goat that was taken to the desert where it was pushed off a cliff.

Yom Kippur Eve was a time to hurry. Before afternoon services (*minchah*) my father and I went to the ritual bath, the mikvah, for our annual baptism by immersion, a ritual act of cleansing. Yom Kippur is a fast day for all males over thirteen and females over twelve. The abstinence from all food and liquid for 26 hours began before sunset and before the evening services, known as the *Kol Nidre*, started. We hastily finished our meal, took our last sips of water, and made ourselves ready for the start of the day of awe.

Yom Kippur, to me, was the most dreaded day of the year. Unlike other holidays, with their sumptuous meals and associated leisure and joyful activities, Yom Kippur is a day of awe, fear, and fasting. The Yom Kippur meal was eaten hastily. The motto that governed that meal was hurry up; we cannot be late for Kol Nidre. As the sun began to set, we lit the *yohrzeit* candles, spending a few minutes to remember those in the family who had died. Then we were ready to leave the house for the Kol Nidre services. Mother was dressed in white, and a white shawl covered her head. Father was carrying his bulging *talith batel* under his arm, because on this day in addition to his t*alith* (shawl) he also carried his *kittl* (the ceremonial white robe) that all married males wear on the Day of Atonement. Following the tradition for this day, all of us, children and adults, wore cloth slippers. My parents, my paternal grandparents, and an uncle shared the same courtyard; so leaving for the synagogue, we would meet them in the yard where I would greet them with the traditional saying, "*L'shonoh tovah und beyt achos a gut yuhr*," which, loosely means, "May your prayers be successful and be granted a good year." It was but a short walk to the synagogue, and on the way we met many people, similarly dressed, women in white and men in their dark suits, with whom we exchanged traditional greetings and good wishes for the year.

The synagogue would be unusually bright. In addition to the regular lights there were literally thousands of memorial candles, some in glasses, others, like oversized Sabbath candles, tall and slim, stuck in sand-filled boxes, all lit in memory of the departed. The floor would be covered with clean straw mats so that the worshipers would not soil their clothes when prostrating themselves in performance of the traditional *korim*. The prayer stands, similar to chest-high lecterns, dark as aged wood should be, were turned over. On this day, like mourners, we sat uncomfortably on the overturned stands, low to the ground. As the sun started to sink, the ark would be opened and three Torah scrolls taken out. These were carried by three rabbis who were also dayanim (judges, at least individuals with the degree of *hatarath haraim*) who approached the *bimah*. These three persons now constituted the earthly court, the *beth din*. The elder of the rabbis would begin to chant, "*B'yeshivah shel maaloh*," declaring that both the heavenly and earthly courts give permission for sinners to enter, join, and pray with the congregation.

Upon completion of the declaration, the *Chazzan* (the cantor) would begin to chant the ancient and haunting melody of Kol Nidre. At that moment, the women in the veiled off-balcony that constituted the *mechitzoh* would begin to cry. After all, Kol Nidre is the beginning of the day in which our fate for the coming year will be determined. On this day, according to traditional belief, not only the fate of the Jews is determined but that of the whole world. It is on this day that the world stands in judgment before God. Surely this is an awesome day, especially for the Jews who since the rule of the Roman Emperor Constantine (350 C.E.) have had to endure atrocities. Most Jews hold firmly to the belief that our fate both as individuals and as a collective is being determined during the ten days of penance. On Rosh Hashanah our fate is being inscribed in the book of life, and at the end of Yom Kippur it will be sealed. Surely one can understand that a people whose collective memories are filled with insecurity will consider the weight of these days, and some will cry from fear of the unforeseeable future. As the sound of the cries would reach the rabbi's ears, he would stop the service and with a loud voice announce: "Shah! Women, be quiet! This is the synagogue."

But even on this day of awe, we boys had our fun. On this day, at least it was a tradition in my city, that we might take our revenge on adults. The word that we most often encountered in our youth was "no." Most of our requests were quite often disallowed by our parents. Of course blocked goals, even such as we experienced in our youth, led to frustration, and in turn, frustration generated anger. On Yom Kippur, we had the opportunity to vent our frustration against adults. On the afternoon of the holiday, we proceeded to the drugstore with tiny bottles that we had procured. The druggist filled the bottles with undiluted ammonia. By late afternoon, most of the elder Jews, who quite often spent the whole night in prayer, were beginning to doze on their low chairs. Slowly and quietly, we approached these people and placed the open bottles of ammonia under their noses. The fumes of the ammonia were so pungent and strong that they could have almost revived the dead. The inhaling of these fumes was quite painful, and the sufferers threatened us, but since it was a tradition, they reluctantly accepted what we had done.

As the days of awe, the *yomim hanoraim*, consisting of Rosh Hashanah and Yom Kippur, ended they were followed almost immediately with *Succoth*. By this time the cold winds, forecasting the coming of winter, had often arrived. This was the time of harvesting the walnuts. This holiday had two aims. First, it was instituted to commemorate life in the desert during the forty years of wandering after the liberation from Egypt. Since life in the desert was temporary, Jews were instructed to construct nonpermanent structures,    (huts, the roofs of which were covered with green branches). These branches must not be so thick that they keep the rain out. Rather, they must be sparse so that at night, the sky, the moon, and stars may be visible. Our *succah* (hut) was a permanent structure constructed with bricks, but with a tin roof that could be swung open so that the covering, woven like a basket made of willow branches, was sparse enough to make the sky visible. The one-room structure was never heated.  As the ritual laws required, we took all our meals in the hut, quite often shivering in the cold of the night. I was always grateful when the meal ended, and I could return to the warmth of our kitchen.

Succoth subsumes three holidays. The other two are *Shemini Atzereth* and *Simchath Torah*. Simchath Torah was important to us children. On that holiday (literally, rejoicing with the Torah), Jewish communities worldwide celebrate both the completion and the beginning again of the annual cycle of reading through the Five Books of Moses. In Munkacs, young children, that is, those pre-thirteen, came to the synagogue with flags and, together with their parents, circled the podium in the middle of the synagogue while the older children carried the sacred scroll. It was a festive occasion, and candies and cakes were distributed to the children. Some adults and children would leave the synagogue to continue services at home incorporating traditional lunches.

I always spent *Simchath Torah* morning with my paternal grandfather in the home of a friend of his. On this day all males, children and adults, were given the honor of having the Torah read to them.  Even at the very young age of six, I already knew how to read Hebrew prayers, and I could see his pride as I read the appropriate Torah blessing aloud. I remember the delicious foods that his friend's wife prepared for all of us, and best of all was the stuffed cabbage, Hungarian style.

Chanukah in Europe, unlike the United States, was considered a minor holiday. In the United States, it has become the Jewish Christmas. The exchanging of gifts and decorating the house were not European Jewish customs. Unlike holidays that are decreed in the Torah, Chanukah was decreed by the rabbis of the Talmudic era and was instituted to commemorate the success of the Jewish rebellion against Antiochos, the Greek ruler of Syria. Judea, after the death of Alexander the Great, became a part of the Syrian Empire. The holiday also commemorates a miracle of oil. When the war was won and the Maccabeans entered Jerusalem, their first task was to reestablish the Temple. Under the Syrian rule, the original building had been dedicated to Zeus and defiled by what Jews considered unclean offerings. After cleaning the building, when the Temple was being rededicated to the service of Yahweh, they searched for pure olive oil, that is, oil pressed by the priests, put in jars, sealed, and set aside for use in the seven-branched candelabra in the Temple. Legend has it that the priests found only one jar, adequate for one day, which miraculously lasted for eight days, precisely the number of days that were required to produce new oil. In Europe, instead of gifts on Chanukah, children received money (*Chanukah gelt*), a few coins that were used by the family to play a game (and this lasted only while the small Chanukah candles were burning), utilizing a special object called a *dreidel*.

Usually at the end of February or in the beginning of March, on the fourteenth day of the Hebrew month of Adar, the joyous holiday of Purim arrived. All of Adar was considered to be the lucky month of the year, and its arrival was announced by a decorated placard, the *mee shenechnaz*, which was nailed above the transom over the door. The placard announced that as the month of Adar begins, we increase our joy. Of the lesser holidays, Purim is far more important because of the preparation. For two weeks before Purim, my mother would begin baking various cakes and tortes to be sent on Purim as *mishloach manoth* (gifts) to friends and relatives. This holiday celebrates the survival of Jews in Persia. On Purim, in the synagogue, the story of the heroic deeds of Esther and Mordecai is recited. It was customary during this recitation for children, only boys, to sneak up behind younger children carrying celebratory paper flags and set them afire. These were just a few of the customs of disrespect to adult authority that served to reduce built-up hostility and subsequent rebellion associated with the frustrations of being teenaged.

Notwithstanding the joy associated with Purim was the recognition that others are in need. It was my grandfather's custom on the eve of the holiday to sit in the courtyard with stacks of coins to distribute to all the poor who came for alms. The holiday ended with the *seudah*, the Purim feast. The family, all my grandfather's sons in the city, came with their families. A huge table was set with a huge and well-decorated *challah* as its centerpiece. It was the day of eating turkey, the "puffed rooster," as it was called in Hungarian. A gypsy band would arrive to provide music so essential for the completion of a feast.

The ensuing month, Nissan, was devoted to preparation for Passover. No other holiday in the Jewish calendar commands the time required for preparation. In our home, preparations for Passover started just after Purim. The first Passover dish that was brought down from its storage space in the attic was an enormous pot in which cooked red beets were placed to ferment. From the beets, borscht was made for Passover. The house had to be properly cleaned; clothes had to be taken out to be aired; and all pockets were cleaned out so that no bread or any other leaven should remain in them or in the house. Passover dishes that were stored in the attic and which were used only during the eight days of the holiday had to be brought down. The first room that was cleaned was my parent's bedroom. In it the *matzoth* and many dozens of eggs were stored. The reader must understand that, unlike today, when eggs are commercially produced and available in vast quantities in the supermarket, in my youth, eggs were bought from peasant women who came to the city with never more than one dozen at a time.

My memories of Passover are always pleasant. It was the holiday that I spent with my maternal grandparents in Talamas, a very small village in the Carpathian Mountains. Because I was their oldest grandchild, I was sent so that they would not be alone, for during this holiday the ceremony called S*eder* begins with a child asking "The Four Questions."

To commemorate Passover, as another new year, it was traditional that on the first day of it we wear something new, and most often it was a new suit. It was a tradition that when one donned a new garment on Passover the wearer was told *titchadesh* (may you be renewed) instead of the more traditional wish, *Tzerass* it *gesunter heit*, loosely translated, "May you tear up the garment in health."

The wish *titchadesh* enthralls me even today because of a beautiful story written by Yaakov Fichman. The story relates an event in the brief life of a poor tailor's son, who never received a new suit and thus has never been wished t*itchadesh*. The child suffers from tuberculosis and dies at an early age, when he is given new shrouds in which to be buried. As the angels lead his soul to heaven, he finally hears the wish that eludes him during his lifetime: "Titchadesh, titchadesh," the angels keep repeating.

Summertime began with the holiday of *Sh'vuoth*, a holiday that commemorates the giving of the Ten Commandments at Mount Sinai. Windows were now opened, and the fragrance of blooming trees permeated the air. The house would be decorated with flowers and the leaves from the walnut tree that grew in our courtyard. Customarily, mother would spend time in the kitchen preparing the various dairy dishes expected for this holiday.

The final holiday of the year was *Tishah B'Av*, a fast day commemorating the destruction of both Temples in Jerusalem. The days were warm, and we knew that summer vacation was almost over, and the cycle of holidays would start anew.

I firmly believe that children today lack the great holiday joys that we experienced. Jewish children today fail to develop attachments to their community because they lack a sense of historical continuity that is essential for developing strong Jewish identities. Just as adults, children too, had traditions associated with each holiday, traditions that were in addition to and independent of religious rites. Surely it was significant that the children's rituals included acts that provided a means to express the hostilities that are so a part of growing up and controlled the expressions of anger and defiance that otherwise could have led to delinquent acts.

Jews' religious beliefs and perspectives in Munkacs were undergoing great change during my childhood. Even fifty years prior to my birth, Jewish life would have been uniform and homogeneous. But, by the 1930s, Jews in Munkacs had formed four distinct groups. The Chassids were still the largest group, followed by modern Orthodox, the Zionists, and the assimilated. Each of these groups affected my own beliefs and views. My Jewish identity, in a sense, is a construct influenced by my association with significant individuals from each of these groups. Let me start with my association with the Chassidim, most importantly with my maternal grandfather.

To be a *Chassid* (literally a pious one) means to follow a particular rebbe. The rebbe, as opposed to a rabbi, is usually a charismatic leader, and in my time, the rebbe of a particular sect usually was either a direct descendant of the founding rebbe or one who inherited the position after the rebbe's death by virtue of his marriage to the rebbe's daughter. This, for instance, happened in Munkacs when the old rebbe's daughter's husband became, by virtue of marriage, the new Munkacser rebbe. Most often, the followers of the dynastical rebbe would identify themselves not by the leader's name but by the name of city where the originator of the sect lived. Thus, we had Vizsnitzer Chassidim, who followed the rebbe who lived in the city Vizsnitz; the Belzer Chassidim; the Szatmarer; the Berditschever; the Brtazlaver; and of course the Munkacser Chassidim. Each of these sects had their own synagogue, and each, of course, claimed the greatness and superiority of their own rebbe over the others. Most Chassidim, however, never met the rebbe whose disciples they were and with whom they identified. Only the more affluent were financially able to make pilgrimages to the rebbe. Like the rebbes who claimed the legitimacy of their status through descent, their disciples likewise followed their father's masters.

The Chassid's belief in his rebbe's charismatic powers was normally fierce. Each chassid, as I said, believed in the superiority of his rebbe and in charismatic powers that gave him greater ability to perceive the future, to have special and closer relationship with God, and, of course, to have greater curative powers than other rebbes. My mother followed her father's belief in the Berditchever rebbe and made me wear as a talisman, a magical amulet, an antique coin which, according to family legend, was *beschprecht*, meaning spoken on by the rebbe. In short, the rebbe, my mother believed, endowed the coin with supernatural powers that would protect me from all kinds of calamity, sickness, and above all else, from the evil eye that others might cast on me. The belief in charismatic powers is universal, because human beings, regardless of religion and geography, have universally similar concerns, hence, the similar ways by which people seek to deal with their problems.

Most sects that believe in the master's charisma also believe that the special powers and leadership are transmitted by inheritance. While the first master had to prove his charismatic powers through prophecies and miracles, his heir's powers were routinely accepted without proof of charisma – but with faith that qualities of greatness are transmitted to descendants. The beautiful ideals that were the common denominator of the Chassidic movements, the elevation of spirit, the essence of joy in their relationship with God, were lost over time. Instead of its glorious ideals, now jealousy, bickering, and pettiness became common. While the ideal of becoming an *eidler* man, a sensitive and saintly soul, was still lauded, the number of Chassids who in practice were sensitive and truly spiritual persons was greatly diminished.

There was one person who in his own way was truly an eidler man. He was my mother's father, my grandfather Rebb Avrohom. Although he occasionally studied the Talmud, he was not a great scholar; he was, however, a saintly and humble person, a contented person who knew what God wanted and sought merely to fulfill His wishes. He never lectured me; he never confronted me; he never preached *mussar* (moral chastisement) to me; and he never admonished me, especially in public. He believed that God merely wants us to do our duties, to be kind to our fellows, regardless of belief and social status, treating all with dignity and honesty. His life revolved around duties to God and family and making a living.

My grandfather lived in a very small village, Talamas, in a valley in the Carpathian Mountains. He rose daily (even on the Sabbath) about five in the morning, donned his boots and his dark clothes, as befitting a Chassid, and went to do his duties. Because of his firm belief in the moral dictum not to inflict pain on any living thing, his first duty, he felt, was to the cow and not to God. God can wait for his prayers, but the cow must be milked and fed and her stall cleaned. The cow must be taken care of, not only because she provided part of his livelihood, but primarily because she was one of God's creatures who could not care for herself. It is only after having taken care of the cow that he turned to his duty to God. Each day he donned his prayer shawl, strapped the phylacteries on his arm and head (alternating between the *Rashi* and *Bal Taam T'filin*), and with great concentration and devotion recited his prayers. On Friday he made sure that the *eruv –halachah* was placed in the proper place. The eruv consisted of an egg and a challah roll (a *bilkeleh*) placed under a stone. Sabbath is of course a day of rest, and on that day Jews are forbidden from walking excessive distances. The limit, according to the Talmud, is two thousand feet from the last Jewish home; this is called the *t'chum shabbath*. But through the magic of prayer, this food became a symbol of a Jewish home, thus permitting an observant Jew to walk an additional 2000 yards. The *eruv* was an essential practice, because it permitted the Jews of Talamas to walk on the Sabbath the mile and a half to Huklivoh, a larger village, to attend Sabbath services in the synagogue.

My grandfather, as I have said, was content with his life. He tended his store, worked the garden that supplied his food, and on sunny summer days, time permitting, he sat on a bench outside his home and store, facing the beautiful mountains and smoking his long-stemmed clay pipe. In his younger days he spent a few years in New York working as a cutter in a garment factory. But he soon returned to his beloved mountains not to leave even to Munkacs, a scant 35 miles from his home, where both his daughters and his grandchildren lived. Today, of course, people might consider him a deviant. They would look at this hard-working and contented man and judge him to be without ambition, without a desire to improve his wealth and status, indeed to violate the work ethic. Perhaps! But in my view, my grandfather achieved what few of us ever are capable of achieving, contentment. He accepted himself for what he was, including his strengths and weaknesses. It was not that he was lazy and shunned labor. He worked hard, perhaps harder than any person I know. But he sought another form of success. He was loved and respected by his community. Rebb Avruhom achieved, even without great wealth, the status that Tevye in *Fiddler on the Roof* sought. He was always consulted and never disregarded. The Talmud raises the rhetorical question: "Who is the rich person?" and the answer is, "He who is content with his portion." This was my grandfather Rebb Avruhom. And because he was a happy and contented person, I, today, with a bigger house and a greater income, envy him. He was at peace with himself and with God. He was truly an eidler man. His greatest joy was to see me called to the Torah in his synagogue; and he took great pride in my knowledge of Judaism. From him I learned the beauty of the spirit and the joy that one can derive from belief in and communion with God.

My grandmother Feige was the epitome of the woman of valor described in the Book of Proverbs. She, like her husband, was also kind, simple, and loving. She was kind to all her grandchildren and generous to everyone, regardless of position or religion. She was kind and generous to the Christian peasant and Jew alike. But, above all, she was a very loving and caring grandmother. She rose early in the morning to bake bread, not only for the family, but also for the store. Without her efforts, there could not have been a store. She came to Munkacs monthly to replenish the store's stock, taking with her on the train many bundles and packages of merchandise. She bore bolts of calico, leather pieces used by the peasant farmers to make moccasins, sugar, salt, and flour. At those times she always stayed with us, and she never came empty-handed. Usually she brought fresh butter of a golden color that tasted extraordinarily good, cottage cheese, or other delights for her five grandchildren. The stress of business often resulted in headaches which she treated with old-fashioned remedies. It was my task to run to the druggist and buy leeches that my mother applied to her neck and upper back as a sure-fire remedy for her migraines. The leeches, she told me, drew out the bad blood and thereby relieved her headache. Like my mother, brother, sister, aunts, and cousins, she perished at Auschwitz.

To me, my maternal grandparents' village Talamas was, and in my memory still is, synonymous with paradise. Long before I had heard of Shangri-La I experienced magic in this little village nestled in the Carpathian Mountains. My life there during my summer vacation in July and August was free from worries, concerns, and stress. Of course, for the most part, the sense of freedom that I experienced in Talamas was due mostly to the absence of stress that came from being at school six days a week and in afternoon studies with the rabbi. But there were also other reasons. First, there was the joy of living in the beautiful Carpathian Mountains where the weather in the summer was just the right temperature with cool nights and warm days. The road that skirted the base of the mountain in front of my grandparents' home consisted of deep dust disturbed only twice a week when the bus from Volovec made its way to the distant villages in the mountains. When it rained, the dust turned to ankle-deep mud. What joy it gave me to hurry out to walk in the mud, feeling it squishing through my toes. Once a day the train from Munkacs to the Polish border chugged along, pulled by two steam engines spouting smoke and exerting great effort to climb the steeper grades in the mountains. Often, when we heard its whistle, we ran up the hill to the tracks to see whether we could beat the train to the crossing. At other times we waited for it, ready with our copper pennies to place on the track and have the heavy wheels of its cars flatten them to thin oval shapes. The cool air that descended from the snow-capped mountains mingled with the fragrance of the tall, majestic pines and provided me, and I am sure every one there, with a most soothing remedy for troubled minds.

There were two streams nearby. The larger one, the Kolobanye, was full of trout, and it was here that I acquired my love of fishing. I did not need fancy gear. I did not have split bamboo rods with tapered lines and leaders. I never saw anyone casting a tied fly or traversing the stream in heavy rubber waders. My outfit consisted of a willow branch and a length of heavy black thread to which I tied a strand of a horse's tail with whatever hook I possessed. Of course, the hook was baited with flies that I managed to catch alive. I became quite agile in catching flies with my hand. Once the hook was baited, I stood behind a boulder and danced the fly above the stream in a quiet pool, imitating the dance of various mosquito-like creatures with gossamer wings that danced on top of the water. The sound of the fast-rushing and clear waters of the stream and the opportunity for solitude led me to explore my inner self. It is difficult to describe the mystical sense of calm that descended upon me, but it was quite different from my normal experiences in the city. In Talamas one experienced a sense of tranquility. There, I never needed to rush. There was no need for a timepiece, and life was not governed by a timetable so characteristic of city life, even in such a small city like Munkacs. I rose when I awoke. Breakfast was always ready, and most of the time it was just a slice of bread and butter. While all this contributed significantly to my sense of well-being, it would have not been the marvelous place that I have in my memory were it not for the Jewish young men and women in the village; after all, a good life exists only through one's association with good people.

Spread out along the dusty road lived about six or seven Jewish families. They, like my grandfather, were Chassidic families, hard-working although poor and with little education and hardly any knowledge of the world and its politics. They lived in two worlds. First, there was the real world of everyday life. This was a world of toil, of farming or some trade like shoemaking or tailoring. Then, of course, they also lived in a spiritual world in which they had a personal relationship with God. This relationship was maintained through their unwavering faith, their meticulous observance of the ritual laws and of the Sabbath, and a fervent belief in life after death and the coming of the Messiah when all the dead will rise to live in an everlasting world of peace.

The daily life of these people took place around their village, where they worked in the fields, growing vegetables necessary for their yearly subsistence and hay for winter fodder for the cows. They planted primarily beans, peas, potatoes, beets, carrots, and cabbage, vegetables that could be stored for the winter. Most had a cow, which provided milk, butter, and cheeses, and chickens. All of them also had some other enterprise, be it a store, a lumber business, a kosher butcher shop, a mineral-water bottling operation from springs on their property, or whatever kind of business fate provided. Their diet, meticulously kosher for the most part, was the same as their non-Jewish neighbors, consisting primarily of bread, dairy food, and hearty vegetable soups.

In some ways Jews and Christians were alike. Both lived in small, often one-room homes, with a plot of land. The observance of the Sabbath, however, made a significant difference between the two groups. First, Jews, unlike the Christian peasants, were devoted to the spiritual world that was associated with the Sabbath observance and its special meals. Tradition required that one had to have meat and fish for that day. When meat was not available, and that was the general rule, there was always a chicken. To comply with the tradition of having fish for the Sabbath, which was a rarity, a dish made of chicken breasts was prepared known as *falshe fish* or false, i.e., substitute, fish.

Huklivoh, a larger village than Talamas and a scant one and a half miles away, was the center of the area's Jewish life. In Huklivoh was situated the synagogue; the *shochet*, the ritual slaughterer; the rabbi who was qualified to judge on matters of ritual and *kashruth*; the *mikvah*, the ritual bath; and last but not least the *Chevra Kadisha*, the burial society. In Huklivoh, in short, were all the institutions that were indispensable to Jewish life. For life in the small villages in the Carpathian Mountains was hard, a constant struggle for survival; nonetheless, Jews and non-Jews alike accepted their circumstances without too much complaint. Both were secure in the belief in an existence of life after death. However, Jews were also sure of the coming of the Messiah, a time when they would be granted the ultimate rewards the revival of the dead and their existence in a world of peace and plenty.

My mother maintained her belief in the world to come and related to me the wonders of that era, a time when no one would have to work, when all foods would be grown on trees, and like the manna that Jews received in the desert, all the fruits would taste as the consumer wished. Of course, there was an additional component to the Messianic Era, and that was revenge. The Messiah would take revenge on those who contributed to our 2,000 years of suffering and humiliation. All the boys in Talamas believed in the coming of the Messiah, and all had their own stories of the wonders of that future world. Till then, as I well knew, they were generous, considerate, and helpful people.

There were in Talamas about eight or nine young people of my age, and I spent a great part of my summer with them.

From them, I learned to distinguish the poisonous from the edible mushrooms and the best places to find them. With them, I went to gather wild strawberries, raspberries, and blueberries, all free for the taking. They shared with me their secret places where the best hazelnuts grew, and it was from them that I learned some Chassidic legends as well as their superstitions. We hunted for bats, which were nailed above the transoms of entrance doors, assuring good luck. They reinforced the belief in the evil eye and how to negate its power. Because of these friends, life in Talamas was never dull. I took part in all of the activities from cutting hay to catching fish, illegally of course, sometimes with our hands alone and some times with homemade traps. Most of them lived in small, one-room, straw-thatched, mud-floored, adobe-like houses with the stalls for their cows attached to the houses. They had their own fun, and sometimes it was at my expense. For instance, the time they induced me to poke a stick into a beehive, and I was attacked mercilessly.

But unlike in Talamas, in Munkacs most Chassidic Jews were not content with their lives. Quite often they were hostile toward the disciples of other Chassidic rebbes. I remember when a group of Chassidim who opposed the Munkacser rebbe came one Sabbath to our synagogue, not to pray, but to throw eggs at the rebbe. The stain of that shame remained on the wall till we were taken away to the concentration camp.

As much as they disliked other rebbes, they all hated the Zionists with a passion. They saw Zionism as a threat to what they considered to be appropriate Jewish life, one that was sanctioned by God. After all, did not God force the Baal Shem Tov to abandon his trip to Israel, indicating that the Jews' return to that land can only be legitimate when the Messiah will take us there? They also rejected the use of Hebrew as a daily language. For them, it was reserved for the study of the Torah and Talmud and for prayers.

Competition ruled most Jews' lives in Munkacs, who sought to make money above and beyond a mere *parnosoh* (subsistence). The rich were not completely selfish, for they did provide for the poor, perhaps not so much because of their moral sense but because they believed in the traditional dictum, charity saves one from death. In its incipient state, Chassidic rabbis had advocated an ideal and utopian philosophy of life and were proponents of humanism. However, by my lifetime, the beauty of its early philosophies had deteriorated into pettiness and hatred. Their beliefs in the miraculous qualities of their own rabbis compared with other Chassidic rabbis were similar to the futile and silly speculation of how many angels can dance on the head of a pin. But I learned from my grandfather the tales of the great Chassidic rebbes, and I was able to derive from his description of their lives the true beauty that was at the center of authentic Chassidism.

Chapter Two
**The World of**
**My Youth**

My parents gave me a wonderful boyhood. I was blessed with a true *Yiddische Mame*, a very understanding and kind Jewish Mother who influenced my emotional being and a father who exerted great influence on my intellectual thinking.

My most memorable times are the Saturday mornings when my brother, sister, and I squeezed into my parents' beds. At such times he talked to me, the oldest son, about social issues. Although he was familiar with Marx and discussed his ideas, he did not accept it as dogma. He was especially skeptical about Marx's view of capitalism. After all, my father was a merchant and by definition a bourgeois capitalist. He owned a book and stationery store located in the central part of the city on Rakoczi Street across from the city hall. His intellectual curiosity had been acquired as an apprentice printer. As he was typesetting, he was also reading, which led to his love of books, a characteristic that I inherited from him. His love of books influenced his decision to open a bookstore.

Most important, his reading led to politics rooted in the philosophy of French socialism, especially Anatole France's ideas. Because of his interest in politics and political philosophy, my father became involved in our city's politics. At the age of twenty, he successfully ran for the position of city councilman. On his advice (perhaps insistence), I read Anatole France's cynical outlook of human history depicted in his novel *The Penguin Island* in my teens.

Through my youth till he returned from the concentration camps, my father led a traditional Jewish life. He observed the Sabbath and all the holidays; yet one already could see the influence of modernity. He shaved and never wore *tzitzis*, the four-cornered garments with wool fringes which were an absolute requirement for the truly Orthodox. His religious orthodoxy, I believe, was not so much a matter of conviction as it was his desire not to hurt his parents or my mother. He was also an ardent Zionist without ever belonging to a particular Zionist party. He called himself an *algemeiner* Zionist, a general Zionist, a follower of the ideals set forth by Theodore Herzl, an advocate for the need of a Jewish homeland as a safe haven and refuge against antisemitism. Still, he accepted all forms of Zionism, including the right-wing Betar movement, which advocated military action to secure Palestine as a Jewish homeland. In fact, he took me along to meet Zhabotinsky, the founder of this revisionist movement, when he visited my hometown in 1934. I doubt that there are many alive who have had the privilege to meet Zeev Zhabotinsky.

It was because of my father's commitment to Zionism that he, together with Dr. Kugel, Dr. Sternbach, and a number of others, started the Hebrew grade and high school that I, as well as my brother and sister, attended. The Hebrew Gymnasium

was a Zionist school committed to two principles: Zionist idealism and academic excellence. The school became noted for its
graduates' accomplishments.

Although the *L'affaire* Dreyfus, the accusation and conviction based upon false evidence of Captain Dreyfus, a Jew, as
a German spy, had taken place a few years before my father's
birth, its impact on him was great. He realized that the history
of Christianity had amply shown that antisemitism was very
much part of it and that the future existence of Jews could only
be assured if an independent Jewish state would become a reality. Together with his commitment to Zionism, he also imparted
a desire for the ideals of justice. By establishing the Hebrew
Gymnasium, my father hoped to change ancient Hebrew from a
language used solely to study sacred texts to a modern language
that would be an essential instrument to modernize Jews and
help them leave the medieval cocoon in which they had existed
for centuries.

Under my father's influence, studying both secular and
sacred subjects seemed to become the central focus of my life.
I began my religious training at the age of five when I was
brought to the *Cheder*. The Cheder, literally room, referred to
the schools in which a Jewish boy began his studies of prayer,
the *Choomosh* (the five books of Moses), and the rudiments of
the Talmud. In the barren room with a long table surrounded by
benches, were about 30 young boys of five and six. At the head
of the table sat the teacher, stern and stoic, who tolerated no
nonsense, no frivolity, no talking, no laughter, not even smiles.
He was in charge of a serious task: to indoctrinate us into the
traditions of our people and to teach us how to read our prayers.
The teacher, the rebbe, often a taciturn gaunt person with a bamboo switch in his hand, ruled the class dictatorially. Intimidation
and shaming were his tools of discipline. An offending student
would have to stand on a chair while the rest of the class was to
pass by and hit him with the bamboo switch. There were other-
shaming punishments as well.

My father did not tolerate my attendance in a school with such a debilitating atmosphere, and I soon switched to study with a semiprivate rabbi. A semiprivate rabbi took only three or four students, most often to implement a meager income. This person also, my father felt, was too narrow in his view and knowledge. My father seemed to be looking for a person who could impart to me a broader perspective of Judaism. He sought a teacher who was familiar not only with traditional Judaism, the Talmud, but also one who at the same time was familiar with the Prophets, Jewish history, and Jewish philosophy. Eventually, I began my studies with Rabbi Jacob, a man who had a profound influence on my thinking.

Munkacs also had scholars who found delight in knowledge, not in rote memorization, but in novel interpretation of the ancient texts and in seeking new understanding. One such person was my rabbi, my teacher, Rabbi Yaakov, with whom I studied for over seven years, that is, till I graduated from the gymnasium. He was a most unusual person. He was a very devout Jew, a *dayan*, a judge (a member of the Jewish court), who like all devout Jews wore the caftan and fur hat on the Sabbath, but unlike others of his ilk, was also a scholar of Hebrew literature and Jewish history. From him I learned not only the beauty of knowledge but also that religiosity and devotion do not necessarily make one a *ch'nyok*, an uncouth and close-minded person. He was different from other hardcore Chassidim. Although like the other Chassidim he wore the straymel and bekeshe (fur hat and caftan), he was not encumbered by the yoke of traditionalism; that is, he was an enlightened person. The combination of Rabbi Yaakov's spirituality and his willingness to explore beliefs and views beyond the borders imposed by Orthodox dicta made him, in my father's view, a good teacher for me.

My father believed in the paramount value of education"Son," he often expressed to me, "One cannot make appropriate decisions, even about religion, without well-rounded knowledge." It was his intention that I become a well-rounded and educated person, which included a religious education. He did not wish that I learn Judaism in the traditional way, to study in a *Yeshiva* (a traditional religious school) where emphasis would be placed on rote memorization of the Talmud with a strict acceptance of the infallibility and inerrancy of both Biblical and Talmudic scripture. In my father's view, proper study must lead to questioning traditional interpretation, to probe beyond accepted meaning. Only by this method, that is, through the dialectic method, can one gain true understanding.

Rabbi Yaakov, because he lived in two worlds, the world of Jewish tradition and the world of Jewish modernity, represented the type of teacher my father sought for my religious education. Like my maternal grandfather, Rabbi Yaakov was a patient man. He was gaunt, a thin body with deep-set, dark, and fiery eyes. His appearance projected, at least to me, the semblance of a saintly ascetic. He loved to study, to seek the meaning in a text. No wonder he loved the ancient Talmudic scholars; he saw in them people like himself who took great delight in learning and not necessarily in piety. One of his heroes was the great scholar, Elisha ben Abuya, who was also known as the different one who dared to challenge the traditional point of view, especially concerning an existential nature of God and offering an interpretation of ritual laws. Because of him I, too, accepted Elisha, "The Different One," as one of my heroes. Rabbi Yaakov's tenderness was one reason why he could impart the joy of intellectualism. With him I studied a variety of subjects: Talmud, of course, but also the fourteen volumes of Jewish and Chassidic history by Dubnow, and later Maimonides' *Guide to the Perplexed*. My most favorite text, however, was Bialik and Ravnitsky's *The Book of Legends from the Talmud and Midrash*. Of course, he prepared me for my bar mitzvah and helped me with my presentation of a *chidush*, the act of finding a new meaning to a Talmudic text. This gentle person, a true representative of an *eidler* man and great scholar, did not survive the Holocaust. His memory is etched in my consciousness.

Compared to the other schools in the city, the Hebrew grade school and gymnasium was small. There were but single classes for each grade, and none exceeded 30 students. Classes were held Sunday through Friday. Although the school emphasized secularism and could not be considered an advocate for the Jewish religion, nonetheless, classes were not held on the Sabbath. We also wore skullcaps so that we would not enrage the Orthodox Jews who constituted the majority not only of Jews but also of the city's population. All these considerations were to no avail. To Orthodox Jews, headed by Chaim Elazar Shapiro, the Rabbi of Munkacs, the Hebrew gymnasium violated a sacred tradition, for the language of instruction was Hebrew, a language which in his view (as well as to most Orthodox Jews) was sacred and to be reserved for the study of sacred texts only.

In my secularly oriented school, we studied Hebrew as a modern language. Subjects like history, mathematics, and physics were also taught in Hebrew. We used Hebrew not as a sacred language but as a secular language, like any other language. We believed the adage coined by Eliezer ben Yehudah, the father of Modern Hebrew: There cannot be a revival of a people without the revival of its language. Modern Hebrew was to be the mechanism, the Zionist believed, that would change the submissive ghetto-mentality Jews into a proud and independent people. Just as the Ten Commandments had given the Egyptian slaves a national identity, so would Modern Hebrew transform the European Jews, whose motto had been don't rock the boat, into people with great courage and daring. This new identity would be rooted in biblical history the heroes of which are indisputably courageous. To the Orthodox, the language for everyday communication was Yiddish and never Hebrew, the holy language used only for the ritual study of ancient texts. Still, there were enough people in the city and the surrounding towns who sent their children to the Hebrew gymnasium to enable it to flourish and expand.

The rabbi of Munkacs sought to stop what he considered the great sacrilege, the secularization of the Hebrew language. He threatened to excommunicate all those who attended the Hebrew elementary school and the Hebrew gymnasium and especially their parents. The rabbi, of course, did not find universal support for his proposal. Throughout the Jewish world, the Zionist movement had begun to grow slowly, providing a substitute for the philosophy and worldview of ancient Orthodoxy. Its followers looked forward to the establishment of modern Israel as a Jewish homeland without waiting for the magic of the Messiah and without reestablishing the ancient Temple and animal sacrifices.

There were clashes between the students of the gymnasium and the students of the Munkacs *Yeshiva* (rabbinical school). The Orthodox rabbis believed that only God could redeem the Jews in the Diaspora where they had languished for almost two millennia. One such clash between the Zionists and the disciples of the rabbi of Munkacs occurred when each group celebrated an important event on the same Sunday. One was the wedding of the rabbi's daughter, and the second was the first graduation from the Hebrew gymnasium.

These two events occurred on the same weekend in June of 1932 and both events were filmed for newsreel. The rabbinical students became enraged and marched to the gymnasium and began to throw rocks, breaking the school's windows till the police stopped them. Even though they never went to movies, the idea that both events would be shown together was completely unacceptable. Intra-Jewish intolerance is not new. It preceded this event by 2000 years in the battles between the Pharisees and the Sadducees.

In many ways my father was a brave man. He dared to declare his political position as well as his commitment to

Zionism. In one event in particular, these beliefs were tested. My cousin's circumcision was celebrated at a well-attended lunch. The tables were set with white tablecloths. Bottles of wine, sparkling water, and of course slivovitz were served at each table. At the head of the table of honor sat the Munkacser rebbe, who was my physician uncle's patient as well as my cousin's *mohel*, i.e., the ritual circumciser. I was a young boy of eight and my father brought me to the rebbe, sitting at the head of the table, surrounded by many of his disciples. As the cousin of the circumcised boy, the rebbe offered me the privilege of eating *sherayim* (leftovers in his plate.) It was a custom that the rebbe would invite his honored disciples to eat out of his plate. As a matter of courtesy, he asked me what grade and school I attend. Being eight, honest, and not knowing the rebbe's extreme hostility to Zionism, I replied that I was enrolled in third grade in the Hebrew-speaking school. The rabbi ended his conversation with me and turned away from my father and me. My father knew that in a city where the rebbe had great influence he could harm my father's business. However, so strong was my father's commitment to the ideals of Zionism that he did not seek to hide his true feelings. But my father's views diametrically opposed the rabbi's. Chassidic Jews' opposition to Zionism was rooted in two beliefs. First, as I have stated, they believed that Jews' legitimate return to Israel could occur only when the Messiah would lead them there. This view was derived, as I have indicated, from a legend associated with the experiences of the Baal Shem Tov, the founder of the Chassidic movement. Secondly, the Munkacser rabbi, like many other Orthodox rabbis, was totally convinced that a school that used the sacred language for everyday communication would lead to assimilation, to the loss of religious identity, and to the rejection of tradition and the ancient way of life. He vehemently opposed the Hebrew gymnasium and strongly urged Jews to send their children to the Russian-language school, which, of course, many did. Finally, the Israel advocated by the Zionist would be a secular land without rebuilding the Temple and the resumption of animal sacrifices. This reality violated the hopes of the Orthodox Jews, who each day prayed for God's return to Israel and the resumption of sacrifices.

My mother was a kind, loving, and a very romantic woman. She, for instance, loved Rudolph Valentino, especially his movie *The Sheik*. She brought love and tenderness into our home, a place that was completely void of strife and harsh words. I did not realize how blessed our home was until I visited a classmate's home.

Probably when I was in the fifth grade in the gymnasium (here, equivalent to the eighth grade), I was invited to visit the home of my classmate Bondi, for according to my mother we were related. His mother and my mother, I was told, were cousins from neighboring villages. It was my first visit to his house. They lived in an upper-class neighborhood in a stately home. I was flattered by this invitation. I was brought into a large living room with tall ceilings and impressive doors and of course a room without beds. In contrast, my siblings and I slept in one room that not only was our bedroom but also served as our dining and living room. Soon, however, I wished I were home. In the next room Bondi's parents began to argue loudly, which both embarrassed and disturbed me. Never in my life had I heard parents argue, though it did not seem to bother my classmate. I was used to peace and tranquility.

Sleeping next to their bedroom, I had often heard my father talk about various problems, some related to the store, others to the family's expectations that he financially help his brother. My mother would listen patiently and then respond:

"Chaim (my father's Hebrew name), you are very wise; you'll know what to do." She divided her time between raising the children, running a household, and working in the store where she served as the cashier. In slack periods she kept herself busy by knitting and crocheting. She had to be productive. As a small village girl, she had not had an extensive education, but married to the owner of a bookstore, she furthered her education by constant reading. She had a romantic soul. "Mother, how was the movie?" I used to ask her after my parents returned from the theater. "It was wonderful; I cried all through it."

Her selection of books to read, like her selection of movies, was governed by romanticism. The authors she admired were Cronin, Broomfield, Buck, and Margaret Mitchell. While the welfare of her children was foremost on her mind, she also extended her protective friendship to other members of the family, particularly to her younger sisters-in-law. She protected them from my paternal grandmother who was a domineering woman, a matriarch who sought to control every part of her family's life. Only once did I experience her wrath when she cursed me. I cannot remember the particulars. This occurred after my grandfather died, and she had all her meals with us. For some reason, she became angry at me and shouted, "Go to hell." (The actual Yiddish expression is "Go into the ground," a synonym for dying and being buried.) Regardless of what I had done and how angry this made my grandmother, my mother would not stand for any one hurting her children, either by deed or word. If we honor the sensitive soul in a man, she was the true representative of a woman's sensitive soul. Indeed, I can truly say that she, like her mother, represented the virtuous woman described in Proverbs chapter 31. The greatest assets of a virtuous wife and mother are love, care, and trust and my mother was the epitome of them all.

As I entered my teens, the question of my future became a topic of discussion between my father and me. His dream for me was that I attain two degrees: to become a modern rabbi who also had a doctorate in philosophy. The persons whom he admired most were people like Samson Hirsch and Samuel Holdheim, leaders in Jewish Reform movements; Martin Buber; and historians Heinrich Graetz and Simon Dubnow. He hoped that I would follow the path of these great Jewish thinkers who sought to modernize Judaism. I, on the other hand, hoped to become a physician. What I sought was both freedom from small-town life and freedom from the forces of tradition. I felt Medicine, because of its high prestige and income, would give me the opportunity to live my life as I pleased. My life, while on the one hand comfortable, was also enslaving. I was bound to tradition. I remember one of my first acts of rebellion against religious autocracy in my preteens. Traditionally, Purim ended with a great feast at which all the family gathered around my grandfather's table. It was a day of joy, and gypsy musicians came to my grandfather's house to provide both Hungarian and Yiddish music, befitting entertainment for a great feast. On the same day one of my favorite Andy Hardy movies was being shown in the local cinema. Of course, I opted to go to the movies. After all, if this was a day of joy, then I felt I should enjoy myself and follow my own sense of pleasure. My father found me at the theater waiting in line to enter and forced me to come home, though he could not force me to eat and be part of the feast.

Throughout my life I lived in two worlds, the world of tradition and the world of reason and modernity. These two worlds have never been nor are they today in alignment. Frequently, traditional ideas and beliefs are diametrically opposed to modernity. Traditionalism and modernity formed the thesis and antithesis in the historical dialectic, and I have often been caught in the middle of these two forces. It has always been difficult to resolve the conflict between my commitment to traditionalism, which has been part of my family life and into which I have been socialized, and modern liberal views and interpretations of historical Judaism. Challenging tradition, I suppose, has always led to battle between the generations. In my instance, this battle was not so much between me and my father; rather, it was a battle between my two self-concepts, between my entity as a historical Jew and my desire to be modern. This battle was the result of my education, between my Talmudic education and modern science, and led to an emotional disturbance that comes from a divided consciousness.

Early in my teens I fell in love with America, at least with the America that I envisaged from the movies. I perceived this country as a great and vibrant land, as lively, energetic, rich, and, of course, the epitome of freedom. I did not know the true America. I fell in love with an ideal, a vision, and not with the real America. The last was unknown to me. I fell in love with what I saw in the movies, especially with a projected image of American youths who were free from the constraints of tradition. I saw America as a country totally committed to the future and far less concerned with the past than European countries. I liked Shirley Temple because she expressed the joy of life and a vibrancy and optimism that was uncharacteristic of Jewish youths in Europe. For this reason I became a card-carrying member of the Shirley Temple fan club. To me, America reflected a can-do attitude that was portrayed by Mickey Rooney and Judy Garland in the Andy Hardy series. I fell in love with Deanna Durbin who dared to challenge the male domination of music. In the movies I saw young people acting freely, unhampered by ancient traditions and ritual laws. This country, I believed, was where my future lay. The vibrancy of this country to me was also reflected in its music. The sound, the tempo, and the excitement of jazz captivated me. I never missed a showing of *Broadway Melodies*; the sound of the trumpets and above all the wailing of the clarinets of Artie Shaw and Benny Goodman captivated my imagination. The term *licorice stick*, a term used by Artie Shaw for his clarinet became an integral part of my vocabulary. I was drawn to this ideal country as a moth to flames.

My brother Benjamin, or as we called him Bejnish in Yiddish, was five years my junior, and my sister Esther, or Edit, was nine years younger. I am sorry to say that I have few memories of them, but I was eighteen and had graduated from the gymnasium when Edit was only nine. The gap between my brother and sister and me was far too great at that time in our lives, and consequently we shared very few experiences. It was only in our last year together that we began to have more in common. My brother who was just thirteen fell in love with the girl I was dating. It was the first time that we had a brotherly heart-to-heart talk. A more poignant memory that I cherish comes from late fall in 1943. Since I could not enroll in the university, I worked in my father's store. I took over the management of both the fiction and nonfiction book sections. I was given a salary, and, hence, I considered myself affluent, at least for a boy my age and living at home. One late afternoon I saw my sister in the company of her girlfriends on her way home from school. I stopped them and asked my sister to join me for cake and a soft drink in a patisserie nearby. She had great pride that her older brother asked her out. She was nine years old, soon to be taken to the gas chambers of Auschwitz.

Munkacs, originally Mukacevo, while part of the Czechoslovak Republic and populated by four nationalities, was nonetheless a tranquil city. Jews, like all other nationalities, had citizenship rights, and although there were many individuals who were antisemitic, unlike some other countries in the thirties, the Czechoslovak Republic did not institute any anti-Jewish laws. But by the mid- 1930s, we had begun to see the signs of change, of impending doom for European Jews. Even in countries not yet occupied by Hitler, such as Poland and Romania, there were attempts to institute anti-Jewish laws. These countries, for instance, sought to outlaw the slaughter of animals in accordance with Jewish ritual laws, in essence disallowing kosher meat. But, of course, the greatest threat to continued Jewish existence was the rise of Hitler. Germany, a country that had prided itself in its high achievements in literature, philosophy, and human rights, turned away from the humanism exemplified by the Frankfurt School of Social Research and embraced antisemitism.

I remember the Friday evening service in the spring of 1938 when, at the age of twelve, I became conscious of a future of foreboding. When my father and I arrived at the synagogue for the Sabbath service, I noticed a change in the mood among those gathered for prayer. The congregation, instead of devoting itself to prayer and to the chanting of joyful Sabbath songs, was talking in low voices. Instead of the joy and calm that usually reflected the peace of the Sabbath, faces now expressed nothing but sadness as congregants discussed their grave concerns for their futures. They were talking about the news of the day, Germany's Anschluss of Austria. Their immediate concern was: Does this event foreshadow dire things to come?

The summer of 1938 was a difficult period in the lives of all Jews in Czechoslovakia. This small country, the most democratic country that I have ever known, was sacrificed on a putative altar of peace. I am speaking, of course, about the infamous Munich conference. The Munich conference consisted of discussions among Chamberlain, Prime Minister of Great Britain; Daladier, President of France; Mussolini, Italy's dictator; and Hitler, German Chancellor. Both France and England conceded to the dictates of Hitler and agreed to accept the division of Czechoslovakia. According to the agreement, Germany would get the Sudetenland, the Western part of Bohemia where many Germans lived, and Hungary would get the Southern part of Slovakia and of the Sub-Carpathian region, Ruthenia. My hometown Munkacs, a city in Ruthenia, would be turned over to Hungary. I still remember the newsreel depicting Chamberlain as he disembarked from the plane that brought him back from the Munich Conference, waving a piece of paper and declaring "peace in our time." As we now know, his well-intentioned appeasement of Hitler did not work. Hitler and the Hungarians were to occupy their territories on November 1, just a week before my Bar Mitzvah.

The news of the change in our status brought sadness to all of us who lived in my city, save the Hungarian nationals. The few months before the Hungarians were to take over the city, the community was in a state of turmoil. All the Czech nationals moved out of the city and returned to the part of Bohemia that they hoped would remain an independent Czech republic. But what mattered most to me is that most of my teachers who were Polish citizens saw the handwriting on the wall and opted to leave to try to find their way to Palestine.

On November 1, Mukacevo, my city, became Munkacs, part of the Hungarian Kingdom. Suddenly, I was no longer a Czech citizen, but was I a Hungarian? Hungary had already established anti-Jewish laws brought along with the occupation of my town. Only those who considered themselves Hungarian nationals were happy about the change in governments. To the rest of us, the Hungarians in the area were, for the most part, illiterate peasants.

There is a story that was told about a ceremony at the bridge crossing the river Latorca. This river marked the new borders between Hungary and the newly created mini-country Ruthenia. At the river, a Czech captain formally turned the city over to a Hungarian colonel. The Czech captain gave a formal speech in his own language. Of course, the Hungarian colonel did not understand what the other was saying. Out of courtesy, the Czech officer repeated his speech now in English; still the Hungarian colonel did not understand. As a last resort the Czech repeated his speech in French, the language of diplomacy, and left. Turning to his soldiers, the Hungarian colonel said, "You see how ignorant the Czechs are? They cannot even speak Hungarian."

A week after the Hungarians took over the city, I became thirteen and performed my rites of passage, my bar mitzvah, which according to tradition marked my transition from childhood to adulthood. Because of my parents' unhappiness with the political changes and their fear for the future, their mood, like those of most Jews in my hometown, had changed. Instead of the jubilant and optimistic spirit characteristic of our community during the Czech regime, the faces and body language of the Jews in the city reflected an overriding depression, a sadness precipitated by a sense of foreboding of evil times. We were already aware of the hostile laws enacted by the Germans in their country as well as the antisemitic laws in Hungary. For this reason, my parents wished to cancel my bar mitzvah celebration. Only because of my insistence, pointing out to them the numerous hours I had spent in mastering the Hebrew texts and in memorizing the chants and the speech that I was to give in Hebrew, did my parents relent and give in to my pleas.

However, it was not the great and joyous celebration that I had hoped for. Compared to the original plans discussed a year earlier that would have included more guests and my classmates, the scale of the affair was drastically reduced. My parents invited far fewer people, excluding my friends, to a *Shalosh S'udoth*. On Sabbath, according to tradition, Jews partake in three feasts: Friday evening, the Sabbath noon meal, and the third meal, called Shalosh S'udoth in Hebrew. This was not a sumptuous meal. It consisted of a chopped fish dish, often called *Gefilte Fish* in Yiddish, cakes, wine, and slivovitz, a plum brandy. In attendance were my family, some of my parents' friends, and two of my gymnasium teachers who had not yet departed for Palestine. Absent from the celebration were my maternal grandparents who lived in the newly created mini-country of Carpathia. This country had a very brief existence; in January of 1939, the Hungarians invaded the country, at which time, my grandparents were reunited with the family.

The main event of the Shalosh S'udoth was my *d'roshoh* and *chidush*, an exegetic interpretation of a passage from the weekly chapter of the Torah. My fraternal grandfather, Elezer Yaakov, sat with a great, pleasant smile on his face. I was his oldest grandson living in our city (the eldest grandson currently live in St. Louis) and he took great pride in my achievement. He bestowed upon me the greatest honor I could have expected. At the end of my recitation, he came to me, took out his gold Elgin pocket watch and chain, his prized possession, bought during his stay in the United States, and gave it to me. Alas, this watch, together with other prized possessions, has been lost, taken from our home when we were deported to the concentration camps.

In spite of these political changes, I went to school the following Sunday. There were very few teachers, and the language of instruction had also changed. Most of my Hebrew-speaking teachers left seeking an opportunity to enter Palestine, and with their departure the dominance of the Hebrew language and the spirit of Zionism also vanished. Instead, the language of instruction, at least for a brief time until other Hebrew-speaking faculty could be hired, became predominantly Hungarian. Although I spoke some Hungarian, it was not my native tongue, and I was hardly proficient in it. Until I was about four, my great-grandfather Reb Beynesh, who spoke only Polish or Yiddish, lived with us. Hence, I grew up speaking Yiddish. At the age of five I started kindergarten where only Russian was spoken and had acquired it as my second language, and then, at six, I began speaking Hebrew. In haste I had to become proficient in Hungarian, now the primary language of instruction. In consequence of the new governmental orientation and the fact that most of the new teachers at the gymnasium were not Hebraists, many of the subjects that had been previously taught in Hebrew were now offered in Hungarian. Needless to say, the school also lost its great commitment to Zionism.

**Chapter 3**
**Prologue to the**
**Holocaust**

The history of yellow badges, yellow stripes, yellow circles, and yellow pointed dunce cap-like hats that were used to identify and denigrate Jews through the second Christian millennium in Europe had become familiar to me in my youth. But I had never thought that, now in the middle of the 20th century, a time that was post-Enlightenment when Europe had experienced democracy, we would be forced to wear a yellow armband, the symbol of shame and denigration.

The Hungarian regime that now ruled my hometown was an ally of Germany. In addition to its standing army, the Hungarians also introduced the Levente movement, an organization that functioned to train boys between the ages of 12 and 18 in military skills. By the age of 18, when they would be inducted into the army, they would then need less training. Every Thursday afternoon, donning our military caps, we started our training with close-order drills, marching, turning right and left and making about-faces, and especially standing at attention. A few weeks after this start, we were introduced to guns. We were issued a .22-caliber single-shot rifle and began our training in marksmanship.

Guns and hunting have never been a part of Jewish culture. Jewish laws forbid the eating of anything that has been killed improperly, that is, not according to ritual law. First and foremost, Jews may eat only those animals that chew their cud and have split hooves. These animals are to be killed by a special knife while they are sanctified by prayer. The eating of animals killed by gun, or even bow and arrow, is not permitted according to ritual law. Hence, guns and shooting never became a part of Jewish life. Guns and hunting belong solely to the non-Jewish world. Nimrod was a hunter, so was Esau, but not Jacob. Instead of being a hunter, Jacob was a scholar, at least so we were taught, and scholarship was the Jewish ideal. We always juxtaposed what was considered the Jewish ideal against the rest of the world, particularly the Christian world. Guns, hunting, and killing belonged to the Christian world. This view has been central to the Jewish culture of the Diaspora. It is not that Jews were always antigun or antiforce. We still celebrate Jewish victories defeating the Canaanites, and especially the Maccabean victories against Greece. The latter is commemorated as the Chanukah holiday. In spite of the many wars Jews had waged when they were still in their homeland, Jews have always stressed the universal value of peace. Peace is a moral value and ideal reiterated by most of the Prophets and repeated by the rabbis in the Talmud. We were taught, for instance, that God did not permit David to build the Temple to His service because he was a warrior. His son Solomon, as the meaning of his name indicates, was a king dedicated to peace who was given the task of building the Temple in Jerusalem. In fact, the rabbis have written that the surest sign that one is a true descendant of Abraham is if one is a seeker of peace (one who runs after peace). Neither my parents nor most Jewish adults in the city considered shooting and the acquisition of gun skills desirable activities.

In spite of the great emphasis on peace, Jews' opposition to guns, at least in my view, was not rooted either in Biblical or Talmudic laws. Instead, antiweapon, antimilitary prowess was a reaction against the values espoused by the dominant Christian culture. Jews' opposition to the acquisition of military skills (and that includes any use of weapons even for hunting) is a form of a *re-sentiment*, namely the attribution of value to qualities that stand in opposition to those of the ruling dominant group. In the Diaspora, Jews' stress on scholarship and opposition to gun culture are similar to the first- and second-century Christian emphasis on meekness, turning the other cheek, and love. These values, enumerated in the Beatitudes, were the consequence of Christian subordinate status in the Roman Empire. However, after Constantine, when Christians gained power and became the ruling class, humility had lost its original value.

Similarly, when the Jewish state Israel was born after World War II, militarism and gun culture again assumed an important part in Israel's life. It is not that the two-thousand-year-old value of peace had lost its moral force. Rather, that meek submissiveness had also died, together with most of the Diaspora Jews, in the Holocaust. We still hope for the coming of the Messianic period to bring a world in peace, but we no longer wait for Elijah the Prophet to come and avenge us for all the injustices imposed on us in the last millennium and half.

Regardless of how my parents felt about guns, the Talmudic dictum stresses that the "law of the land is the law," so the other Jewish youths and I accepted the gun. The idea of shooting a gun excited me. Perhaps that was because as a young Jew I was already imbued with a reaction against the submissive

philosophy that was at the center of Jewish-Christian relationship. Even though I had only a single experience with shooting,
it was sufficient for me to acquire a taste for firearms. First, to
my own surprise and that of the rest of the group, I had four
bull's-eyes out of five shots, which gave me some prestige.
Second, because the government gave me a gun, I thought that
I was to be equal to non-Jews. But my sense of equality did
not last long. In fact at the next week's Levente meeting, we
no longer were issued guns for practice shooting. Instead we
were given shovels, and with it my experience of humiliation
began. We were issued and ordered to wear yellow armbands
and were brought to military stables with instructions to clean
them. Notwithstanding our continued use of army caps, the yellow armbands that we were ordered to wear became, in our eyes,
precisely what they were meant to be, badges of shame, and the
loss of gun privileges were an official sign of distrust. For the
first time in my life, I was confronted with hostility of Christians
toward Jews.

The Hungarian government quite rapidly began institut-
ing various anti-Jewish laws. I soon became acquainted with
*numerus clausus*, an impressive Latin word which is a euphemism for quotas. Unlike some who in America today argue for
the inclusionary character of quotas, I see quotas as exclusion-
ary social devices. They do not reflect the ideals of universal-
ism, the treatment of all people according to the same standard.
To the contrary, quotas demand that some people, for whatever
reason, should be treated differently, either to be given prefer-
ences (as, for instance, the privileges given to the nobility) or
to be systematically denied their constitutional rights and privileges. The numerus clausus with which I became familiar were
of the latter. In my community, where the Jewish population
was over 60 percent and most stores had Jewish ownership, the
law of numerus clausus limited Jewish ownership to a scant six

percent of stores. Consequently, a great number of stores were forced to close. Three uncles and many of my father's cousins lost their right to earn a living because under the law they were denied merchants licenses. Many Jews tried to circumvent the law and started to do business sub rosa from their homes. Of course, such business enterprises were limited to intra-Jewish economic exchanges.

The same quota system was applied to University attendance. First, universities had to limit the attendance of Jews to seven percent. But in a short time the laws of numerus clausus were changed to *numerus nullus*, meaning the total exclusion of Jews from universities. With this edict, my chances to attend the university and my hopes to become a physician were, at least for the time being, eliminated.

These edicts were issued in 1939. The future for Jews was clearly visible, and it was a future of doom. Why didn't we leave? Although I was just 13, the future for Jews in Munkacs looked bad even to me. In January of 1939, I wrote to my Uncle Saul, in St. Louis, asking him to bring me to America. I sent him my birth certificate and informed him that conditions in Munkacs for Jews were deteriorating. I even confronted my father, who still had his store. I begged him, "Father let us leave; let us go to America." But, of course, neither of these was possible. The gates of the United States were shut and guarded by an immigration quota system instituted in 1924. It strongly limited immigration to the United States, particularly for people from Eastern Europe.

My family, like other Jewish families in Munkacs, and for that matter in all of Hungary, settled down to wait out the storm that was soon to become World War II. History has shown that such antisemitic flare-ups have frequently occurred in European countries. These historical events, at least as my parents interpreted them, taught them to become invisible, to be quiet, not to make waves, and to wait out the storm. In colloquial terms, we need but hunker down, and this too shall pass. Life will continue.

September 1, 1939, the Germans entered Poland from the west; Russia began its occupation of Poland from the east; and World War II began. Chamberlain's attempts to appease Hitler had not worked. No one, at least no one whom I knew, believed that appeasement would work. No one wanted war, but in this instance war was seen as the only means to our liberation. Huddled around the radio, with me as the guru and master of the controls, we listened to the BBC and hoped for prophetic encouragement. Every evening, till our radios were confiscated, my family, friends, and I huddled around the instrument, hoping for good news. "This is London calling" and "This is Radio Free Europe" were our watchwords. We followed the war news, hoping for a quick victory, but to no avail. War, at least for a while, settled down to stalemate with occasional exchange of gunshots between the French at the Maginot and the Germans at the Siegfried lines. In May 1940, the Germans, as they did in World War I, entered France from the north. They subdued both Holland and Belgium, and by June, after the tragic events at Dunkirk, France became a vassal state of Germany. Our hopes for a quick resolution of the war were shattered.

When Russia had occupied the Eastern half of Poland in 1940, it became Hungary's neighbor. The two countries now shared a border. At the same time, Stalin and Hitler entered, at least for a short while, into a covenant of peace and friendship. This friendship also affected the Russo-Hungarian relationship. Hungary, a member of the Axis and a friend of Germany, also benefited from the peace-and-friendship treaty. As a gesture of friendship, Russia returned the battle flags it had captured in 1849 when the czar came to help his cousin Franz Joseph subdue the Hungarian Revolution. In turn, Hungary added a third rail to the track between the Russian border and Volovec, a larger village just past my grandparents' home in the Carpathian Mountains. By widening the tracks, Hungary accommodated Russian trains. This friendship did not last long, for soon Germany attacked Russia, and Hungary allied itself with Germany and joined the war on the Axis side. Conditions in 1941 seemed, to us Jews, quite devastating. On the Western front, German bombers were hammering England; London was being destroyed; and at the same time Russia was forced to retreat almost to Moscow.

It was about this same period that my family first experienced the Holocaust. We received a letter informing us that most members of my mother's family living in Lemberg (Lwow) had been killed by the Germans. More so than before, we kept listening to the BBC, daring to disobey the law. More than ever before, we surreptitiously listened to the Hungarian edition of the news, hoping for some flicker of something positive. Alas, nothing in the news could cheer us. By this time, Jews could not leave the country, and many young Jewish men of military age were conscripted into work service. They were taken to the Russian Front, not to fight as soldiers, but to construct bunkers and quite often to clear minefields. On the High Holidays, our prayers became more desperate. "Oh Lord how long must we suffer?" we asked God and petitioned, "Our Father, our King, hasten our redemption."

The first event that brought us any hope came with Pearl Harbor and America's entry into the war. Most of the middle-aged Jews and older remembered that it was America's entry into the First World War that had brought it to a conclusion with an Allied victory. We were quite sure that Hitler's days were numbered and salvation was at hand.

Perhaps my parents were right about our course of action in the meantime. Perhaps, if we kept quiet and did not draw any attention to ourselves, the storm generated by Hitler would blow over and we would survive. For the next three years, we continued to live an almost normal existence. These were my late teen years, and my studies at school and with the rabbi continued. Spring 1943 came, and I prepared for my Matura. The Matura is the last examination, which covered all the subjects ever taken in the eight years of gymnasium study. One could achieve passing grades in all his classes but still, to receive a gymnasium diploma, the Bacheloriate, one needs to pass this last examination. The Matura consisted of four days of written examination; essays in Hungarian, Hebrew, and English; and the translation of a text from a selected Roman writer, in my instance, a selection from Marcus Tullius. A week later came the oral examination in which three students faced an examination board consisting of my gymnasium teachers and a chairman, usually a representative from a university, and at my examination this was a professor from the University of Debrecen in Hungary. I still remember all the questions to which I had to respond on my oral examination. I had to derive the formula for the solution of the quadratic equation, to discuss Boyle's law of gasses, to examine the Turkish invasion of Europe, to compare Madach's play The *Tragedy of Humanity* with Goethe's Faust, to speak on Achad Haam's philosophy (in Hebrew), to give a brief resumé of Keats, and to recite ten lines from *A Thing of Beauty*.

European high schools levels of achievement then far exceeded those in the United States. The struggle against the remnant of the feudal social system still continued. Social status was still rooted in the tradition of family name. True democracy, however, cannot be achieved unless and until the individual is given a chance for social mobility. A new social system, one rooted primarily in meritocracy, can rise only from educated classes. Hence, schools and education must be open to all regardless of family background. Admission must be guaranteed to all, but it is each person's responsibility to succeed.

Demand for quality is the sine qua non for mobility, and thus performance in class must be the means to mobility.

With great joy I was informed, a week after completing my examinations, that I would be awarded the Matura. Christian students with their Matura were heading for various universities or inducted into the military as officer candidates, but my fellow Jewish students and I were barred from the university. All we had to look forward to was being taken into the Hungarian Army for forced labor on the Russian Front. Meanwhile, I went to work in my father's store and continued to hope. My role in the store was to manage the book department, that is, all the books except textbooks. I had a steady job and an income that far exceeded the allowance I received as a student. As manager of the store's book section, I had to keep myself informed about all new books, fiction as well as nonfiction, a task that required continual reading.

There is a vignette I can recall from my very brief relationship with my sister Esther. Whenever I think of her, my memory reverts to this episode. My relationship with her had just been beginning to develop as she approached her 10th birthday. I mentioned it earlier, but now I shall describe it fully.

It was a late afternoon on a weekday when I accidentally met my sister together with all her girlfriends coming home from school. On this street was a Jewish bakery, a *cukrazda*, in Hungarian, a confectionary where people came to have a piece of cake, coffee, tea, or other refreshment. As I stopped to say "hello" to her, it suddenly occurred to me that it would be nice to ask her to come with me to the confectionary and be treated to a piece of cake, something that she had never done. "Esther," I said to her in front of her girlfriends, "Would you like to come with me to the cukrazda? You can have anything that you want," I added. Her eyes lit up; a pleasurable smile came to her face. I could see the great pride that enveloped her. I could see the envy on the other girls' faces and her joy that her older brother, older by nine years, had asked her to a treat that other children of her age seldom if ever got. I doubt that this memory, my only significant memory of Esther, will ever be eradicated from my mind.

I worked and hoped for the end of the Hitler-generated nightmare and to be freed from the oppressive antisemitic laws, as we heard about each Allied victory. The victory at El Alamein, the German defeat in Stalingrad, and the successful invasion of Italy, each was taken as a sure sign of the forthcoming freedom. However, all our joyful anticipation of a new era soon turned to unspeakable tragedy.

**Chapter Four**
**The Holocaust**

Hungary had been Germany's ally and sent troops to support its war effort in the invasion of Russia. In 1938, Hungary was rewarded for its pro-German stand. With Hitler's support, through various treaties and Chamberlain's and Daladier's submission to the Axis demands, Hungary reclaimed the territories it had lost to the newly created Czechoslovakia and Romania. Perhaps Hitler's affinity for Hungary reflected their common misfortunes and shame under the terms of the Treaty of Versailles.

It is true that Hungary, like other central European countries, had become a German ally out of a reluctant accommodation under duress rather than a belief in Hitler's ideology. I am sure that if Hungary had refused to join the alliance, it most likely would have been invaded and occupied by Germany years earlier. It would then have shared the fate of Norway, Belgium, Holland, Greece, and many other countries who felt the yoke of German occupation.

Despite this previous alliance and affinity, in March 1944, Germany invaded Hungary. Just before the Hungarians began commemorating their revolution of 1848, an attempt to become free from the Austrian Empire, they were again invaded and occupied by another Germanic country, ending Hungarian independence.

Perhaps in 1944 Hitler felt that Hungary, with Horty Miklos at its head, did not provide adequate support for the German war effort; and perhaps by this time Hitler had become paranoid and did not trust lesser allies like the Hungarians. Hitler might have felt that, given the first opportunity, Hungary would defect from the Axis. In any case, in mid-March, the German Army occupied Hungary and took Miklos as a hostage to Germany. The Hungarian parliament was dissolved, and the Hungarian Nazi party, the Hungarian Nyillas Party (meaning the arrow party) the symbol of which was two crossed arrows, took over the government. Hungary became Hitler's vassal state. No sooner had it taken over Hungary than the new Hungarian Nazi government, jointly with the Germans, started to implement Hitler's plan of the Final Solution, namely, the extermination of Hungarian Jewry. The first step in this plan was to create a ghetto and to force all Jews in the city into the fenced-off enclosures.

All Jews in Munkacs were ordered to move into the ghetto. The ghetto consisted of two separate areas in the city, both of which had a high density of Jewish population. These two areas were isolated from the rest of the city by a high barbed-wire fence. Many members of our family whose homes were declared to be outside of the ghetto had to move in with us because our home and that of my Uncle Michael, who lived in the same courtyard, were inside the ghetto walls. Mattresses were laid on floors and, when it did not rain, even outside in the courtyard.

Life in the ghetto was, at least as I remember it, a waiting time, merely a preamble to things unknown. Each day was punctuated by new rumors that seemed to have one common denominator, conditions will not be bad. These rumors, I have later been told, were initiated by the *Juden Rat*, the Jewish council in the ghetto that became the arm for carrying out German wishes, mainly German propaganda. All German orders were disseminated through this council. Members of the council, later rumors had it, were promised to be sent to Budapest where they would be safe from deportation, but I cannot assure the veracity of this information.

I tried to read during this period, but my mind was not at ease. My greatest diversion and occupation was dating the daughter of my Uncle Nathan's former brother-in-law, whose family had moved in with us. She was about one year my junior and I had tried to date her, unsuccessfully, earlier. Now the conditions made her captive in our house. My brother Benjamin, who was a few months shy of his 14th birthday, fell in love with her, the older woman. This was his first crush, a most difficult condition for a boy just entering puberty. He was tormented by his hopeless love, first, because she was older by three years and, also, because I, his older brother, dated her. Of course, dating is not the right word for the relationship. We kept company with each other since, in a sense, we were sharing a common prison cell. It was at this time that I had my first heart-to-heart conversation with my brother, which I mentioned previously.

We stayed a few weeks in the ghetto. Even though the future of the Jews in Munkacs seemed bleak and the destruction of our Jewish community was clearly inevitable, nonetheless, the Jews of the city remained passive. The thousand-year-old Jewish motto remained the same, "Wait and this too shall pass." We entered a period of anomie, of social disorganization. This disorganization was evident in the breakdown of all normal life. My mother, for instance, who was very Orthodox and all her life adhered stringently to laws of *Kashruth*, the ritual pre- and proscription pertaining to edible food, was now forced to violate these religious laws. To her sorrow, she now surreptitiously frequented the black market and bought pork products, the only meats that were available. Bacon, ham, and sausages were now stored in the pantry of our previously glat-kosher home. She justified this action to herself by saying, "Children need food." The violation of the ritual act was legitimized by the Talmudic reasoning of *pikuach nefesh*, namely, saving a life takes precedence over all ritual laws. Jewish law not only permits but mandates disregarding all ritual laws that will save a life. Based on this thesis, we stocked our larder with various nonkosher (*treyfa*) meat products, to be consumed only when kosher food was no longer available. "Dear God," she kept repeating as she hung the meat in our impeccable kosher pantry, "The children must eat. Isn't pikuach nefesh more important than being kosher?" And for a very short time in the pantry of our home that previously contained only food that would have satisfied the *mehadrin min hamhadrin*, the most observant and pious of all Jews, pork products hung. And of all treyfa food to have in one's home, the possession of pork was, perhaps, the most disturbing. Pork is not only treyfa, but it is the epitome of all forbidden foods, the sine qua non in a person's rejection of his Jewish identity. Life became a period of constant waiting for the next event. All routine was suspended, and no one knew what to do.

The Christian world outside the ghetto permitted and in some instances even took advantage of the Jews' misfortune. I am quite sure that there were many who began to move into the vacated Jewish homes and who looted the closed Jewish stores. The closing of all Jewish-owned businesses meant that my father had to pull down the steel shutters on Henryk Schönfeld's book and stationery store for the last time. While we were in the ghetto, Sarkadi, a long-time salesman in my father's store, came to our home with an outrageous offer. He wanted to buy my father's store although he did not have any money. If my father would transfer to him the store with all its contents, he offered to give my father a monthly stipend. My father felt betrayed by one whom he had for many years employed but who did not come to offer any help. To the contrary, Sarkadi came to take advantage of the situation. My father refused the offer. He would rather see the store destroyed than be blackmailed.

It was early one Friday morning in the beginning of April, about six a.m., when we heard the sound of gunfire. Immediately, we ran to the window overlooking the market, the direction from which the shots had come. From our window we could see police and soldiers shooting their rifles in the air. We soon learned what this commotion was all about, for shortly thereafter the police came into our home and told us that we were to leave. To emphasize the command, they proceeded to shoot into the ceiling or strike at us with their rifles butts, all the while shouting, "Gather up only those belongings which you can carry yourself, and be outside on the street in fifteen minutes." Of course, we were ready. We placed some clothes into suitcases, but above all else we packed food. We knew that food would be the most important item that we would need.

From our homes we were taken to a brick factory some miles away that was owned by our neighbor Kalus, in whose home I had spent a lot of time. The Kaluses had two daughters and a son and were wonderful people. The factory was the only place where thousands of people could be placed under a single roof. The brickyard had a large covered space where the raw bricks were placed to dry and be kept safe from rains before they were fired in the kiln. We stayed in this place about five or six days, that is, until the Hungarian police force gathered all the Jews from the outlying areas. Soon, my grandmother from Talamas, my Aunt Lujza, her husband, and two daughters were also brought there.

During these days there were many rumors. Most of them proposed that we would be shipped to Germany to become a labor force. Families, the rumors assured us, would remain together. These rumors, we found out later, were fabricated and spread by the Germans. Again, as in the ghetto, the Germans were using the members of the Juden Rat to spread the German-initiated rumors in exchange for better treatment and exemption from shipment to the camps. These rumors, a part of the German big-lie technique, served as the soma, the tranquilizer by which to minimize any possibility of rebellion. Had the Jews known what was in store, that most of us in that brickyard would be gassed, that we would be part of a holocaust, I am quite sure there would have been at least some attempt at a rebellion. But we wished to believe the rumors, even when deeply in our hearts we doubted them. It seems that people would rather believe falsehood if there might be a glimmer of hope. We would rather take a chance on an uncertain life than fight when the outcome is certain death.

The day came when a long train made up of freight cars arrived at the siding of the brick factory. Soon the shouts in German were heard, "Zusteigen," and we were herded onto the train. The four little windows on the corners of each car were covered with barbed wire to assure that no one would escape. As each was filled, the doors were shut and padlocked. My extended family of uncles, aunts, cousins, and grandparents managed to occupy more than half of a freight car that was filled with about 50 persons.

Soon we were off to an unknown destination. We spent about three nights on the train. It was at this time that I saw my mother cry. Like Rachel, in Jeremiah's prophecy, she was crying for her children and could not be consoled. Based on the letters she had received from her aunts in Poland, my mother knew that there was little, if any, chance that we would see each other again after we reached our destination.

For two days we traveled in the freight car with pad-locked doors and barbed-wired windows. No one in the car knew our destination. Now and then through a window we glimpsed a name of a city when the train was shunted to sidings awaiting a clear track. Now and then voices of prayers could be heard as time for *minchah/ma'ariv* approached. Needless to say, the mood in the car was somber. All through the trip, we hoped that the propaganda we had been fed was true; that we would end up in a work camp where families would live together while the men and women worked in German industry. Deeply in our hearts, we knew better. Still, the power of hope was so over-whelming that we encouraged ourselves by our forlorn hopes.

It was late afternoon, about sunset on the third day, when my mother opened up one of the packages containing bread and some smoked meat. She cut off pieces which she handed to us, to my 10-year-old sister Esther, to my 13-year-old brother Benjamin, and to me. As she handed the food to us, I heard her sigh. There were many reasons for her sigh. But one reason, I am sure, was that she, Yocheved, the daughter of Avrom, a pious Berditchever Chassid, was handing her children treyfa meat.

You understand that, to my mother, the keeping of a meticulously kosher home was an important foundation of her Jewish identity. However, when our home became a part of the Munkacs ghetto, we soon became aware that food in general and kosher food in particular would indeed be very scarce. And when we were driven out of our home, she made sure that the sausages and hams, the most nutritious of all foods at our disposal, came with us, for after all, "Dear God, the children must eat." Now, imprisoned in a cattle car on our way to an unknown destination, she handed each of us, her children, a portion of bread with a portion of sausages. In the dim light of the car, I noticed tears in her eyes and heard an almost imperceptibly soft cry. "Mame, far wus wineste?" ("Mother, why are you crying?") I asked her. She turned her teary-eyed face to me, responding "Oy kinderlech. Oy, my children, I cry for you. I am scared for you. I have lived, and I have had a good life, but you haven't started to have a life yet. You haven't had time to experience the joys of life. Oy gotteny! Oh dear and merciful God help them..."

On the third night, more specifically early morning while still dark, the train stopped. Through the barbed-wired window I could see only three huge flames burning brightly in the sky. The air that filtered into the freight car had a peculiar odor, an odor that I had never smelled before. Where were we? What had the Germans in store for us? These questions danced around in my head without finding any answers.

As soon as the morning sun came out, the gates of the freight cars were opened and our questions were answered. With the first rays of sun and the opening of the doors of the train, the command was given clearly and harshly, "Heraus!" As I exited from the train, I noticed a number of buildings with slogans painted in big letters on their roofs. One slogan stated, "Arbeit macht frei" (work liberates) and another stated, "Arbeit macht das Leben suss" (work makes life sweet). These slogans are perfect examples of Nazi cynicism and their propaganda technique, the big lie. Life in the camp was definitely not sweet, and work there never created a path to freedom.

Now, standing on the tarmac, we were ordered to form two lines, one for men and the other for women. We lined up in the men's line, my father; my brother; my uncles Alexander, Nathan, and Fabian; my cousin, Gus and I. Some distance away was the women's line. Among the many that were standing in that queue were my mother, my sister Esther, and my grandmother. There were others from my family, my Aunt Illi, carrying her six-month-old baby in her arms; her mother; my Aunt Louise and her two daughters; Nathan's wife and two daughters; my mother's sister, my Aunt Rebecca, and her daughter and young son. I took a last look at the women's line, directing my gaze at my mother. Good-bye, mother, zei gesund, Mame, Esther, Babe, "Geit mit Got," I shouted into the wind.

As I stood in line, an inmate in a striped blue-and-gray uniform looked at a passing plane in the sky. "Dear God," he sighed, "Wouldn't it be wonderful if he would drop some bombs and kill us all?"

"Why do you wish for all of us to die?" I asked.

"You'll soon find out. You'll soon find out," was his cryptic reply, and we soon did.

The men's line slowly moved forward. At the end of the line stood a solitary figure in a leather coat who, I later found out, was the infamous Dr. Mengele. He stood there quietly, and as people passed in front of him silently he moved his index finger either to the left or to the right. I found out later the meaning of the right or left direction. Being sent to the right meant that the person was judged young and strong and capable for work, and being sent to the left meant dispatched to immediate doom. As we came more closely to that figure, we were told that we would be asked the ages of the two younger persons in our family, that is, my brother Benjamin and my cousin Gus. We were told that they had to be over 16 years to remain with us. My father and my Uncle Alexander calculated the appropriate birth year so that both would be sixteen. The year they arrived at, namely that both were born in 1928, was correct. What they did not anticipate being asked was the month of birth. Alexander gave Gus's birth month as April, making him sixteen, but my father gave my brother's actual birth month, which made him four months shy of being 16. To the Germans, my brother was therefore not old enough, and he was taken from our midst. Similarly, I found out later that when my mother and sister came before the leather-coated Mengele, they were sent to the left. It was different with my Aunt Illi, who was a young, tall, beautiful, and a strong woman. When she came before Mengele, carrying in her arms her six-month-old baby, my little cousin Shalom, one of the Germans asked her whether there was an older person to whom she might entrust the baby. Illi gave the baby to her mother, and both the baby and his grandmother were sent to the left.

My father and I and my uncles Nathan, Fabian, and Alexander and my young cousin Gus were sent to the right.as we entered the camp, we were told to get undressed, to leave our clothes on the ground, but to keep our shoes. All our belongings that we had packed and carried to the brick factory were left in the train. We were naked. The next step was to be de-haired. We walked in line like sheep to be shorn before men with large electric shears, who cut our hair, including our pubic hair. Next, we came before men holding pails of a dark, foul-smelling liquid, a creosol-like substance, which they dabbed around our genitalia and under our arms, which, according to the Germans, was supposed to destroy the lice that we might have brought with us from our previous residence, the ghetto. After all this, we were marched to the showers.

Later, during my stay in Birkenau, I learned the significance of the shower. We who were still fit to work were given showers, but those who were considered unfit for work, those who were either too young or too old for labor, were gassed in similar shower rooms and then cremated. Now I understood the sight and the odor that permeated the place. The night when the trains stopped, indicating our arrival, I looked out the little window in the freight train and noticed four huge flames while my nostrils detected a peculiar odor. The Polish Jews, who were brought to the extermination camp years earlier, explained to us the realities of the camp and the meaning of the flames.

What I am about to tell you is most likely untrue; there is no evidence of its veracity. However, I want to relate it because of the rumor's pervasiveness in the camp.

Before entering the shower, we each received a small bar of soap. In my memory it was small and rectangular, similar to those one gets in a cheap motel. The inscription engraved on the soap was RJS. The same people who told me about the flames and the crematoria also told me what, at least in their opinion, the letters RJS stood for. RJS, they proposed to me, is an abbreviation for "Rheine Juden Seife," that is, pure Jewish soap. A main ingredient in making soap is fat, and speculation in the camps, however unproven, was that the cremation of bodies would provide an ample supply of rendered human fat.

After I showered, I returned to the place where I left my only possession, my shoes, but, instead of finding the pair I had left, I found two right shoes. Someone mistakenly had taken my left shoe. I immediately faced two problems. First, my shoes had a built-in arch support for my flat feet, without which I constantly had aching feet. Secondly, I had no other shoes to wear. I approached a capo, an inmate supervisor, and asked him what I should do now. He showed me a window and told me to knock on it, and when it opened to ask for a pair of shoes. Someone there might, he told me, if approached properly, give me a pair of wooden shoes. Wooden shoes would be better than none.

So I approached the window. Before leaving the capo, he further advised me that I must begin my request for shoes with the following statement, "Ich bette gehorsam," meaning, "I humbly request." I knocked at the window; it opened to reveal a room with two persons, a German in an SS uniform and an inmate with an armband identifying him as a capo. Before I had a chance to make my request, the capo hit me on the head with a stick that he carried as though he were an Irishman armed with a shillelagh. Then, having demonstrated to the SS officer that he was adequately cruel, he asked me, in German, "What do you want?" I began my request, as instructed, with the words "I humbly ask for a pair of shoes." Before I had a chance to tell why I needed the shoes, he hit me again on the head and closed the window. I returned to my father, crying, not from hurt but from rage. "How can it be," I asked my father, "That such inhumanity still occurs now in the middle of the 20th century?"

This was the beginning of my education into man's inhumanity to man. It was here that I learned one of the tragic facts of human civilization, which is that humankind, in spite of the development of philosophy, morals, ethics, and technology, is, sadly, still a naked ape. He is still governed by his most ancient of all mental forces, the id. Contrary to my previous belief in the benefit of technology for the improvement of human life, technology also provides the means of more efficient techniques for human destruction. War is the major contributor to technological advancement. Governments are most likely to spend their resources for war materials and technologically more efficient ways of killing than for developing the means to solve genuine and pressing social and human problems. Any social benefit that we derive from technology is only a matter of serendipity, a byproduct of humankind's main occupation, war. About my shoes, well, the man who took the wrong shoe found me, and we exchanged shoes.

To complete our dehumanization, the Germans changed our names to numbers. I was no longer Eugen Schönfeld; instead I was known as #90,138. This number was sewn on my inmate uniform right above a little yellow cotton triangle, which indicated that I was a Jew. Because I did not remain either in Auschwitz or in Birkenau, my ID number was not tattooed on my arm. After the war, many people were skeptical about my claim of being a survivor. They all believed, erroneously of course, that all who were in the camps were tattooed. Officially, we were called "schutz heftlingen," meaning protected incarcerates. I always wondered from whom the German were protecting us. Moreover, why in the world did the Germans give us their protective service?

The uniforms we were issued were a cotton pajama-like suit, with alternating blue and gray stripes. When they cut our hair, they also gave us a reverse Mohawk hair cut. By this, I mean that they shaved about a two-inch stripe on our head, which was referred to as the *lausen strasse*, that is, the lice street. This was an additional mode of taking away any semblance of human dignity.

I was assigned to a barrack in this camp, which I was told was Birkenau. This was the extermination camp located right next to Auschwitz. The inside of the barrack consisted of a series of platforms, like three-tiered bunk beds. These platforms served as sleeping places for about six persons; their dimensions were about seven by seven feet. We slept on the bare wood, and we were very cramped. We were forced to stay in the barracks and could go outside only for a certain period of time. At night, the Germans provided buckets to be used as latrines, and each morning people were assigned to carry them out to empty them into the latrine, and to clean the buckets. Thus, the dehumanization continued. It was also in Birkenau that I witnessed my first death. A middle-aged man from my city who was diabetic went into a diabetic coma. Nothing could be done for him.

We stayed about a week at Birkenau. I do not remember now much about the place nor what we ate nor what we did there. My next memory is being on a train to Warsaw, Poland. On that train I encountered the meaning of human individuality. The train, like the one that brought us to the camp, was made up of freight cars. A freight car has three equal areas, and the door area takes up the central one third. We, the inmates, all 60 of us, had to stay on the left or on the right side of the car.

In the door area were two field cots reserved for two SS guards. One was a tall, blond, truly Aryan type, the kind that Hitler wished that all Germans resembled. The other was shorter with dark hair and a dark complexion. He was a Ukrainian who had joined the German SS not only because he agreed with the Nazi philosophy but also as a way of rejecting the Soviet Union. It was he who epitomized German brutality. The blond German guard often tried to protect us from the other's verbal brutality. The Ukrainian threatened us with his gun while the German kept indicating to us, behind the other's back, to let him alone and not to worry about him. At every stop, the German would leave the car to gather whatever containers he could find to bring us water and sometimes even sweet coffee. Both were SS; both were in the *todskopf*, the skull division (their emblem); and yet they were very different individuals. Twice I have encountered individual kindness in the midst of destruction and utter hatred. Such experiences taught me the importance of judging each individual on his or her own merit, not as members of a particular group. Individuals can on more than rare occasions transcend their own group's philosophy and its norms.

My sense of humor did not leave me, even when facing life's most grim conditions. It seems to exist in us even in the most desperate conditions. Perhaps, if we could maintain a sense of humor, unbearable conditions might possibly be made more bearable. On the way to Warsaw, I encountered something that not only made me smile but made me laugh out loud. En route, we passed many cities the names of which I did not recognize on the rail-station marquees. Others were recognized because of an association with an event in Jewish history. But the one city that we passed with a name that brought laughter among a number of us was Chelm. This city is immortalized in Yiddish tales because its Jewish inhabitants are characterized as bumbling idiots, ne'er-do-wells, whose activities are contrary to common sense. In their bumbling inertness, they become humorous characters. All of us in the car who had ever read the tales of the wisemen of Chelm could not withhold our laughter, even in the conditions in which we found ourselves.

We, that is, my father, my three uncles and my young cousin, along with a thousand more, arrived in Warsaw. The train stopped near the infamous Warsaw ghetto, now lying in ruins. A year earlier Jews in this ghetto revolted and fought the Germans for eight days. The end, however, was inevitable. When the rebellion was quashed, the survivors were taken to an extermination camp. Subsequently, the Germans systematically blew up all the buildings in the ghetto and built a concentration camp in the midst of the rubble. We were brought to Warsaw to participate in "Project Berlin Aufbau," that is, a work project designed to help rebuild Berlin, which by this time was being bombed daily. Our job was to clean the bricks of the destroyed buildings and stack them for shipment to Berlin.

After a march, we arrived in the camp which consisted of brick buildings with indoor plumbing and single beds with straw mattresses. The buildings in which we were now being housed were luxurious compared to the barracks in Birkenau. I thought that maybe camp life would not be so bad after all. Maybe we could withstand it and survive. Our food, although bad, was adequate in volume. Most often, as I remember, we got beet soup and bread. I always tried to position myself in the line in such a way that when my turn came to receive my ration of soup it came from the bottom of the barrel. The bottom of the barrel always had the greatest amount of food solids. Sometimes, I even found pieces of meat, and quite frequently the volume of solid beets exceeded the liquid broth.

We began to work. Our work hours were eight in the morning till six in the evening with a half-hour break for lunch. The routine of work provided structure to my existence to the extent that my life assumed some semblance of normalcy.

This sense of normalcy, even though it was founded on a false consciousness, coupled with rumors of German losses in the battlefield, gave me hope that Nazi rule would soon be over. I may have even deluded myself that I was seeing the beginning of redemption, and soon I would be back to pursue my dreams.

Before the ghetto, before the German takeover of my hometown, I had had a dream. True, it was the dream of a teenager, but it was a dream that gave my life some excitement. I dreamt I would visit Western Europe by bicycle. This dream was founded on my reading of the travel experiences an author had during a year of bicycling all over Europe and North Africa. I wanted to duplicate this feat. Toward this end, I had begun to study French to complement the two other major languages that I already spoke, English and German. I began to study French on my own, in the same way that I had learned German. I took a French-language book home from the store and began to memorize words and grammar. In Warsaw I found a person who, like my bicyclist hero, had traveled all over Europe and who also spoke French. At work, I managed to sit next to him, and as we both cleaned bricks, I began to study French grammar under his tutelage, to decline nouns and conjugate verbs, and memorize a few conversational phrases. This act focused my thoughts on the future, and, for the brief time when I studied, the grim reality of the present did not matter.

When we arrived in Warsaw, the camp already had an inmate population, most of whom were Jews from Saloniki, Greece. It was the first time that I had met Jews different from the Central European Jews of my culture. They spoke Greek and also a Spanish jargon called Ladino, instead of the German/ Yiddish jargon spoken by Central European Jews. Many of them also spoke Hebrew, giving us a common language and hence an opportunity to communicate. Each morning we were marched from the camp, surrounded by SS storm troopers, to our workplace, a destroyed house on Novolipcki Street, just a few city blocks from the camp. We were given the hammers that brick masons use and settled down to our work, cleaning and stacking the bricks. Lunch was brought to the workplace, usually consisting of soup. Across the street from where I worked was the Machorka cigarette factory. The women who worked there often threw cigarettes to us.

Our life in this camp soon came to a halt. One evening in the middle of summer of 1944, we were told that next morning we would leave this camp for another one. There were already many rumors that the Russian army was getting close to Warsaw. This announcement reaffirmed these rumors. Next morning, we lined up for *Appel*, which is the daily routine of being counted. The Camp Commandant, in a very pacific voice, told us that the whole camp would be moved by train. However, he pointed out that we would have to march 100 kilometers to where the trains to transport us to the next place would be waiting for us. Again, in a calm and concerned tone, he asked those persons who felt unable to walk 100 kilometers to step out. In a sincere manner he informed us that they did not have adequate transportation to move all of us by trucks, but he was quite sure that he could manage to secure a few trucks to ferry those who were physically unable to march to the embarkation point. I knew that they would never take transport from the war effort to ship weak Jews who could not march that distance. Still, there were some who, in spite of all of our experiences, believed the commandant. One of the believers was my classmate, Friedman. I tried to dissuade him from stepping out, but he would not listen to me. I warned him, "You cannot trust the Germans." It was a lesson that I had learned the hard way, the lesson of the big lie. By lying, they were able to maintain a sort of order. People always wish to believe that others would treat them humanely. But, that was not true of Nazi Germany where people lied and took advantage of human hopes. Friedman did not believe me and stepped out. All of those who believed the German stepped out and were marched outside of the camp walls. Soon we heard the sound of machine guns. I never saw him or the others again. Till this day, I am not sure whether Friedman believed the German commandant, or if he succumbed to depression and saw this as a way out, a form of deliberate suicide.

The rest of us waited. I had a feeling that we too were to be shot. The rumors were that the Germans were retreating. The few highways leading out from Warsaw were clogged with the retreating military, and there would be no room for us. But there was nothing we could do. All of us were sitting on the ground, four abreast in a long line. At each two steps along the line stood two SS guards with automatic weapons, one on each side of the line. So we waited. A few hours later a messenger on a motorcycle came to whisper something to the camp commandant, after which we were told to return to the barracks.

Next morning we rose early. The Germans gave us our breakfast, a cup of substitute coffee, and we marched out of the camp. It was a hot summer morning. It had rained the night before, saturating the air with humidity. We marched on back roads that were paved with broken rocks, the sharp ends of which made the marching difficult. Occasionally, there were large puddles of water that were too large to step over. As the day progressed, it became hotter and we became thirsty, but, of course, we were not given water. By the afternoon, the heat and the thirst were taking their toll. Some older persons began to fall down from fatigue and thirst, and were shot. Sometimes, I found a water puddle in the road, and leaned over to scoop some of it as fast as I could with the tin soup plate that hung from my waist on a rope that served as my belt. I did not care whether it was clean or not, whether it was sanitary or not; all I cared about was that it was water.

That evening we arrived at the banks of a large river. Some younger persons, who broke ranks and without having permission ran into the river seeking to quench their thirst, were shot. The rest of us stood in front of the river while the Germans counted us again. The ritual of Appel, the ceremonial counting, would be performed regardless of conditions. Finally, the commandant stationed guards in the middle of the stream, and then he permitted small groups, one at a time, to walk into the river to drink. They permitted us to stay for a very short time (maybe less than five minutes), and then it was another group's turn. Each group was given a five-minute water break. In retrospect, our mode of drinking reminds me of Gideon's test. Standing in the middle of the stream, some of us would bend over and drink directly from it, as though we were at a water fountain, while others used their hands as cups, bringing the water to their lips. The five minutes allocated us was not an adequate time for our rehydration. While at the time we left the water, we might have felt some relief from our thirst, I still remained dehydrated; I knew instinctively that without additional water I, and perhaps most of us, would not survive the next day's march.

We were told that we would spend the night at the river's bank. While our guards were on dry rations, we were not given a thing. It did not matter. We sat down on the ground; better yet some of us were lying down. By the commandant's order, no one was allowed to stand. All of us were in a hopeless situation. We had received neither food nor water with another full day's march ahead of us. When I closed my eyes, my mind wandered to an image of our bathroom at home, where all the faucets were wide open with water gushing from every one of them.

My immediate problem was a renewed thirst. How was I to find water without being allowed to search for it? I am not sure why, but I thought about Moses who had produced water in the desert with his staff. Indeed, why could not I? Why could I not dig a well? A foolish and unrealistic thought, after all, for the only tools I had for such an undertaking were my spoon and my metal dish. Nonetheless, I began to dig.

"What are you doing?" asked my father.

"I am digging a well" I replied.

He did not stop me. Was this a foolish dream of a nine-teen-year-old boy, desperately seeking a miracle? I kept on digging. It was not difficult to dig, for the soil at the riverbank was primarily sand. Soon the color of the sand became darker and moist. I could feel the water in it. I kept on digging, and to my amazement and joy, at the depth of about a foot and half, water started to seep into the cavity. I filled my tin cup with the precious moisture.

In my teens I had ceased to be religious, at least what conventionally was thought to be religious. I had long ago stopped reciting the appropriate blessing over food. But lying on the ground in the Polish steppes about to drink a cup of water that seemed at that moment to be a response to an inarticulate prayer, I felt that a blessing was in order. Perhaps my feeling was merely a variation of the old adage, "There is not any atheist in the foxhole." Whatever the reason, I recited the blessing, *shehakol*, and I gave my first cup of this precious liquid to my father. When the others saw what I did, they too began to dig wells, and the place assumed the Biblical description of "wells upon wells."

Suddenly, I heard heavy footsteps. The camp commander was standing right at my well looking down at me. I remember his arrogant stance. His gray coat had a Persian lamb collar. Feet set wide apart, his arms folded around his chest, he presented himself as the image of complete power over us. Looking up at him from the ground, where we had to stay either sitting or prostrate, he loomed tall and formidable. "Well," he said, "Since you found water you may as well have it."

Of course, some people may argue (and probably will) that finding water was nothing but a series of coincidences. After all, being at the bank of a river with a sandy soil increases the probability that there may be water underneath. But I submit to you that, in my view, this was but one of the many miracles that occur daily which we take for granted. To me, a miracle is an improbable and unanticipated event that saves one's life in an otherwise hopeless situation. Indeed, there is no doubt that we were in a hopeless situation, and death appeared to be quite imminent. There in the Polish steppes, I, a fledgling agnostic, felt obliged to give thanks to the infinite and recite the traditional prayer for experiencing a miraculous event, the *birchat hagomel*. I am not sure whether others will consider my experience a miracle or just a series of coincidences. And, perhaps, miracles are nothing more that unanticipated coincidences that occur at the precise times when they are needed most, when one's life is totally dependent on the event. In such a case, one may call the occurrence a most welcomed coincidence, or if one has an unquestioning belief in the existence of a personal and benevolent deity, what happens may be perceived as a miracle. This is what happened to me, and each of you may choose your own term, coincidence or miracle. I, for one, am happy to consider this event a miracle.

It seems that this miracle or coincidence on the banks of the river affected others who were there, too. Early in 1999, on a trip to Sydney, Australia, I looked up a Mr. Grunwald, recommended as a "landsman," a person from near my hometown. I tried to phone him, but I was able only to speak to his answering machine. Three days before my departure, my wife and I visited Sydney's Holocaust museum. One of the docents asked me whether I knew any Jews in the city.

"I am sorry but I haven't met any Jewish people in the city, though I have been trying to contact a Mr. Grunwald," I said.

"Oh, I know Jimmy very well; we are close friends," the docent replied. "He owns a summer home in the Blue Mountains, and he spends a great amount of time there. I will try to contact him." The docent left us, and we continued to tour the museum.

Shortly, the docent found us again. "I just contacted

Jimmy; he is on the phone." He led me to an office and handed me the phone.

Mrs. Grunwald answered, "Jimmy has already left to pick you up," she told me, "Be at the front door, and he will meet you there in about ten minutes. Look for a blue Volvo."

We left the museum and waited at the entrance. Jimmy soon appeared, and after a few minutes of introductions we were on our way to his home. In the car I asked him from which city he hailed.

"I am from Nagy Szolos," he replied.

"Did you by any chance know my uncle and aunt, the Fabians; he worked in a bank?" I asked.

He confessed that for some reason he was unable to recall anything about his city.

"Have you been in camp?" I inquired further.

"Oh yes, I've been in Auschwitz, Warsaw, and a few others."

You were in Warsaw? Were you part of the Berlin Aufbau project?"

"Yes," he replied.

"Then we were there at the same time." After reminiscing of our experiences, I asked, "Do you remember the miracle of the water?" Suddenly he became quiet; his facial expression changed, and he suddenly assumed the blank stare and the air of sadness that people bear when they recall a very painful event.

"Was it really true?" The words came out quietly and softly. "I always believed that it was merely a figment of my imagination. I was so sure that it never happened that I never told any one about it. I believed that such a miracle couldn't have happened." By this time, his eyes were moist, and tears appeared on his face.

"Yes, it did happen," I assured him, and my eyes too welled up with tears.

That evening sixty years ago, on the banks of the river, we hardly slept. Most of our time was spent in drinking, rehydrating ourselves, and preparing for the next and equally difficult day. I do not remember most of the events of the second day's march except one incident. We were walking near some trees that bore fruit resembling cherries. One person in the group plucked some of them and started eating. Soon he began acting peculiarly as though he had lost his senses. My Uncle Alexander, a physician, informed us that the man had eaten a poisonous fruit called belladonna. It is a fruit similar in appearance to cherries but that contains atropine. I do not recall what happened to him. At the end of the day, we arrived at our destination, an empty field near a rail line.

Unlike the previous days, which had been dry and hot, now while waiting for the train, we endured rainfall. I believe it took two days (or three) for the train to arrive, and all that time we had to lie on the soggy ground in a continual rain. We were completely soaked. The morning of the train's arrival, the sun came out. The day promised to be hot. We were hastily fed canned meat, the nature of which was unidentified, which was very salty. Still, it was meat, something that we hadn't had for a very long time. Again, we, the *schutzheftlingen*, as we were called, were forced to get on the train, occupying only the left and the right sides of the freight car with the middle third, where the doors were, left free for the guards. Unfortunately, because there were few cars, 90 persons were forced into one car. In order for the guards to have greater control over us, we were forced to sit. With such crowded conditions, we had to pile our legs on one another.

While we had been waiting for the train, a young person who had managed to escape during our march reappeared. Why would any person return willingly to his enslavers? What compelled this person to give up the freedom that he had achieved through a daring escape? He told us. Once he was free he sought help from the local Polish population, but no Pole wanted to help him. No one whom he asked offered him food, not even a drink of water. Nor would anyone help him to join with the partisans (the guerilla fighters). He was not sure whether their reluctance was the result of antisemitism or fear of German reprisal, but the consequences of their refusals were the same. He had not had a place to sleep; he was tired, starving, and thirsty. Most importantly, he was afraid that, were he to be caught, he would have been summarily executed. He felt that he had no other choice but to return.

This story confirmed what I had already suspected: Poles traditionally hated Jews. Even before Hitler, the Polish government had established such anti-Jewish laws as forbidding our traditional way to slaughter animals for kosher food and limiting our access to education.

The three days that we waited for the trains to arrive were very difficult. As I have said, for three days we endured rain, and three days and nights we sat and slept on soggy ground. Once a day we were allowed to rise; it was when we were fed. But as soon as we embarked, the sun came out; the temperature rose, and the day became hot.

It was even hotter in the closed cars where the air could not circulate. On top of this, the air in the enclosed space became very humid as our extremely wet clothes and blankets began to dry. The four small windows in the freight car, two on each side, were covered with boards and nailed shut. Yet, all the while, we were forced to sit. The salted meat that we had been fed prior to embarkation, the heat, and the stifling humidity increased our thirst. But, true to German cruelty, we were not given anything to drink.

We faced again a desperate situation that led us to take desperate measures. We started to collect our own urine. First we used it to dampen ourselves and reduce our body temperature, but then slowly and reluctantly, we began sipping the collected urine. When this occurred, the Germans reluctantly brought us some water.

I do not remember how long it took to travel from central Poland to Dachau. Suffice it to say that many of the internees died and others lost so much weight that I could not recognize them. As we disembarked at Dachau, I heard a familiar voice calling my name. I turned to the speaker; I hardly recognized him. Just a week ago he had taught me French, and now he looked almost dead. I do not think that he survived the ordeal.

Dachau was one of the first German concentration camps. Initially, it was used to intern Germans considered anti-Nazi, and perhaps for this reason it had some modern conveniences like indoor toilets. We were assigned to barracks. The only water available to us was in toilet bowls. No one was permitted to visit the bathroom and take water from the faucet in the sink or shower. I stood at the toilet flushing it and letting the water run into my tin soup plate and continued to drink, trying to rehydrate myself.

Dachau was not to be our final destination. After a week there, we were again put on trains and transferred to a newly created work camp in the foothills of the German Alps, only five kilometers away from the city of Muhldorf. The camp was called Muhldorf's Forest Camp, in German, *Muhldorf Wald Lager*. The proximity of the camp to the city, coupled with the fact that we had often been taken to work in public places, like the train station, leads me to question German civilians' claim of ignorance about the existence of concentration camps.

Muhldorf Wald Lager was a brand-new camp located in a forest in the foothills of the Alps. Unlike the major camps with permanent buildings, Muhldorf had been hastily built. The huts that served as our residences consisted of round, thin, cardboard structures similar in appearance to miniature grain silos, about ten feet in diameter with conical roofs about ten feet at their apexes. The floor of each cabin was mud and covered with straw. We were brought there to erect a factory for the manufacture of planes. We now know that this was to be a factory to build Messerschmitt Me-262 fighter jets. Luckily, the factory was never finished, because the introduction of jet planes even as late as the summer of 1944 could have influenced the final outcome of the war.

Living conditions there could at best be described as ultraprimitive. Sleeping on a straw floor presented a number of problems. First, of course, it was cold and hard. Second, there were not clearly delineated private spaces. One merely eked out a space on the ground, which varied each day. Also, we slept in our clothes. Last, the proximity of our bodies and the straw was conducive to the infestation of lice. We became lousy, so much so that we could reach under our armpits and gather up handfuls of lice. The constant biting and itching was one more discomfort to tolerate. Quite often as we stood, we hit and scratched each other's backs to alleviate the constant itching and biting. In July and August, while still warm, we tried to boil our meager clothes, but to no avail. The straw on which we slept was already infested, and we had no means to control the infestation.

Our routine was as follows: We rose about 4:30 a.m. and went out to the yard where we lined up according to our barracks and were counted. The capos, that is, inmate supervisors, called out our numbers to which we had to answer. After both the counting and roll call by numbers verified that no one had escaped, we were allowed to have breakfast. The morning meal consisted of what the Germans called *erzats kaffee*, namely, substitute coffee. This I believe was made of roasted grain which was ground and boiled like coffee. No other food was given. After this sumptuous repast, we lined up again for Appell, in which we again were counted and lined up in companies to be sent out to work.

There were two different work camps. For the most part, I was sent to the forest camp as a part of the work group whose task was to build the airplane factory. We marched two kilometers to the work area with the SS guards flanking us on both sides. Escape, of course, was impossible. Not only were we guarded by the SS with great diligence, but by now we were in the middle of Germany. At work, the SS guarded the perimeter of the building site, and the paramilitary construction company known as *Organisation Tod* supervised the work area itself.

I was assigned to carry cement to the mixing machine. The cement mixer was a tall machine, about 15 feet high, which mixed gravel with cement. Two people hefted a sack of cement weighing fifty kilograms (about 100 pounds) onto my shoulders. My job was to climb the wooden planks to the top of the machine where others took the bags, cut them open, and dumped the contents into the mixer.

We began work at seven in the morning and worked till noon when lunch was brought. Lunch consisted of some sort of soup. Sometimes, we were lucky and got bread soup. This concoction made of old, stale military bread was somewhat sweet, because, I assume, it contained sugar. This was the most desired and best of all of the lunches. Most of the time, however, lunch was an almost empty soup. I am not sure what it was made of; all I remember is that it had no solids. We were given about a half hour for lunch, after which we returned to work.

At other times, I had an easier job. I was placed on top of the scaffolding, that is, the wooden frames into which the cement was poured that would become the walls of the factory. We were handed long wooden poles, and as the cement was poured, we were to continue to stab the liquid cement. I assume this was done to eliminate air pockets from the cement and make sure that the walls were properly made and were strong.

It was fall and the Alpine air was getting cold. In spite of all our troubles and torments, some of us constructed a facsimile of a Jewish calendar, which revealed that the holy days of New Year (Rosh Hashanah) and later Yom Kippur had arrived. Although while I was still at home, in my late teens, I had begun questioning the validity of religious beliefs and what I considered in my youthful rebellion senseless ritual laws, I nonetheless had strong emotional ties to my history and to my people. I observed religious holidays, not because of fear of heavenly punishment, but as a reaffirmation of my ethnicity. For instance, I had always fasted on Yom Kippur (and still do today); therefore even in the camp I joined other Jews in fasting; that is I didn't eat my lunch. At the same time, while I was working with the poles, jabbing the poured cement, others who remembered various parts of the Yom Kippur services recited them aloud, and we repeated them. Praying was not only the way by which we renewed our hopes for liberation but also our attempt to humanize ourselves.

Work was usually over by seven. Again we had to line up for another Appell, again to be counted, before we marched the two kilometers from work back to camp. By the time we arrived, it usually was past eight. Back in camp, we again had to line up to be counted, and thus we never had our dinner before nine in the evening. Dinner usually consisted of a bowl of potato soup and a loaf of bread. Lucky was the individual who got some potatoes in his bowl. At first, four persons shared the military loaf of bread; but over time, as the end of the war approached, the Germans reduced the size of our bread portion. Toward the end, eight persons shared a loaf. Since bread was so precious, all of us who shared the loaf supervised the cutting of the bread, lest one's share be bigger than someone else's. Having eaten the meal, we went into our plywood tent with the lice to sleep till we were woken next morning at 4:30.

By the fall of 1944, I decided that I would not work. Carrying cement was hard, and since our food was not enough to support our bodies, many people died. While most died at night, some died at work, and we had to carry them back with us to the camp. Every morning, we examined our ankles to see whether they were swelling. Edema was a sure sign that the heart and kidneys had weakened and that soon death would follow. I decided to risk death by being shot for shirking work rather than to die slowly while working for the Germans. Thus, when I arrived at the working place, I hid among the bushes that were growing right in the middle of the work area. Although the work area was surrounded by military personnel, within the area there was some degree of freedom of mobility. In the middle of the work area, the dense bushes provided a seemingly good hiding place. Because early fall brought with it chilly weather, I needed some insulation from the biting chill. The thin cotton outfit I wore was hardly adequate when the temperature went below 60o F. By late September, in the foothills of the Alps, the temperature even in midday was quite low. For insulation, I gathered discarded empty paper cement sacks and stuffed them under my jacket. These paper sacks served to insulate me both from the chill in the air as well as from the cold ground. One day I made the mistake of inviting a boy from my school to stay with me in the bushes. On that day I was quite miserable, for he constantly expressed out loud his fear of being caught. Indeed, were we to have been discovered, we probably would have been shot. As for myself, I accepted the possibility of death. I was able to hide not because I was brave, but because if one constantly faces death, as I did, one ceases to fear it. I accepted death, and I knew that if I were to continue to carry sacks of cement I surely would not survive.

I must relate here one incident that occurred when I was carrying cement on a night shift. This experience reinforced my earlier realization that I should not judge people as a class but as individuals. The night supervisor was a member of Organisation

Tod. As I was carrying the cement bags, I started to shake and became unable to walk straight. I was becoming very weak. I saw the supervisor coming toward me, and, from experience, I expected to feel the pain of the stick on my back. Instead, as he reached me, he took the cement bag from my shoulders and told me to follow him. He went directly to his knapsack, from which he took out a piece of bread, and instructed me to sit down to eat and rest. A little later, he approached me again, giving me a broom, and told me to sweep the floor. Why he singled me out for special treatment I did not know.

Of all the members of my family who were with me, I was the only one engaged in hard physical labor. Uncle Alexander was working as a physician in the makeshift hospital. He kept his son Gus with him as a messenger boy and later took my father into the hospital as a patient. He employed both my uncles, Nathan and Fabian, as clerks. The Germans gave him these privileges because they used him as their personal physician. Because of my youth, he could not get the Germans to exempt me from labor.

In the late fall, we began to construct our winter homes. In the foothills of the Alps, the winters come early, and the temperature drops precipitously. Our winter homes consisted of rectangular holes dug into the ground. They were approximately four feet deep in the ground, 15 feet wide, somewhat longer across, and a total of about eight feet tall. The roof was made of wooden planks constructed in an inverted V-shape and were topped off with earth. Packed earth served as insulation against both cold and rain. The floor was covered with straw to serve as our beds. We slept on both sides of the room with the middle left open for a walkway. The place was never heated nor was there ever any wood to burn. On Christmas Eve, 1944, another young inmate and I sneaked out from our subterranean bunker to seek wood. We found some large logs, which we carried into the bunker. We also stole a saw with which to cut the acquired logs. Since we did not have lights, we had to saw the wood in darkness. The saw jumped out of the log and cut my left index finger. The cut did not heal because my body did not have enough nutrition for it. The wound remained open and festering until I was freed by the U.S. forces and given food and vitamins.

It was too cold to work with cement so they put us to cutting wood. Winter in the Alps was quite cold, and since we now had wood, we made an open fire, which was against regulations. On one cold day working as lumberjacks, I began to build a bonfire. At all times, we posted a lookout away from the fire to warn us of the approach of a capo. However, one lookout chose, instead of watching for an approaching capo, to stay by the fire. The head capo, a German who was brought from a prison where he was serving a sentence for murder, found us all standing around the fire. When we were asked who made the fire, the failed lookout pointed to me. The capo began to beat me with a heavy stick till I fell on the fire. Out of both pain and fear, I involuntarily urinated in my pants and passed out.

In the spring of 1945, the war became directly visible to us. Twice daily, we noticed the airplanes that were on their way to bomb Munich. At eleven in the morning, the planes of the U.S. Air Force flew directly over our camp, and at night, British planes were on similar missions. There were times when the planes also bombed the freight trains in the nearby city of Muhldorf. On such occasions, some people from the camp were dispatched to help with clearing the debris caused by the bombing and also repairing the destroyed rail lines.

On one such occasion, the returned workers brought with them, stuffed under their jackets, both uncured tobacco and sugar. I was able to procure a portion of each. Because both the sugar and the tobacco were kept together in a pouch created under their jackets, the sugar acquired a tobacco taste. Nonetheless, for the first time since my internment, I had the pleasure of putting sugar into my morning coffee. We tried to cure the tobacco leaves by boiling them and then hanging them to dry. We shredded the dried leaves and rolled them in newspaper to form cigarettes. They were extremely strong and made us cough. Still, we kept on smoking till the tobacco supply was exhausted. Of course, these cigarettes were harsh and gave us no pleasure. Why then did we smoke? I do not know why others did, but in retrospect, I smoked because it re-humanized me. It brought me back to my past, to my time at home when I smoked. Any activity that broke the routine of camp life, any activity that was perceived by me as contrary to German authority, any activity that gave me some degree of individualism, I perceived as desirable. This was, in a minor way, a form of rebellion, of my daring to challenge the status quo.

These bombing raids also gave me my closest encounter to battlefield death. Near the camp was a community cemetery, and occasionally some of us were assigned to dig graves for dead German civilians. It was on one such occasion that an American bomber missed his target and released a bomb that fell directly in my vicinity in the cemetery. I wedged myself between two mounds of dirt that formed two graves, listening to the ever-increasing whistle of the falling bomb, awaiting what I considered the inevitable, death. The bomb fell about ten yards from where I pressed myself to the ground. I was lucky. I was too close to experience the bomb's direct effect, too close for the shrapnel to hit me. This event, that is, the possibility of dying, did not frighten me. By this time I had long anticipated my death, and hence, death and I were no strangers to each other. In short, I became immune to the fear of dying.

In the spring of 1945, the rumors reached us that the Germans were losing both on Eastern and Western Fronts. Still, the SS in the camp acted as though nothing had changed. When Roosevelt died, I had an opportunity to glance at a newspaper read by a German, which declared in very bold headlines, "Roosevelt Dead, Victory is Ours." We knew better. We knew that the German fortunes were turning because the food rations were becoming smaller. Our daily ration of bread was now down to ten persons per loaf. It was the end of April when we came back from work and standing at Appell were informed that next day we would be shipped elsewhere. Only Christians and those in the hospital, declared the commandant, would remain in the camp. I knew that the safest place would be with non-Jews. That evening I surreptitiously sneaked out from my barracks and joined my family in the hospital.

Chapter Five
**Liberation**

It was a crisp, sunny morning when I was awakened in the hospital by the sound of rifle, machine gun, and cannon fire. The date was May 2, 1945, the day the surviving members of my family (my father, three uncles, and a cousin) and I were liberated from Muhldorf Wald Lager, the last of the concentration camps in which we were interned.

For two days prior to my liberation, I hid in the camp hospital. I was not ill, that is, other than being a 90-pound weakling, suffering from malnutrition and scurvy. It was a hospital in name only. It was a small building with bunk beds for the sick, most of whom never got well. The absence of nutritious food and medicine assured an inevitable fate of being dumped with the other dead into a mass grave. Most people were never hospitalized. Frequently, we had to strip before a Nazi physician who determined the usefulness of the inmates for labor. Those who in his opinion were too thin or lacked any strength were sent away to be gassed.

We, that is, the members of my family, believed that our safest place, at least for the moment, was to remain in the camp together with the Christians. Of course, at that time we did not know that the Germans planned to pour gasoline on the hospital and burn it together with its occupants. But for the moment, we felt that being together with Christians gave us some degree of safety.

Next morning, I believe it was May 1, the notorious freight cars arrived, and all the clearly located Jews were taken away to an unknown destination and fate. Of course, regardless what reason the Germans gave for transporting the Jewish inmates, we all knew that their plan was to implement the Final Solution, the extermination of the Jews. As it turned out, most of the Jewish inmates on the train were not fated to die by German hands. They became the victims of the war's collateral damage. After liberation, I learned from some survivors what happened to that train in which many friends and schoolmates met their deaths. It was an ironic fate that the train, in which a day earlier German soldiers had been taken to the battlefront, was now loaded with Jews. Customarily, trains that carried soldiers to the battlefield were decorated with flowers and colored streams of crepe paper. So, this train, decorated from its earlier mission, was now transporting the German Reich's victims rather than its soldiers. One of the survivors of the train related to me that, in their hearts, they knew they were being taken to the Alps where the Germans intended to kill them. To the Germans, the killing of Jews seemed to take precedence over even the war itself. Toward the end of the war, they had even diverted sorely needed transportation from the war effort itself to the killing of Jews. To French pilots who patrolled this part of Bavaria, a decorated train, or for that matter, any train, was fair game. French fighter pilots swooped down and began strafing the train, now filled with Jewish captives. As the shooting began, the inmates jumped out of the train, which by now was not guarded, waved their striped jackets, and the strafing stopped. It was too late. Half of the Jewish inmates had been killed or seriously wounded.

Meanwhile, I was hiding, not knowing what my fate would be. But at least I was with my family. The thought of death did not frighten me. I had lived with the idea for over a year, and death and I had become friends. I accepted my grandmother's dictum: "Wus ist beshert ist beshert" (what is preordained is preordained).

I cannot remember my last night in captivity. I remember waking up and hearing the thunder of distant big guns. "Were these the Americans?" I wondered to myself. My excitement for my anticipated liberation was, however, short-lived. Into the room walked a young SS officer, his pistol still in its holster strapped to his overcoat belt. He was wearing a class A uniform and his boots were polished to a mirror-shine. His demeanor and his meticulous uniform belied the reality, namely, that both he and I were experiencing the end of the war, I soon to be liberated and he, the loser.

He walked directly to me. "I understand you speak English." His words did not sound like a question, more a statement of fact, and still spoken with the arrogance so characteristic of SS officers.

"Yes, I do, a little." I responded hesitatingly. In truth, my English was the result of six years of gymnasium education.

He handed me a piece of paper with a German text. "Translate this into English and sign it, and have the others in the room sign it, too" he commanded. The text he handed to me was an affidavit written in German, asserting that he, whatever his name was, had been good to Jews and treated them with kindness.

"I am sorry," I replied, "I cannot translate this. It is far beyond my knowledge of the language." The truth was that my English was adequate, but the sound of nearby guns gave me the courage to refuse his demand. To say that I was afraid is to minimize my feelings; I was extremely frightened. However, I was not about to give this German, this SS, an easy way out for his evil doings. Thus, I dared to refuse him and waited for the consequences. There were none. He turned around and walked out of the room.

For a while, no one dared to open the outer door and walk out the hospital. This, as the Germans would have stated, was strictly *verboten*. But soon, since it seemed very quiet outside, we opened the door a crack. To our astonishment, there were no soldiers in sight. The bastions that just a while before had been manned by German soldiers with machine guns stood empty. Was this the end of our enslavement? Was this freedom? These questions raced through my mind.

Here we were in Germany, a strange people in a strange land. Where did we go from here? For over a year, we lived like livestock. While we were aware of our situation, there was nothing that we could do. Earlier in our internment, my father and I would dream of a better time in the future. We made postwar plans. But we soon had forgotten about the future. We could not plan for a future because we did not know whether there would even be a future. We were not in control of our lives, and, hence, we had never made any decisions. We – and I am generalizing for all the inmates based on my personal experiences – lived for the moment. We ate when food was given and did as we were told. And now, suddenly, we were free. We could, theoretically, make decisions, but how could we implement those decisions, even if now we could make them?

The next few hours all of us moved aimlessly, waiting for someone to take charge of our lives and tell us what to do. Surely, I thought, we would not be abandoned.

We were free; the hated enemy was defeated; and yet no one cheered. There was no expression of joy or jubilation among the survivors. Surely, one might have expected that the long awaited freedom would be welcomed with cheers or some form of vocal expressions of joy. But nothing like this occurred. We were in a state of confusion. No one knew what to do. In short, we needed help.

It was not till early afternoon that we heard the clatter of a tank. I ran outside the gates of the camp, happy that now someone knew of our existence. I was sure that help was on its way. There they were; one tank, one jeep, and a squad of American soldiers. "Does any one speak English?" A young man with a silver bar on his shoulders looked at us with inquiring eyes.

Hesitatingly, as one who was not accustomed to speak to authority figures, I replied, "I do."

The leader of the group introduced himself, "I am Lieutenant Schwartz. I am sorry that we didn't come earlier, but we became aware of this camp's existence about a half hour ago. A German we interrogated mentioned that there is a camp nearby. In fact, we took the city of Muhldorf [only three miles from our camp] by nine this morning."

In turn I introduced myself. For the first time in over a year I said, "I am Eugen Schönfeld," instead of identifying myself as *Schutzheftling* #90,138. My introduction was my regeneration as a human being. A year ago, my name had been taken from me and replaced by a number. I was, till now, a numbered object, a thing. This was my renaissance, my rebirth, as a human who was, like all humans, endowed with a name.

I looked at this young officer who, I assumed because of his name, was a Jew like me. I was grateful to him for coming and liberating us from a sure fate of death. I was also very happy that here I was standing before a Jewish officer. Can you imagine, I thought to myself, a Jew in command? I wanted to mark the occasion by saying something extraordinary. But what could I say to this liberator? How do I thank the one who freed me and all the other remaining Jews in the camp from deprivation and captivity? What profound words were there to be uttered at a time like this? It was simple, "Lieutenant," I asked, "Do you have a cigarette?" He laughed and handed me a pack of Camels.

Suddenly, I found myself surrounded by a group of inmates who now called themselves my friends. "Can I have one?" The inquiries came from all sides. So I handed out cigarettes till I found that I had only one left. "This last one," I told my new friends, "I'll keep for myself."

Lieutenant Schwartz, a member of Patton's Third Army 14th Armored Division, was curious. He had heard about camps from others who liberated them, but he had never seen one till now. This was his first experience with people half dead. I do not know what he thought upon encountering his fellow Jews. In the camp there were still piles of dead who had not yet been thrown into the common grave. In retrospect, were I in his place, the experience surely would have conjured Ezekiel's vision of the valley of the dead bones with God's voice asking, "Son of man, will these bones ever live again?"

I, instead, responded to the volley of queries he sent my way. I told him where we came from and about our lives, our starvation, our tortures, and, of course, the dead and the dying. I explained to him our reduction to subhuman existence, of being just one level above livestock. After all, no human, still conscious and endowed with thought, could endure the mental and emotional anguish that we had to endure. To have a chance to live, to exist at all – at least in my own case and I am sure this held true for others – thought and conscious belief and hope in a future had to be abandoned. Perhaps Dante's statement would have most apropos, "Ye, who enter here, abandon all hope." It is not that we had lost all hope of survival and of liberation. We just had had to reduce those hopes to a subconscious level. For, harboring hopes of liberation and survival, which most of the time seemed to be unattainable, coupled with the physical pain due to hunger and beating, would have been even more unendurable.

I described to him our daily lives and the cruelty of the capos, and the particular brutality of the main capo who at times beat us mercilessly.

At that moment, that selfsame capo, who had beaten me till I was unconscious, passed us. His physical appearance was ample evidence for his being a residual from an earlier, subhuman species: five-foot-three and completely simian; low brow, with arms, visible because of rolled-up sleeves, extremely long and hairy and dangling below his knees. His arms were also bloody from having just butchered a cow. The sight of this depraved and sadistic man, together with my description of his character, made a profound impression even on this battle-hardened soldier.

Lieutenant Schwartz drew out his service revolver and handed it to me. "Shoot him," he told me. "No one will mind if you kill him, and no harm will come to you."

But how could I kill another human being? I had never even held a pistol in my hand. My only experience with a weapon consisted of that brief encounter with a O.22-caliber rifle when I was given military training by the Hungarian Levente. But it was not my lack of experience alone that kept me from shooting and killing this archenemy. Of course, I harbored great anger towards him, who had beaten me senseless with an ax handle because I dared to make a fire on a very cold January day in the Alpine foothills. My reluctance to kill another human being, even though my whole being at one level cried out for vengeance, was rooted deeply in my psyche. My opposition to violence, particularly to killing animals from the position of a hunter, let alone to killing another human being, was rooted in the values my parents had instilled in me. In Freudian terms, opposition to violence was a core of my superego. Thus, neither the anti-Jewish laws that had made my life difficult even before being taken to the camp, nor the camp experience itself, succeeded in erasing the values that I had internalized. I could not kill, at least not at that moment when this simian-like man no longer threatened my life. I could not kill for the sake of vengeance. At that moment I realized that my humanism, rooted in Jewish values induced into me by my parents, had not been erased by German brutality.

"Thanks for the offer," I replied to the lieutenant, "but I cannot do it," and I returned his gun.

I have often felt I was a deviant compared to other survivors. It seemed that I did not have the capacity to hate the Germans with the same intensity and ferocity that other Jews manifested right after liberation and that many still do today. Do not misunderstand me. I did not love them either. Of course, I hated the regime and its philosophy that was the direct cause of my bitter experiences. They were the primary reason for the loss of all that was important to me. I hated the Germans and Germany and the philosophy promulgated by Nietzsche. I also hated the religious philosophy and beliefs that led to centuries of irrational antisemitism. At the same time, I was not capable of hating the German individual with whom I came into contact, unless, of course, I knew that they were part of the system that brought on this calamity to be called the Holocaust. But even then, I could not have inflicted physical vengeance on them.

My refusal to shoot the capo and my lack of a capacity to hate the Germans with the ferocity that I detected in others were not the result of conscious decisions or a thought-out philosophy. At the age of nineteen, I lacked neither the insight nor the experience necessary for a philosophy of life. My feelings and responses were, I am sure, the product of my childhood upbringing, a subconscious attitude introduced to me by my father. I believe that my decision to become a professor of sociology and my concern with understanding the nature of morals and the concept of justice also had, similarly, its roots in my early childhood discussions with my father. It was during Saturday morning talks with him that I became inculcated with his French Socialist perspectives, rooted in the writings of Anatole France. His *Penguin Island*, for instance, on my required list of reading, gave me an early understanding of human foibles.

As I was talking to the lieutenant, another one of the liberated inmates approached us. "Tell the soldier that Obersturmbandfuhrer Weiss is hiding somewhere in the soldiers' barracks."

"Who is he?" I inquired.

"Don't you know? He is the head of the Dachau region camps." Our camp in Muhldorf was part of the Dachau complex.

I informed the lieutenant, who relayed the message to his headquarters. Soon, more soldiers arrived, and a systematic search of the premises began. Weiss was found hiding in the basement of one of the military barracks. His trip to Muhldorf was not pleasant. I was informed the next day by my new friend, the lieutenant, that Weiss had been made to run ahead of the jeep, encouraged by occasional pokes from a baseball bat. He was later tried in Nuremberg and found guilty and hanged with other war criminals.

The word must have spread about the liberation of a concentration camp, for shortly, a full-bird colonel came to inspect the camp. Since I was the only person who spoke English, I was pressed into service as translator and guide. He was a tall man, as I recollect, but I could hardly understand his accent. At school, I had learned what is generally referred to as the King's English, but this colonel's language was strange and unfamiliar to me. It prompted me to ask, "Colonel, are you speaking English?"

"No, son," he declared laughingly, "I speak Texan." He also told me, "Son, I speak all the languages of the world except Greek, but all the languages are Greek to me."

Later in the afternoon of my day of liberation, we broke into the German warehouse. Its contents revealed that it had stored officers' rations. The bread there was white and not what we had been given, which, I could have sworn, had been made of equal measures of sawdust and ground-up straw. There was also an ample store of butter and eggs. I, together with others, helped myself to the loot. I proudly brought my liberated treasures to my father. Yet, in spite of his hunger and decimated condition — his weight was less than 100 pounds – he refused to eat it and cautioned me not to. "This food is too rich for our stomachs. You'll become ill," he informed me. But, in my youthful arrogance and impatience, I believed that, having survived the camps, I could not be hurt by a mere trifle, like food. I ate a magnificent meal of toast, butter, and scrambled eggs. Later that night I paid the price; I was struck with diarrhea.

The morning after liberation, all the survivors were deloused. For over a year, all of us had suffered from lice infestation. In the beginning of our imprisonment, we had tried to control the spread of these parasites. Whenever the weather and the Germans permitted us, we not only washed the clothes that we wore but we also boiled all of our garments. But all our efforts were of no avail. The straw that was strewn on the floor of the bunker where we lived and slept was filled with these creatures. After a while, we had gotten used to being lousy and accepted the itching and biting as a normal part of life.

Through the gate came several trucks with barrels of white powder and pumps. I was again recruited for translation duties. Speaking in Yiddish, I informed the inmates to line up for delousing. I remember the process well. Soldiers with operating-room-like masks inserted the nozzle of the pump into our shirt and jacket sleeves and proceeded to pump and spray white powder. The same process was repeated in the front and the back of our shirts and pants. The effect was incredible. Suddenly it felt as though all hell had broken loose. For a few seconds, I felt the lice scurry all over my body and then quit. This quiet, this absence of the usual itching and biting, made me feel as though something normal was missing.

Were this a script for a Hollywood movie, it would end right here. The bad guys lost; the righteous survived and were freed with the presumption that they would live happily ever after. True, we were freed from the death camps; we no longer were under a previously ever-present death sentence. However, hardly any of the survivors of the Nazi atrocities had that happily-ever-after outcome. For the majority of the survivors now faced the almost insurmountable and insoluble problem of finding the balms that would alleviate the pains from the loss of family, home, and hope. We were a people sans hope. In the following chapters, I attempt to present my own life and my views as I struggled to regain some degree of normalcy.

Chapter Six
**The Hospital**

The day after liberation, any sense of jubilation or elation that I might have felt the day earlier was now completely gone. This seems to have been true for most Jewish survivors. I did not hear any jokes or any cheerful conversation. Above all else, no one seemed to have any plans for the future. My father and I did not discuss our future, for neither of us was sure what to do. For us, the main question was, should we return to Munkacs, or should we just leave Europe for America?

It was not that we had not thought about the future. Early in our internment, in an effort to lessen the impact of the experiences of people dying in the camp, my father and I thought that if we diverted our attention from the present to the future by talking about life after the ordeal, our spirits would be lightened and our depression lessened. We did this by discussing and projecting our lives after liberation. The plan for our future was built around the family's immigration to the U.S. We would go to St. Louis where my father's brother Saul resided. St. Louis was the place that the whole family had agreed, prior to our internment, would serve as the contact point for all of us who survived. There, in St. Louis, my father proposed to open a bookstore that would serve the literary desires of the various ethnic groups that make up America. I am sure now that these dreams of the future were nothing but escapism, the kind of dreams that Freud called *schnorer träumen*, beggar's dreams.

Now, after the liberation, most of the survivors in the camp, including my father and me, were ill, both physically and spiritually. We had neither the energy nor the clear mind necessary for decision making, let alone to make life-altering decisions. We all suffered from various degrees of malnutrition. In addition to being a ninety- pound weakling, I also had scurvy. My gums were turning white from infection, which led to a loss of bone holding my teeth. Wounds that I had sustained in the camp, due to the lack of nutritious food, had not healed fully all during my internment.

Our bodies lacked the strength, or for that matter any capacity, for healing. It was only after our liberation, when we began to receive nutritious food supplemented with vitamins, that the wounds we had sustained earlier started to heal. And, as our bodies started to heal, we hoped that our wounds of the spirit would also start a healing process.

For some, liberation came too late. In spite of the great care we received from the liberating forces, many liberated inmates continued to die. Their physical condition was so deteriorated that even the medical remedies that were now available to us, such as antibiotics, could not keep them alive.

The day after our liberation, the U.S. Army's medical branch took us to a makeshift hospital. It was in a large building, a nunnery which the army had converted into a medical facility and rehabilitation center. The nuns who had lived there were still there, albeit in smaller quarters, and they also served as nurses in this newly established hospital. Again, we were in the care of others, and again we did not have control over our lives. The fact was that there was nothing that we could do for ourselves. Our first task was to gain strength, and this we did by eating mostly cream of wheat or other cooked cereals because, after long months of starvation, our digestive system could not tolerate anything else. I was still suffering from diarrhea, the result of not heeding my father's advice and indulging myself with rich food the day of liberation. We were also given massive doses of vitamins to overcome past deficiencies and to supplement the extremely light diet of the present.

Because of my knowledge of English and other languages, I was put to work in the hospital's office. My job was more than just that of translator. I also dealt with day-to-day problems and patients' complaints. What I did would today be called customer service. My task was to talk to the patients to try to explain the need for various directives, to listen to their grievances, and to bring them to the attention of the major in charge of the facility.

One of the great problems that I tried to solve was caused by American fraternization with German women. About a week after our arrival at the hospital, a delegation of survivors headed by my Uncle Alexander came to see me.

My uncle confronted me. "Tuli, [my nickname]" he said, "You must speak with the major. We are angry." The problem that they lay before me was twofold, one more severe than the other.

The war was over, and the physical and psychic energies that had previously been devoted by the members of the U.S. Armed Forces to fighting and staying alive, had now been freed and were directed instead toward the most basic of our male drives, sexual gratification. And, opportunities were everywhere. The GIs' relationship with the German Fräuleins, at least at that time, was solely directed to the satisfaction of their libido. Right after the war, Americans' association with the Fräuleins led neither to love nor to marriage. As members of the conquering army, having at their disposal surplus food while the German population was going hungry, the soldiers had ample opportunities to satisfy this basic drive. With cigarettes, food, and chocolates, the coin of exchange, sexual gratification was easily attainable. The soldiers' sexual relationships with German women, with the people that enslaved us and murdered our families, was perceived by the survivors as an affront to their sensibilities.

Hence, it is quite understandable that about a week after having been in the hospital, the delegation supposedly representing the patients came to see me. Their complaint was that the American soldiers working in the hospitals were providing food, candies, and chocolates to the German women, and, thus, in their view, the GIs were giving comfort and succor to the enemy. Also, in their view, Germans, all Germans, regardless of age and gender, deserved to be punished. The motto was, "Let them suffer!" While their complaint, from a reasonable point of view, was not justified, at the same time, the law of antifraternization gave the case a legal status. It was against military orders for Americans to fraternize with the former enemy.

Still, I felt that the delegation was making a mountain out of a molehill. In my youthful opinion, I considered the GIs' violation a minor offense. I tried to argue with these delegates that giving food and chocolates to German women was purely a business exchange. In fact, if anything, I considered the arrangement to be a form of mental and emotional punishment. It was a part of the dehumanization of German women and a form of retribution against German males. Many German women, because of their need for food, preferred the company of GIs to German males.

The other complaint was, however, far more serious. According to information they had gotten, the major in charge of the hospital had diverted penicillin, a scarce drug, from the hospital stock to treat his German girlfriend. This was far more than mere fraternization that the army forbade. The diversion of drugs could have meant that a survivor would have to forego life-saving treatments.

I tried to convince the delegation that it would be foolish to dwell on the issue of chocolates. After all, I argued, this was merely a business exchange, payment for services rendered. Moreover, is not the need for women to offer themselves for food and other commodities a form of punishment? Is not the exchange of one's body for food a diminution of self-worth? "Imagine," I argued, "What the German women must feel when they, the master race, not only have to face the shame of defeat but compound their shame by seeing their daughters becoming dependent on a form of prostitution. Is it really worth," I asked, "Diluting the greater issue of the drugs with such minor infractions as fraternization and the giving of chocolates?"

I was faced with the problem of finding the best and most reasonable and judicious way of handling the major's infraction. In my view, based on the little experience I had had with the military, bringing formal charges against the major would be of little use. The war was over, and the troops had been given some slack. I was sure that a formal charge would not only be whitewashed but it would also, most likely, lead to a resentment of the complainers for having caused difficulties for an officer. It would be considered biting the hand that fed us. I proposed to the delegation that the preferred solution would be to speak with the major informally. And this is what I did. In a private conversation, I informed him of the survivors' great concern about his use of penicillin, and it was never mentioned again.

The major and his German girlfriend, recovered from her pneumonia, remained together. Whether he continued to provide her with any provisions or medicine from the hospital I do not know. In my studies of Latin in the gymnasium I came across the phrase: *Quod licet Jovi* non *licet bovi* (what Jupiter is allowed to do the ox may not), or in military parlance: Rank has its privileges. I accepted the reality, if not the morality, of this adage. I suppose that my uncle and other members of the delegation also realized what folly it would be to pursue the major's infraction. At least from my point of view, our most formidable task was our recovery of body and spirit.

How should I feel about and toward the Germans? Every one around me publicly and frequently declared utter hatred of the German people. I never discussed my feelings, my lack of hatred of Germans, with anyone, not even with my father. With the exception of known Nazis, I could not develop the intense hatred for all Germans that others were manifesting. The consequence of my feeling differently from other survivors resulted in an overwhelming sense of guilt. I felt guilty because it seemed to me that there must be something deficient in me. Shouldn't I, a survivor of the Holocaust, one whose family had been killed by the Germans, have an intense sense of hatred for all Germans? Why did I differ from other survivors in the hospital whose hatred was intense, vocal, and vitriolic? Of course, I was angry at Germany, but I could not place the guilt for murder on individual Germans. I felt that, in this regard, I stood alone, as a deviant in the community of survivors. From their perspective there were no good Germans; collectively or individually, they were all guilty. On the other hand, when I interacted with a German, unless I knew that he or she was directly related to the atrocities, I could not regard the individual German as the "enemy." I could not divulge this feeling even to my father, let alone to any one else. Being angry and hostile to Germans was the norm, the sine qua non of being a survivor. Many survivors then and even today considered hating Germans and Germany a moral obligation. And yet, as I interacted with Germans, regardless of with whom and in what capacity, I did have a sense of apprehension and foreboding, caught in the midst of an approach-avoidance conflict. Because of this inner dilemma, I had, and continue to have, difficulties interacting with Germans.

Of course, no one should forget what the Germans have done. The Nazi regime, even if it was true, as postwar Germans claim, that Hitler ruled without the total support of his citizens, could have not accomplished the atrocities it did without the population's acquiescence. The Germans, not only the Nazis, were therefore guilty. Still, and in spite of all that I knew about the Germans during the Nazi regime, I could not generate the same degree of hate expressed by other survivors. In retrospect, I surmise that this was due to the values that my parents and my Talmud teacher implanted in me. I had been indoctrinated into the rabbinic values that I believed (and still do) constitute the core of Jewish moral philosophy. Judgment should always be mitigated with mercy. Nonetheless, I always had and continue to have difficulties making friends with Germans, but at the same time I cannot carry a grudge forever. Because of a perspective that differed from most of the survivors, it has been difficult for me till this day to join various voluntary groups and associations of survivors.

My knowledge of English, although adequate, was by no means fluent. But the few weeks that I worked in the hospital improved my English, my American English. At the age of 19, I made friends with the GIs, and because of their generosity in giving me cigarettes, re-acquired a bad habit, smoking. My friends supplied me with enough cigarettes that I could share with others, which made me a very important person.

**Chapter Seven**
**Repatriation**

With care and proper diet, I gained weight and strength. I knew that soon we would be discharged from the hospital and would have to go somewhere. But, where would I go? Foremost in my mind was this question, how do my father and I find the rest of our family? During this time, I always wondered, were they alive? Since my brother and sister were so young when they were taken from us, where would they be? Did they remember our uncle's address? The best that I could do was hope that they would be alive and that once again we would be a unified family.

Most of the survivors, at least those with whom I talked, were sure that they would not return to their hometowns. How could we return to our hometowns where we had experienced the hostility of non-Jewish neighbors who never protested when we were shunted into ghettos and who stood gleefully by when the Germans took us to the infamous trains? It seemed to us that many non-Jews could not wait to usurp our homes and possessions. Most with whom I talked did not wish to return and live again among such people. Most survivors decided to settle in other countries and not to return to their erstwhile homes in cities where their neighbors had been their tormentors. Others, particularly younger people, having lost their families and lacking attachment to the past and to the cities of their birth, sought new horizons. In short, the past and its way of life ceased to hold importance.

This perspective was exemplified one day when a bus arrived to repatriate the French survivors. I do not recall if there were French survivors among us, but two young men, originally from Poland, stood at the hospital entrance looking at the bus. I overheard the following conversation:

"Do you want to go to France?" asked one of the other in Yiddish.

"Why not," replied the other, "I don't have anything to go back to."

And I did not wish to return to Munkacs either.

The idea of repatriation was abhorrent to me. I could not imagine returning to Munkacs, resuming my life there, or making that city my home. Early on in the camp, when our spirits were not yet completely destroyed, my father and I talked about the future. Back in Munkacs we had our book and stationery store, and, of course, he believed that he would continue this occupation. But instead of Munkacs, our home would be somewhere in the U.S.A. Coming from a town with five different ethnic groups, each with its own school system and culture, my father felt that the U.S. would be similarly diverse.

Sitting at our workplace in the Warsaw Ghetto, my father commented, "Isn't the U.S. a country of immigrants? Wouldn't the people of the U.S. be interested in books written in people's native languages? Wouldn't they be interested in the English translation of the many books written by their compatriots?"

My grandparents' and my father's roots were in Munkacs, and as far as I knew, our habitation both in Slovakia and Carpathia went back to at least the beginning of the 16th century. Now, our life there had come to an end. Two of my uncles who also survived refused to return Munkacs at all. They were not even interested in seeing what had happened to their property. They felt betrayed by a great number of non-Jews who had been jubilant in our misfortune. Most of the Christians had seemed disinterested in our misfortune and did not care what was happening to people with whom they and their ancestors had lived for hundreds of years.

Working in the hospital office, I knew that soon the time would come for me to be repatriated. By repatriation, the authorities meant to return us to what one may call civilian life. In anticipation of being returned, officers from the United Nations Relief and Rehabilitation Administration (UNRRA), a division of the United Nations in charge of the housing and feeding of displaced persons, distributed clothes right out of barrels, donations from Americans. I was given two shirts, shorts, and a pair of shoes. But what I remember most vividly was the suit I was given: a single-breasted, pink, houndstooth check wool suit. Since I had nothing, even this atrocious outfit had to suffice.

The distribution of clothes was a clue to us that it would soon be time to leave. And so it was. We were given Displaced Persons' identification cards that could be used as railroad passes. My father decided to return to Munkacs, and I would keep him company. He wanted to see what was left of our home and store. But most important, he hoped that we might find there other members of our immediate family and be reunited. Surely, I hoped, one of the three – my brother, sister, or mother – would be alive. I had little hope for my sister, who was ten when we were taken to camp. My three uncles who were in camp with us, unlike my father, adamantly refused to return to their hometowns. Instead my two uncles – my father's brothers, Nathan and Alexander with his son – went to Prague, Czechoslovakia. Fabian, my father's sister's husband, who was sure that no one from his family (his wife and two very young daughters) had survived, went to Budapest, Hungary, to join his brother there.

I do not remember much about the trip home. I do not remember what provisions, if any, we were given for the trip. I do remember, however, one event. Other survivors seem to have a far greater recollection of all events in that period of their lives or, at least, claim to have. My memory is limited only to those events that must have had a great emotional or intellectual impact on me. The following event is one of these.

The first night in our journey of repatriation we spent in Bratislava, today the capital of Slovakia. This overnight stop was forced on us by the lack of a train connection to Munkacs. We were taken to a school that had been converted into a makeshift dormitory for survivors solely for an overnight stay on their way home. When we arrived, mattresses and blankets were strewn on the floor of a large classroom. An ad-hoc kitchen had also been created on the premises, and we were provided a much-welcomed hot meal. It seemed that we were the first transport of repatriates to have stayed there. But, from the number of mattresses that were on the floor, the organizers must have expected a greater number of people.

What was foremost in our mind was to find out what had happened to our families. At every opportunity when we met survivors from other concentration camps, my father and I always asked the inevitable question, "Do you know Bejnesh Schönfeld? Do you have any information about Schönfeld Jolan?" We were hoping to hear some positive news. But alas, no one had any information; no one knew anything; no one had a positive response to any of our queries.

But miracles do happen. There were a number of

family members who, in spite of the odds against survival, had managed to stay alive and eventually reunite. Such a miracle occurred in Bratislava. Late that evening as we were preparing to go to sleep, settling down on the mattresses on the floor fully dressed, another transport of survivors arrived at the school. We all jumped up and surrounded the newcomers, peppering them with the same question, "Have you seen?" or "Have you heard?" For most people, this was an exercise in futility. Instinctively, I knew that, given their ages, the rest of my family most likely didn't survive; still we did not give up hope. Each of us in the room was hoping for a miracle. We were hoping that, in spite of all the negative odds, we would find and be reunited with our family. This hope was reinforced by a most heartrending event.

Sometime about ten that night, a new transport of survivors arrived, mostly women. We all jumped up, not only to welcome them and share our joy in their survival, but also to inquire whether they knew anything about our family. I hoped that perhaps women might have encountered my mother, who at the time of incarceration was only 45 years old and might have had a chance. My father and I approached the group to seek information. Another man from our city, who, I believed, was in his mid-forties and who was resting on a mattress next to us, also arose and approached the newly arrived survivors. Suddenly we heard a great cry, a cry of both anguish and joy, coupled with loud sobbing. Our mattress neighbor was hugging a woman, who, we were informed, was his wife. This reunion affected us all. There were tears in most, if not in everyone's eyes, and I knew that while we were joyful in his good fortune, we were also envious. Is it possible, I was thinking, that this could also happen to me?

Around midnight, another transport arrived. Eagerly we rose to meet them and again to ask the same questions. The newly reunited husband and wife also approached the group. Suddenly the wife let out a shriek; it was neither the sound of horror nor of fear. It was a peculiar shriek, a cry of joy and anguish combined. There among the newly arrived were their two daughters. Such a sight affected all of us. By this time, there were tears in everyone's eyes. How does one react when witnessing a miracle? I too cried. My tears were not of joy arising from the empathy of seeing a great rarity, a reunited family. I cried because their reunion reminded me of my own loss. I knew well not only that I had lost my family but also that I had lost the world that I knew. The world of my youth had vanished.

Chapter Eight
**Back in Munkacs**

The word "repatriation" means to be brought back to one's fatherland (*patria*). I was born in Munkacs, and thus by definition it was my hometown. Being on my way to the city of my birth, meant by definition that I was being repatriated. I, however, had ceased to identify myself as a Hungarian, and Munkacs, while it was the city where I was born, had ceased to be my hometown. How could I ever see myself as a Hungarian, as part of a country that sent me to concentration camps? Nor was I a part of Czechoslovakia, the country in which I was born and whose political ideals I admired. Munkacs was no longer a part of Czechoslovakia. And I never could be an integral part of the Soviet Union, the country to which Munkacs now belonged. How could I be repatriated? How could I be sent back to a homeland that I had never had? I had never considered myself a Hungarian, nor had the Hungarians considered me as one of them. How could I define myself as a Hungarian when all I experienced under a Hungarian regime was oppression and rejection? If I did not feel a part of Hungary, where I lived for the last five years before being sent to camp and whose language I spoke, how much less could I have considered myself a Russian or a Ukrainian, let alone a citizen of the Soviet Union? I was, in fact, a stranger, a homeless person, in its truest sense. I would have been a stranger, even were I to have stayed in Munkacs, a city in which both my father and grandparents were born.

The fact is that we Jews in Munkacs were always strangers. A stranger is not necessarily a person who comes for a visit. A stranger is not the immigrant who comes and within a few generations is integrated into the country and culture of his newly chosen homeland. Strangers are people who come and stay for centuries and who at best are grudgingly tolerated. Strangers, like me, may even be given citizenship rights but are never perceived to be an integral part of the society and its culture. Most Jews in Europe were strangers, dwellers in a land that was not theirs, a people without any historical attachment to any European country. Jewish history in Europe is a history of frequent deportation, of forced ejection, of cruel treatment, and of victimization. With this history and with my awareness of that history, how could I call either Hungary or Russia my home country? How could I call the people in Munkacs my kindred? I had no historical claim on the land or on its people and, now that it was U.S.S.R., even on its government.

There is a Yiddish saying, "When a worm eats itself into a horseradish, it thinks that it is in heaven." For hundreds of years, my family and thousands of other Jewish families lived in Munkacs, and, like the proverbial worm, we thought that Munkacs was heaven. We lived in a gilded ghetto, but it was a part of the Diaspora nonetheless. The city to which I returned was not even the same city that I left; it no longer was even a gilded ghetto. The Munkacs to which I returned was very unlike the one from which I was forcefully ejected. It was devoid of the people who were significant to me, my extended family, my friends, my classmates.

As I got off the train and entered the station that I knew so well, I met a number of Jews standing on the platform. They were not a welcoming committee. They were camp survivors who waited for incoming trains, hoping to meet surviving family members. There was no laughter or joy expressed as we met them. The prevailing mood was not even somber but deep depression and excruciating sorrow. Their slouching bodies expressed sadness, and their deep depression was etched in their faces. One could not see a spark of hope in their eyes. They were, however, a source of information. From them, my father and I learned that my aunt and cousin were in the city, and they gave us their address.

Leaving the rail station, carrying with me the small valise with the few shirts that had been given to my father and me in Germany, we went to seek these two remnants of the family.

We found them in the apartment where they resided. My aunt and a second cousin had been liberated earlier than we had been, and hence they had already been in Munkacs for a few weeks. They shared an apartment that they were given by the city. None of us who returned to Munkacs could return to our homes, because as soon as we were taken away, our homes were occupied by squatters. Like me, my aunt and cousin were ready to leave the city. They stayed there hoping to be reunited with remnants of family and friends. My aunt waited for her husband and her oldest son to return while my cousin prayed for the return of her fiancé. They, like most of us, were now at a loss as to what to do. They did not work but waited for news that they hoped would give a direction to their future.

The reunion was not a happy one. The tears we shed were not from joy. We continued crying as we talked about all those who did not survive. My father and I were informed by my aunt that for a few weeks after having arrived in Auschwitz she saw my brother across the electrified fence. My mother and my younger sister were sent, by the infamous Dr. Mengele, to the left, which meant to the gas chamber. Although my mother was only 45, her premature gray hair had made her appear older than her actual years, and thus I assume that she was considered too old for labor. Most of the day and night we spent in retelling our individual stories. We informed my aunt of her husband's decision not to come back to Munkacs but to stay in Prague. He knew that Jewish life in Munkacs had come to an end, that those Jews who remained in the city would become nothing more than the guardians of a cemetery in which our former lifestyle, the shtetl life, was buried. Most of those who returned to Munkacs left within a few days of their arrival, leaving their homes and all their real and tangible properties. No one seemed to have been concerned about the value of the home, the farms, or whatever else was theirs prior to their deportation. I know that I cared little for the properties in Talamas that I, as sole survivor of my mother's family, could have inherited. The quest for material possessions, at that time, never entered my consciousness.

Later in the day, my father and I proceeded to visit our home on St. Martin Street. The city, even on first glance, appeared to me like a haunted town where the ghosts of the past took over my consciousness of the present. There was not a place that I encountered that did not bring to memory my life with my friends and family. There on the main street, across from the city hall, was our store, seemingly intact, with the rolled-down steel shutter guarding its entrance. Not far from the store was Hamdi, the confectionary and dessert place where, in front of my friends, I committed my first rebellious act. It was in this store where, at the age of 15, I violated the Jewish food code, *kashruth*, and ate my first ham sandwich. I walked in front of the Csillag (star) coffeehouse on the *corso*, the wide main street where my friends and I had walked, not for the sake of exercise but to look at the girls, who in turn looked us over. Of course, the joy and laughter of light-hearted teens was not there. It was merely another street to traverse on our way to St. Martin Street and my home.

Finally, we could no longer escape the fearful visit to our home. With anxiety and trepidation, my father and I walked over to St. Martin street, No. 7, to our home in which I had spent my first 18 years, the place in which my brother, sister, and I were born. The house was not empty and waiting for our return. Instead, it was occupied by Gypsies, who had moved into the house, kept the furniture, but discarded all our pictures, books, and personal items. Standing guard at the front entrance to the house was the Gypsy family, telling us by their demeanor: "This is no longer your house." Neither my father nor I could take the emotional disturbance generated by seeing strangers in the house in which, once upon a time, just a scant year ago, we had lived with our dreams and hopes for the future as a happy family. Without a word and without entering the house, we turned around and left. The courtyard, which in addition to our home also contained both my grandparents' and my uncles' homes, was also occupied by Gypsies.

As I left the courtyard into the street empty of my neighbors and my friends, I felt an emptiness of spirit. I felt empty not only of their physical presence but also of the sound of Yiddish, the continual music that used to come from Bronsteins', the bottlers of "sour water," and the smell of fresh bread that came from the Weiss bakery. I felt as though I was in the middle of a nightmare, soon to wake up and all would be well. But, alas, this was reality, and my sense of alienation, my feeling of emptiness, continued. Munkacs, to me, had become a cemetery filled with the ghosts of the past without a glimmer of hope for a future. Right then I decided to leave; "I cannot and will not stay in Munkacs," I said to myself.

Throughout my life, my mother had cautioned me, "Don't trust Fonye (Ivan), the thief." Russia, with its history of antisemitism, the frequent state-sponsored pogroms that Jews had had to endure, the peasants' hatred of Jews denounced by priests as Christ killers, would not be my home. Munkacs, even though now belonging to a theoretically secular Communist government, I was sure, would not be a kind and accepting home for Jews. Russia, by any name and political system, never had and never would accept Jews as full citizens. I decided to leave as soon as possible.

I told my father of my decision, that if circumstances were right, that is, if the borders were still as fluid as yesterday, the day I arrived, I would posthaste leave it. The questions foremost in my mind were, Where would I go? What will I do? And how could I resume my life? I wondered whether, indeed, I could have a normal life at all. I had heard that Molnar, my art teacher and the principal of the Hebrew gymnasium, after learning about the death of his family, committed suicide. To him, the loss of his family deprived him of life's meaning, and existence seemed purposeless. There must be meaning to life. Without meaning, work is nothing but drudgery, and such an existence is a difficult way to pass a lifetime. My life, too, must have meaning, and I must seek it. I decided to seek again the goal that in my youth had always been central in my plans for the future. I was going to become a physician.

To connect with my past and my life prior to the Holocaust, I reached back to my dreams and hopes of my earlier years. At the age of 12 I had read Paul de Kruif's book *Microbe Hunters*. It contained biographical sketches of famous researchers such as Pasteur, Koch, Semmelweis, Ehrlich, and many others. These were men whom I admired and whose contributions to humanity were great. They were my models and constituted my reference group. Their work and lives excited me and influenced my decision to study medicine. But, my desire to study medicine was not rooted solely in its nobility. Medicine, I knew, was also an occupation that bestows upon the practitioner wealth and high social status. Even more important than wealth and status, I believed that medicine would become my path to personal freedom. Being a good physician, I believed, would give me the freedom from social and familial control and the constraints that I had experienced in an extremely religious community like Munkacs. In my youthful view, it appeared to me, a great and successful physician is independent of his patients and the collectivity in general. Rather, the members of the community become dependent on him. It is not that I wished to be separate from the community in which I would eventually reside. Possessing the skill of healing would, however, give me control over a scarce resource and the power associated with it that would free me from the tyranny of the community. Of course, at that time, my view of the community was Munkacs, where the Orthodox Jewish community was rigid and unforgiving of those who did not conform. Individual freedom and the prestige concomitant with the practice of medicine were my primary reasons for wanting to become a physician. Before the concentration camp, it was understood that I would study in Debrecen, Hungary, a town fairly close to my hometown, and that my father would support me. But of course the destruction of my hometown and the loss of family and business changed all previous plans. I, therefore, needed answers to two new questions: Where would I study medicine? And, how would I finance my studies?

To study in Hungary would be the easiest course of action for me. I spoke the language fluently, and I was quite sure that, now in the post-Holocaust period, I would have no difficulties being admitted to the university. In addition, there were opportunities for a scholarship. I decided to leave for Budapest in search of my future.

My Aunt Illi gave me the address of her Aunt Rose, who lived in Budapest. She assured me that I would find lodging with her for a few days. Next afternoon, I returned to the railway station, this time to leave my hometown permanently. I now embarked on a quest to find a new life for myself. At the station, as I was saying my farewell to my father, he assured me that after he liquidated the store, which miraculously had not been plundered, he would follow me to whatever city in which I had settled. I left with high anticipation, looking for a new future. I remember distinctly the feeling of sadness that descended upon me when I realized this was the last time that I would see Munkacs. My life that I had there had now ended. My dreams and the plans for a future there that I had conjured in my youth would never be realized. This, I thought to myself, was the end of a phase of my life.

The train to Budapest was full. Most people in it were ethnic Hungarians who had lived in Munkacs for six or seven hundred years, that is, throughout the time the city had been part of Hungary. Now, since the city had became part of the U.S.S.R., they too, felt disenfranchised and were migrating to what still remained of Hungary, wishing to settle among their own people. Luckily for me and the others in the train, the Iron Curtain had as yet not separated the U.S.S.R. from the West, and the borders, at least for a little while, were still open with travel to other countries still possible. The identity card that had been issued to me in Germany, written in three languages, attesting to the fact that I was a concentration-camp survivor, gave me free travel. In eight hours, sitting upright through the night, I was gone from Munkacs and my past and had arrived in Budapest, hoping for a new future.

My stay in Budapest was brief. When I arrived, it was quite evident that Hungary was an occupied country. Russian soldiers were everywhere. For whatever reason, the Jews living in Budapest had not been deported to camps. They were spared. Still, the Jewish community was in disarray. Synagogues were closed; personal freedoms were being denied. Russian dictatorship was evident almost everywhere. This was not the kind of country that I wished to live in. I took a streetcar to Rose's apartment. Rose was a widow in her 60th year, and I was sure that cleaning for and feeding an extra person would be difficult on her. Still, she agreed to allow me to stay for a few days while I decided on my next steps. In Europe, many homes had kitchen tables that could be opened and extended to form a bed. These beds were most frequently used by live-in maids. I was given such a bed to sleep in. That evening, as I turned the lights out, I soon experienced the discomfort of being bitten. As I turned on the lights and threw back the covers, the source of my discomfort became evident. Under the sheets, the bed swarmed with bedbugs. I slept the rest of the night and an additional two nights sitting up.

I had decided that the political conditions in Hungary, a country governed by the Communist party and occupied by Russian forces, would make my stay there short. This decision meant that I had to seek another place in which to settle and another university at which to pursue my dream. My stay in Budapest was indeed short. Three nights of sleeping sitting upright and resting my face on the table hastened my departure. Thus, on the third day, I left for Prague. My identity card describing me as a homeless person to be repatriated was still valid. I embarked on a train for Prague, the city that I had hoped would become my permanent residence, if not my home. I chose Prague for a variety of reasons. First, the Czech government, as I experienced it in Munkacs, was always very liberal. That country's liberal ethos was the result of its presidents, Jan Masaryk and Eduard Benes, both former professors of sociology. Because of their liberal political ethos, the Czech Republic was also my father's favorite country. But even more important, I had two uncles and a cousin who lived there, and I took comfort in the idea that I would not be alone.

Chapter Nine
**Prague**

The trip from Budapest to Prague required an overnight train ride. I arrived in Prague with my very few possessions, most of which had been given to me when I left the hospital in Germany. My first impression, which was etched into my consciousness when I arrived in Prague, was of a large number of people, each wearing a white armband, which reminded me of the yellow one that I wore in Munkacs. In fact, the white armband had a purpose similar to that of the yellow one that we Jews had worn. The white band indicated that these were the Sudeten Deutsche, the Germans who resided in Bohemia and in 1937 had begun agitating to become a part of the German Reich. Now, after the war, they had had their wish granted and were being forcibly removed from the Czechoslovak Republic and sent to Germany. It was indeed a matter of justice, to have their wish granted, to become Germans in a German country.

At the station, I inquired at the information center regarding shelter for the homeless. I was told to go to a public school where displaced persons could receive free lodging and meals. I took the tram to the address of a vacant school in which classrooms had been transformed into dormitories. Most important, it had a kitchen that served two meals a day. In retrospect, it seems to me that there must have been very few homeless displaced persons because I was the only person occupying the classroom, though it contained a number of beds. Mine was an old, white, wrought-iron hospital bed and mattress. Having had the bad experience with bedbugs in Budapest, I immediately proceeded to clean the bed with turpentine and other chemicals, hoping to make my nights restful and comfortable. Between my precautions and the school's general cleanliness, I found that sleeping alone in that big room was quite comfortable. The school was not too far from Hradcany, the ancient Prague castle, and the little Golden Street where alchemists had tried to perform magic, turning lead into gold.

Soon after my arrival, I met up with my uncles. First, I found Nathan, the youngest of father's brothers, who lived in Prague and who had already gotten a job as a sales clerk in a bookstore. Alexander, my other uncle, had secured a position as a physician in a noted TB sanatorium outside of the city in Plesh. The sanatorium provided him with a home and meals. I related to the both of them the news I brought from Munkacs. I informed Nathan that there was nothing left of his store, and to the best of our knowledge his wife had not returned from camp. To Alexander, whom I called Uncle Sandor, I stated that his wife was well and would soon join him in Prague. He did not inquire about his home or any of his other material possessions. Only recently have I found out that he foresaw the troubles and before the advent of the war had deposited money both in Swiss banks and in the United States.

I discussed with Uncle Sandor my plan to attend the medical school at Charles University, his alma mater. In the late 1920s and early 1930s, he had attended Charles University where the language of instruction had been both Czech and German. He was quite happy to help with my endeavors to enroll, help which I needed since I hardly spoke Czech, in which he was fluent.

I also needed work, and as a medical student (and again with Uncle Sandor's help), I obtained a position in Bulovka hospital. The work in the hospital was more than pleasant. When I donned a white coat and strung a stethoscope around my neck, I felt that I was on my way to fulfill my dream to become a physician. My job was to obtain a patient's medical history and then to do a work-up, which consisted of analyzing the patient's urine and blood, testing reflexes, and performing many other examinations required by the attending physician. Compared to the present, what I did was primitive medicine. I drew blood from patients to determine type, to count both white and red blood cells, and to determine sedimentation rates. I also examined the patient's urine for albumen, blood, and sugar. In addition I took blood-pressure readings and, when ordered by the resident physician, electrocardiogram (EKG) readings. The EKG was primitive by today's standards. It was a two-lead EKG, which registered its reading on a light-sensitive photographic paper. As soon as I finished taking a strip, I literally ran to the darkroom where I developed the strip and dried the paper before I handed it to the physician. The task that I liked least was to extract stomach acids from patients. This was a routine examination for people with gastric pain or discomfort. My task was to determine the degree of acidity of their stomach juices. To accomplish this task, I had to help the patient swallow 70 centimeters of a small-radius rubber tube. Most often, this procedure made the patient nauseated, and most of them ended up gagging during the procedure. When the tube was finally in place, I extracted the patient's stomach juices using a large syringe. I then took the fluid to the laboratory where I determined the amount of base it required to neutralize the acid.

Twice weekly, I was entrusted with a more important task. Its import derived not from its difficulty, but because it made me the professor's assistant. On Tuesdays and Thursdays, the professor of internal medicine at Charles University made the hospital rounds, followed by his students. On those occasions, I was selected to operate the primitive fluoroscope, a forerunner of today's X-ray. I did this without lead-lined apron or gloves.

The work in the hospital was quite therapeutic for me, and I started to feel somewhat better about myself and hopeful about my future. The dream of becoming a physician and through it gaining status was reinforced one day when a young woman stopped me on the hospital grounds. "Aren't you Dr. Schönfeld from Munkacs?" she inquired.

"Yes, I am Schönfeld Jeno (my Hungarian name) from Munkacs, but not yet a doctor," I had to confess.

A week after my arrival in Prague, my Aunt Illi and my cousin Charlotte arrived from Munkacs. I took them to stay with me at the displaced persons shelter. Charlotte came to Prague to meet her former fiancé Fred, who had been captured by the Russians while serving as a forced laborer for the Hungarian Army. After his capture he had been imprisoned by the Russians. Even though the Russians knew that he was Jewish and that he was part of a forced labor battalion, they nonetheless kept him imprisoned. After a great ordeal, Fred had been given the opportunity to join the Czech legion, fighting as a part of the Russian Army. It was there that Fred met a Jewish female soldier with whom he had established a liaison and with whom he now lived in Prague.

In Fred's defense, I must point out that in those years no one knew whether life would ever attain normalcy and whether wives, fiancées, or any other relatives would have survived the Holocaust. Most people, like Fred, lived for the moment, without thinking of the past and having little concern for the future. Therefore, I never considered Fred's association with the other woman as an act of disloyalty or betrayal. What Fred sought was to stabilize his life, which included a shared emotional relationship with another person.

However, Charlotte wished to reestablish their old relationship. They had been engaged, that is, the conditions for marriage had been declared. Now the problem was how to communicate her feelings and wishes. She was reluctant to talk to Fred face to face as long as he lived with the other woman. I was enlisted to carry messages from Charlotte to Fred and vice versa. Fred assured her that he still loved her, and that his feelings for her had not changed. Charlotte understood that one could not blame him if he had altered his life in the two years that he had lived as a soldier in the Czech/Russian Army. Still, Fred had a hard decision to make. To return to Charlotte, he had to leave the woman with whom he had shared an intimate relationship for almost two years. It was a push-pull situation, and the pull to return to Charlotte was greater than his other feelings, so he left the other woman. In a short time, Charlotte and Fred were married.

While my father stayed, all my cousins and uncles left Munkacs. I even met some members of the Neuman family, my mother's cousins from Talamas, who had survived. They and I were the only survivors of my mother's family. To my shame, I lost contact with them, and the older I get, the greater is my sorrow at not having kept in touch.

My Aunt Illi informed me of my father's decision to stay in Munkacs for a while, at least till he was able to sell the merchandise that he had found in his store. With the money, he planned to start another business, he hoped, in America. Indeed, he sent me money with my Aunt Illi and with other messengers. I considered that money to be my father's. It was the foundation on which we might build a new future. I never used any of that money, even though I sorely needed it. I held it in trust for him.

But the fates were against us. On November 1, 1945, the Czech government declared that all old money must be exchanged for new bills. All old paper currencies must be turned in at designated banks where new currencies would be issued. True, new bills were issued, but, instead of crediting me with the amount I turned in, all monies were declared forfeited. However, because I was a student without full-time employment, the government permitted me to withdraw 1,500 korunas each month for living expenses. This amount was far from sufficient for food and lodging. So now, soon after being freed from slave labor, from the starvation in the camps, I again started to feel the discomfort and the pain of hunger.

Although the work in the hospital was hard, what made it even more arduous was that, in addition to my eight-hour shift, I also spent almost three hours commuting to work. Nonetheless, the work was very satisfying. There was an important bonus, namely, that I also had one good meal a day in the hospital's dining room. I rose at four in the morning, had a piece of bread for breakfast, shaved and dressed, and then made a fifteen-minute walk to catch the tram. I had to be at the tram station by five-thirty. The tram took about an hour and a quarter to arrive at the station near the hospital, and then I had to walk to the building housing the men's wards. My shift began at seven and ended at three. I arrived back at my dorm at five in the afternoon and had my evening meal by six. I hardly did anything in the evenings. First I was too tired, and, second, I had no money for entertainment. Occasionally, however, I went to the movies; it was my sole diversion and entertainment. On one occasion, the auditorium for the seven o'clock feature was filled, and I foolishly decided to wait for the next feature, which started at nine. I sat down to watch the film only to be awakened by the custodian. The theater was empty; the lights were on. "Don't you think it is time to go home to sleep?" he inquired of me, mockingly.

My love for the United States has been a constant aspect of my life. If anything, the friendships I made when I worked in the military hospital after the war reinforced this feeling. In the summer of 1945, many U.S. soldiers came to visit Prague, a beautiful city with ancient architecture that had not been touched by war for centuries. It was the city that Mozart loved most.

I joined a group of English-speaking people who acted as hosts to visiting GIs. I enjoyed this task. Not only did I have a chance to show them one of Europe's most beautiful cities, but I also was able to maintain my language skills. During one of my visits to the "Friends of America" office, I was given another assignment. I was handed a number of tickets to a football game, and I was required to sell them. These tickets were for a game to be played in Prague by two Army divisions. Of course, I purchased one ticket for myself. I have always been a football fan, and in fact I had been on my high school's "B" team. With great anticipation, I went to the stadium that Sunday afternoon. When the two teams took the field and I saw their uniforms, I knew that this was not the football I knew and loved. It was a peculiar game, a game I neither knew nor understood. I was perplexed as the 11 men on one team formed a tight circle, putting their heads together, and then lined up in a formation that I had never encountered. Instead of a round ball, they used an oval-shaped ball that was handed by one player to another. The players ran at each other and hit each other with great ferocity. At other occasions, the ball was thrown, but the hitting continued. For two hours, I watched in amazement without knowing what in the world was going on. This, I was told later, was American football.

By late summer of 1945, my temporary residence in the displaced persons' housing ended. The school was to be refitted for classes. I moved to an old college dormitory. It was a wooden structure that seemed to be a relic from the turn of the century. Each room, although very small, was designed for two persons. It contained a wooden bunk bed and a washstand. Since the dormitory was not filled, I had the pleasure of a room to myself.

I still had the same clothes that had been issued to me in Germany at liberation. One could say I traveled extremely lightly. My worldly possessions consisted of the pink suit given to me in the hospital in Germany, two shirts, two pairs of shorts, some socks, and a pair of very tight-fitting light summer shoes. For the first time in my life, I experienced the pain of a corn and learned to cut it out. I was glad to have had a single room because I could strip naked and wash my few items and hang them to dry in the room.

I was not aware of what the color pink symbolized. I knew that homosexuals in the camp had been designated by a pink triangle sewn to their jacket above their numbers. But in regard to the practice for which they were imprisoned, I was naïve. I soon learned the meaning of wearing a pink suit. My Czech language skills were extremely poor, and I needed to have one of the medical students in the hospital who spoke German serve as my translator. Thus, I needed a Czech-Hungarian dictionary and sought a bookstore. In my best Czech, I asked the salesman for a dictionary. While handing me the book, the salesman looked at my pink suit and rubbed my palm with his finger. Although I did not know for sure what he meant, I surmised that the salesman had propositioned me sexually. Disturbed, I hastily retreated from the store. That evening, I related to my friends what had happened. They informed me that I would, most likely, receive more such propositions because of my pink suit. Not having the means to purchase other clothing, I had to endure my fate till I could do something about it.

I fell in love with a beautiful red-haired Jewish girl who lived in the dorm. There was nothing that I could do about my feelings, not only because I lacked any money, but also because I realized that my education must come first. Soon my dilemma was solved. One day, she asked me to accompany her to Kosice, a city in the Slovakian region. I could not leave at that time. A week passed by and she did not return to the dorm. I received a letter from her in which she informed me that while in Kosice she had met someone and married him. Fast marriages were quite common among survivors. People were lonely. Single persons without any family married as a means to dispel their loneliness. Whether these marriages lasted, I do not know.

I wanted to study and pass my course work. But how could I pass my courses when my knowledge of Czech was minimal? I did not even have an adequate vocabulary for simple conversation. When I began to work in the hospital, I found someone who could speak English who helped me to slowly acquire conversational Czech. (Of course, I would have preferred to speak German, but at that time both Sudeten Germans and the German language were hated entities.) I purchased a used anatomy book and decided that I would underline the words I did not know. Through hard work and the use of a dictionary, I hoped to acquire the knowledge to pass the courses. But after attempting to read the first page, I became quite despondent. The page had more words underlined than not. How long, Oh God, I thought to myself, how long must I suffer?

My suffering extended beyond my academic struggles. I was constantly hungry. Because I hoped to spend most of my time in study, I gave up my work at the hospital and missed the one decent meal I received there in the cafeteria.

It was paradoxical that now after liberation I should continue to suffer hunger. Throughout my internment, I accepted hunger as an unalterable condition, hoping, of course, that after liberation I would no longer feel the constant pangs and pains of hunger. Now, I was liberated, and I still continued to lack the basic necessities of life: decent shelter, food, and clothing. Almost everyone suffered, to some degree or another, the consequences of war. Food was scarce for everyone in the city, and such items as meat and butter were still rationed in Czechoslovakia. But native Czechs, even those living in cities, were able to manage. They had various connections and resources in the country from whom they could secure food without ration cards. I, living in one room in a wooden dorm that was an extreme fire hazard, not only lacked the resources and money for black-market food but also cooking facilities, and I had to rely solely on restaurants. These were not only expensive, they also required food coupons. The coupons that I received entitled me to a monthly ration of 500 grams of meat (about 1 pound) and 100 grams of fat. An average portion of meat in a restaurant required at least 200 grams of meat and 50 grams of fat coupons. My coupons did not last long. They were used up within the first week after receiving them.

Was there a solution to my problem of hunger and loneliness? I contemplated two solutions. Neither, however, suited me. First, I could give private language lessons. For instance, I was hired by a family to teach Hebrew as part of their preparation to immigrate to Palestine. The pay was not much, but I managed to schedule the lessons close to dinnertime, resulting in frequent invitations to join the family. While I accepted an occasional invitation for dinner, I was ashamed to accept more meals, or for that matter to schedule my courses too close to dinnertime. In my view, to have done either would be tantamount to begging. That would reduce even more my already low self-esteem. My second solution was to find restaurants that were both inexpensive and served food that did not require food coupons. I found a number of such restaurants. The cheapest meal without rations was fried blood and potatoes. The idea of eating blood was, at first, downright abominable to me. It went against everything that I had been taught in childhood. It was not that I kept Kosher; one eats almost everything when hungry. But eating blood, especially the blood of pigs, was perhaps equal in distaste to eating dog. But hunger is a formidable force. One soon changes his values and perspectives when hunger is strong enough, and in my case it was.

Fall comes early in Prague, and still I had nothing else to wear besides my pink suit and a pair of light summer shoes. I was cold. Luckily, my father sent me a short coat. It was not warm enough for the upcoming winter, but it was far better than being without it.

In September, I began my studies. If I progressed at all, it was very slight. First, my lack of the necessary language skills handicapped me. Second, in my self-alienation, I was estranged from everything. As beautiful as Prague was, I could not think of it as home. I could not develop a commitment to anything. I was in limbo, in a terrestrial purgatory, neither in hell nor in heaven, a no man's land in which I lacked attachment either to people or to the country. My class attendance was infrequent.

My only joy was to visit my cousin Charlotte and her husband Fred. They provided me with a sense of being home, a sense of belonging. For a few months after Fred's marriage to Charlotte, he was still in the Czech army for which he served as a movie projectionist. In this capacity, Fred had access to American movies, which he brought home. In their apartment on one such occasion, I heard again the wonderful sounds of big band. He showed us the film Sun Valley Serenade, and I fell in love with the sound that all America loved, the sound of Glenn

Miller's band. His music influenced me just as it did countless American youths. The big-band music was not only different from the chamber music that was popular in Prague, but it also spoke eloquently of a new way of life, the American way. It was the music of a different world. It was a stimulus for my imagination to dream of a world not only very much unlike the shtetl of my youth but also quite unlike staid Europe.

In August, just before the beginning of the fall semester, I moved into a new dorm. This one was a large brick building, and I had a room set up for four students. Luckily, I now met three friends, boys who had been my schoolmates in the Hebrew gymnasium, two from my class and one a class below us. All four of us Holocaust survivors now enrolled in medical school, our pre-Holocaust dream. I hoped that living with my friends, sharing the same dream, would alleviate my depression, my inability to study. But, alas, such was not to be. My friends suffered from the same malady. We all felt restless, unable to concentrate on our studies. Above all, we felt rootless, as though we did not belong in this city or in this country. None of us felt that our future would be either in Prague or in any part of Czechoslovakia. Life, at least the one we lived, was unreal. We were constantly on edge, waiting for something to happen, for some event that would give meaning to our lives and perhaps magically make us aware of our destiny. Perhaps, if my father had been with me, it would have been different for me. Perhaps, his presence would have anchored my life, and I could have accepted it as more or less a continuation of my earlier existence. But, of course, this did not happen.

Mail from my father had always been addressed in care of my cousin Charlotte. In his letters, he assured me that he had not forgotten me nor our plans to immigrate to the U.S. and open a bookstore. One day I received a letter from my father, who informed me that someone, whose name I now cannot recall, would give me some diamonds and U.S. 20 dollar gold pieces. I was given the messenger's address. When I went to seem him, he denied that my father had entrusted him with the gold and jewels. Since this transaction would be an illegal act, there was nothing that I could do but to suffer the loss without informing my father.

I was always hungry, and Charlotte insisted that I take some of the money that she was keeping to buy clothes for the winter and occasionally even black-market food. I had refused to draw upon the money my father sent me, but in spite of wishing to guard it, all of it had been lost when the country exchanged its currency. The loss of the money was a harsh experience, but the next letter from him brought me news that was even more devastating.

In one of my visits to Charlotte, in the beginning of November just before my 20th birthday, I received three letters from my father. Prague was already cold, and a penetrating wind made it feel even colder than the near- freezing temperature registered on the thermometer. The letters were waiting for me on her kitchen table. I opened the first letter and read it. Its content and tone were the same as earlier ones I received from him. In this letter, as in all previous ones, he lamented the death of my mother and my siblings. Again, he informed me that at the first opportunity he would smuggle himself out of the Soviet Union to join me in Prague. The borders were no longer in a state of flux and relatively unguarded, as they had been when I had left the Soviet Union. By the fall of 1945, the Iron Curtain had descended, and legal emigration from behind it was impossible. Still, there were people who found ways to escape, and my father, at least in his letter, was confident that he could find a way to get out to join me. Again, he assured me that we would immigrate to the United States. I opened the second letter, and its content was similar to that of the previous one. I began to get a feeling that, in spite of his earlier plans, the opportunity for our reunion had passed. I turned to my cousin with a sense of resignation. "I've had enough of his doom and gloom. He writes the same lamentations in all of his letters. There isn't any need for me to read the next one. I am sure it will be the same as the other two."

"Come on, Tuli," she responded, "Read the next one; it may contain some good news."

Yes, the third letter was different from the others. It contained news, but it was not good, at least for me. In this letter, my father did not start by depicting his state of sadness and his sense of loss. In this letter, he no longer recited his life's disappointments or our collective tragedies. He did not eulogize my brother and sister. Instead, he informed me that he had gotten married. Now that I am 79, I can understand his loneliness, and, of course, his sexual needs. He was only 47 years old, a young person. But at that time, the news of his marriage did not fill me with happiness for him. To the contrary, I felt only anger. Not only did I feel rejected, that he chose a wife to be with instead of me, but I took his act as an affront to my mother's memory. I judged him as an adulterer. My hopes for having a normal life were now completely shattered. It was just a few days before my 20th birthday, and I felt alone. My plans for the future had always revolved around our being together. I had not used the money that he was able to send via messengers. It had been kept in Charlotte's closet, waiting for him. This was his seed money for a new life. Since I was always hungry, my cousin had urged me to use that money for food. I had refused. In rejecting the use of the money, I always commented, "This is my father's money; he will need it to have a fresh start when he joins me." Now, the money was gone, and I had to face the stark truth that I was alone and penniless. My feelings toward him had changed. I was utterly disappointed in him; I was hurt by his callous disregard for my feelings. I felt devastated that he had abandoned me and that I came second in his life. This experience taught me, unfortunately the hard way, that my life had to be my own, that one cannot count on anyone else, and that each of us responds to our own needs and desires first. I learned the true meaning of Rabbi Hillel's adage in the collection of teachings titled *Ethics of our Fathers*: "If I am not for myself then who is for me?"

Where were my uncles during this time? They had their own concerns and problems. I seldom saw them, nor was I invited to see them. Alexander lived outside Prague with his wife and son. Nathan was trying hard to normalize his own life. My hope was in America. So I turned to my uncle Saul in St. Louis for help. To have a chance to immigrate to the United States, I needed an affidavit and a ticket. He sent them to me and quite quickly. The affidavit attested that, when I would immigrate to the United States, he would take responsibility for my welfare. He further assured the government that I would not become dependent on state welfare. Together with the affidavit, he also sent me a one-way plane ticket from Paris to St. Louis.

But immigration to the States was difficult. These were the days of quotas, and the quota for Czechs seeking entrance to the U.S. was filled, and it seemed there would not be an opening for a number of years. I was informed that I had two problems. First, my place in the quota system would not come up till at least 1948. Second, to be able to exit the country, I would first to fulfill my military obligations to the Czechoslovakian Republic.

I was about to become a Czech citizen. The Czech government offered two options to persons born in Carpathia, a part of the Czechoslovak Republic prior to 1938, an option to apply for Czech citizenship or one to return to the region, which now was a part of the Soviet Union. I opted to become a Czech rather than a Soviet citizen. But Czech citizenship also came with military obligations.

The political mood in Czechoslovakia after November of 1945 was becoming repressive. Both the American and Russian occupation forces, in accordance with the Yalta Agreement, had been withdrawn by the fall of 1945. But it did not take long for the Soviet Union to repudiate its agreement. Two weeks after it left it started to return, and once again Soviet soldiers could be seen on the streets of Prague. The withdrawal was a ploy. The Soviets had never intended to free Czechoslovakia from their sphere of influence. The free and democratic country that I had known in my early youth was being replaced by a harsh totalitarian regime. The Czechoslovak Republic was becoming a part of the Eastern bloc.

Life in the dormitory was hard. It was winter, and there was little and sometimes no heat all. From somewhere, my friends acquired resistor wires which they strung, illegally of course, across the room. By the surreptitious use of electricity, we managed to keep the room, if not completely comfortable, at least at a tolerable temperature.

December was the beginning of the Farshing, a period of merriment that lasts through Fat Tuesday, the day before Lent. This is observed in most Roman Catholic countries. In Brazil, it is Carnival time, and in the United States we know it as Mardi Gras.  According to local traditions, the time from Christmas through March is the time of masquerade balls. The dormitory's masquerade ball was also an annual tradition. I decided to attend it, dressed as an American GI. As a sociologist today, I would refer to this desire as *anticipatory socialization*. America and Americans were becoming my point of reference. I was beginning to identify myself as a future American. I was slowly transferring my allegiance from Europe to the United States. I was leaving the past and looking ahead to the future, which to me was synonymous with being an American, the Golden Country, as Jews referred to it. To become an American GI, I needed a uniform, but I knew someone who had a complete uniform, and he was kind enough to lend it to me. I also needed two additional items, props, which I thought were the sine qua non in playing the American soldier: American cigarettes and chewing gum. These I acquired on the black market. I was ready.

This was the first dance that I had ever attended. Dancing was not considered an appropriate activity for Jewish teens (or adults, for that matter), and there were not any dance parties in Jewish homes. Although there were some dances, as in the local hotel and coffeehouse, traditional Jews, as my family considered itself to be, would not attend them. It is not that Jews were kept out of these places. Simply, the community would look askance at any Jew who would violate this norm. Most adults in Munkacs would not dare to go to a dance even on New Year's Eve. But it was time to change. I was free from the constraints of tradition.

When I entered the ballroom at my dorm dressed in an American Army uniform, with American cigarettes and chewing gum, I attracted the attention of those present, especially the young women. That was my desired effect. I was seen as an American, and I also pretended that I could not speak Czech. Some of the young women there spoke English, and from my few months of association with Americans, I now spoke with enough of an American accent that my disguise was believable. I enjoyed listening to the women discussing me, especially as they were working out agreements among themselves regarding who would dance with me. For a young man of 20, all of this fuss over me was more than gratifying. It was ego enhancing. Toward the end of the evening, I chose to stay in the company of one young woman. After midnight, following tradition,

I revealed who I really was, and everyone accepted me, with no one really angry at my deception.

That one particular young woman and I began dating. While I took her to the movies and for a hot dog at an outside stand, she took me to the theater and to restaurants. She justified her extravagance with the explanation that she had a well-paying full-time job in an office. I was grateful to attend the theater, particularly Mozart's *Don Giovanni* at the Estate Theater. I did not know who my date really was. I knew her name, but the family name itself did not mean anything to me. I took her word that she was from a middle-class family and that her father was a businessman. In fact, I did not have either her address or her phone number. We had what Europeans at that time referred to as a rendezvous, that is, an agreement to meet at a certain designated place, usually at a coffeehouse on Prague's main street, Vaclavske Namjesti. Consequently, I never met her at her home and did not get an opportunity to meet her parents.

A few months after our initial date, the woman whose name I have by now forgotten, gave me a letter to read. The letter was a response to one she had written to an uncle. In her letter, she wrote about me and my desire for and difficulty in attending medical school. She informed him that I was a Holocaust survivor and that we had been dating for a while. Most surprisingly, she told him that she had fallen in love with me and that she wanted to marry me. Her uncle's response was very surprising. He informed her that it would be nice if we could join him in his new home in Brazil and there become a part of the family business. The letter was signed "Bata."

I was surprised and astonished that all this time I was dating Bata's niece. Bata was a name associated with the largest European manufacturer and distributor of shoes, socks, hosiery, and many other related items. His factories in Czechoslovakia were located in Zlin, and it was said that in 1938 his company had more airplanes than the Czech Air Force. When the Germans occupied Bohemia, he escaped to Brazil, and his company became a worldwide manufacturer and distributor of footwear. The offer to marry into a family of great wealth was tempting, but my youth kept me back. I was barely twenty and did not have any desire to settle down into married life. Also, I had a deeply rooted and unshakable belief that I must not, under any conditions, marry someone non-Jewish.

The mere fact that I dated a non-Jewish woman was itself a deviation from my inculcated norms. Never in my life in Munkacs would I have dared to date any one but a Jewish girl. Even in my little shtetl, status considerations were very important. In a search for status honor, all Jewish families hope that their children will marry well, with wealth and connections to a desirable family. A good marriage brings *yichus shat* (status honor) to both families; honor is extremely desirable. The parents of a child who marries well become the object of envy. But no marriage, regardless of wealth and family status, is a good marriage if it is exogamous. Not only would the violator of the norm of endogamy be sanctioned but so would the extended family. The pressure for intrareligious marriage in my town, in which the Jewish population was the majority, was enormous. The violator of endogamy was cut off from the Jewish community and ostracized. Most frequently, the family of the exogamous person would declare their son or daughter dead and perform the rituals associated with death.

In Munkacs, fortunately, it was easy to stay within the bounds of expectations. Consider my case. I lived in a town that was primarily Jewish, on a street in which but one family was non-Jewish; I went to a school in which the language of instruction was Hebrew and hence attended by Jews only. My only contact with non-Jewish girls was when I helped as a salesperson in our store. For all practical purposes, I was cut off from most associations with non-Jews.

In Prague, conditions were different. My association with Jews in Prague was limited to uncles and to Charlotte. I lived in a dorm that, with the exception of my three roommates and me, was occupied by non-Jews. I worked in a hospital in which, to my knowledge, there were no other Jews. Hence, the necessary propinquity for intrareligious marriage was absent. The young women I met at the hospital and at the university were non-Jews. There is a sociological dictum "interaction varies with sentiment," and my interaction in Prague was mainly with non-Jews. Moreover, a large city also affords the kind of personal freedom that one does not experience in small towns. In Prague, I was not subject to communal pressures to be endogamous. Why then did I not marry this rich, good-looking young woman? The answer lies in my education, my Holocaust experience, my continued association with my uncles, and, perhaps most importantly, my desire to be free.

It is only now, in retrospect, that I can understand my decision not to marry a non-Jew. Of course, I cannot totally discount my anticipation of the severe negative sanctions my surviving relatives would have imposed on me. I was fearful of alienating myself from the few surviving members of my family, even though I suspected that their concern for my happiness was not genuine. In fact, later experiences in the United States, especially when it came to their recommendation as to whom I should marry, were ample evidence that their wish was to have control over me rather than a genuine concern for my happiness. One particular uncle who sought to act *in loco parentis* told me that he would find me a wife from a wealthy and socially important family. My interpretation of this desire is that it was perhaps more for his benefit than mine. Were I to marry into wealth, he could then have divested himself from any sense of responsibility for my welfare. In fact, should I have married someone with wealth and high status, like Bata's niece, even if she were not Jewish, he most likely would not have objected too much.

But my decision not to marry Bata's niece, in addition to the reasons I've given, was rooted mostly in my worldview and most importantly in my overwhelming commitment to my Jewish identity. This identity did not reside in religion. In my teens, I had started to rebel against unexamined faith. I could not understand the need for unquestioned obedience to God or the dutiful performance of rituals just because such obedience was justified as God's will. Religious rigidity seemed contrary to reason. I sought understanding rather than blind faith. Even though there were synagogues in Prague, I cannot remember having attended any, even for High-Holiday services. I did not obey the kosher dietary laws; to the contrary, I ate food that would have been considered abominable by even non-Orthodox Jews. Instead of religion and cult, my Jewish identity was rooted in my commitment to Jewish moral philosophy, to Jewish culture, and to Jewish history. I felt bound by a golden chain to my people's destiny, although, as I have stated, I did not agree with the Orthodox view that we must perform rituals because God demands it, more specifically, as His Torah ordains it.

Still, I did not reject in Prague, nor do I now reject, all rituals. I observe some rituals because I see them as necessary for maintaining my Jewish identity. My performances of Jewish rituals, then, as they are now, are symbolic acts and overt declarations of my ties with my people. By performing the rituals, I declare that I am a part of my people and that their fate is my fate. Curiously, my Holocaust experiences, my suffering because of being Jewish, did not diminish this sense. To the contrary, it strengthened it. Not too long ago, someone asked if I fast on Yom Kippur. I replied in the affirmative.

The interrogator was astonished. "Why do you do it? After all, I know you don't believe in the magical efficacy of fasting."

"True enough," I replied, "But I choose to fast as my affirmation of being Jewish, of being a part of my people."

In this manner, I tie myself to the worldwide Jewish collective. Being Jewish, being a member of this historical people, was then, and is now very important to me. I could not conceive of marrying and living with someone who did not share this view. And after the Holocaust and the destruction of a great part of my people, the need for endogamy is indeed crucial and central to Jewish survival.

There may have been a third reason for my reluctance to marry this rich woman, and this arose, perhaps, from my desire to be free and to seek my own goals. Marrying into wealth would have subjected me to her family's pressures. The family would have tried to make me conform to its view of what my life should be. My mother, a romantic, often remarked that marrying for the sake of wealth is to invite problems. She taught me a Yiddish saying which proposes that when one marries for wealth, "eventually the money will disappear but the *klipotoh* (the problem, i.e., the wife) will remain." She often told me about cases where marital disharmony was related to marriages of convenience. I am not sure that my rejection of this opportunity and later similar opportunities were solely the result of my mother's teaching. Still, I did also reject other such opportunities to marry into wealth. In my mind and in my view, marrying for the sake of gaining wealth is tantamount to giving up one's freedom. And this I was extremely reluctant to do.

My sense of impermanence in Prague and my perception of being a stranger in a strange land constantly haunted me.

Although I was proud to have been born in a country whose presidents were intellectual giants like Masaryk and Benes, still I lacked both the emotional and intellectual ties that could connect me to the country and its people. I did not have and I could not develop a sense of belonging. I came to Prague not because I sought to be a part of this country but because I wished to escape from the Soviet Union, and there was no other place, at least at that time, where I could have gone. I knew that my life in Prague was temporary, that I would stay there only till I could immigrate to the United States. My aim since I was 13 years old was to go to the U.S., the country that the Jews in Eastern Europe called the "golden country." In fact these were the same feelings expressed by both my uncles. I think most survivors lost their desire to remain in Europe with its history of both official and sub rosa antisemitism.

To emigrate, to leave one's country of residence, one must experience both push-and-pull forces. First, one must feel the pressure, a stress, which compels the person to want to leave his country. Second, one must have positive images of the country of destination to desire to become part of it.

I made my decision, and the country to which I sought to immigrate was America. The United States was my ideal. I did not know much about its history nor about the real America. What I knew about the United States was derived from the movies I had seen and from the GIs with whom I had worked at the hospital after my liberation. At that time, I perceived America as a democratic ideal, as the country where any person is free to achieve his dreams. It was the land of Horatio Alger. England was not an option to me. I could never become, or would want to become, a part of a country that had reneged on its agreement with the Jews. England was a country that, in my opinion, was, and still is, without moral integrity in its politics. In its view of its own national superiority, the English do not have to be moral since they are quite certain, and have made it abundantly clear to everyone, that God is an Englishman. As a Jew imbued with Zionist ideals, how could I live in a country that lacked the moral courage to carry out the promise of its Prime Minister, Lord Balfour, to make Palestine a Jewish homeland, Israel? Neither was France my ideal. This was a country which, although espousing the slogans of liberty, equality, and fraternity, was also guilty of the Dreyfus affair.

My compulsion to immigrate to the United States made me jealous and envious of any person who gained the permission to immigrate there. I was asked to attend a farewell party given by some students for a young woman who was leaving for the States. I reluctantly accepted, only to make a fool of myself. I usually do not drink alcohol. I am not a teetotaler; after all, in my father's house we always had wine on the table on Shabbat. I just never had the urge to drink as a means to enjoy a party or as an escape mechanism. But in this instance, because of my envy, I sought to escape my own reality, to disguise my hurt and jealousy. I drank brandy, the only alcohol available. Since I did not like its taste, I sweetened it with sugar. The combination of sugar and alcohol not only made me drunk, it also made me sick.

In early 1946, we heard a persistent rumor, which like all rumors in those days, one took seriously. This one had severe political implications if it was true. My experiences in the concentration camps had led me to take rumors at face value, for life in the camps and the experiences before camp made me fearful. Hence, in hearing a rumor, I never thought, "Oh, it's just a rumor and it doesn't have any factual basis." Instead, I thought, "Suppose it is true." I felt that it was better to anticipate problems than to be sorry if the problems, which the rumors predicted, were true and I had not prepared a defense. For instance, in November of 1945, I had heard rumors that the old Czech korunas (the old bills) would be exchanged for new ones and that the government would not necessarily make an even exchange. Although I could have exchanged the old money on the black market for dollars at a devalued rate, I chose not to heed the rumors. Consequently, I lost the money my father sent me.

I had learned the hard way that one must consider that rumors may indeed have a factual basis. The rumors that we now heard persistently from a number of different persons could, if true, literally destroy my life. It was rumored that the Russian secret police (NKVD), operating in the Czechoslovak republic, was gathering and sending back to the Soviet Union all those who came from Carpathia and had applied for Czech citizenship. The Communist Party in Czechoslovakia, with Soviet help, was becoming emboldened. This was the period when Jan Masaryk, the son of the founder of modern Czechoslovakia, supposedly committed suicide by jumping out the window of a tall building. No one accepted the legitimacy of the suicide report. We all took it for granted that he had been murdered. In this atmosphere, we believed most rumors we heard, especially about the possibility of being arrested and taken back to the Soviet Union. The four of us, friends and classmates – Chaim, Dudi, Hershi and I – living in the same dorm and hailing from the same region in Carpathia agreed that we must leave Prague immediately.

Since we could not go to the United States, we felt that there was but one place where for the interim we could go. A place that, because of being occupied and governed by America, could provide us safe shelter: West Germany. But how did one get there? How could we cross the Czech-German border without any documents? How could we enter Germany surreptitiously? To solve the problem, I sought help from Prague's Jewish Federation. Its people were willing to help us, but with one condition; we must take with us over a dozen children, aged 12 to 14. The children were survivors of the Holocaust, and they too were seeking to settle in another country. I agreed. Of the four of us, only Chaim Sternbach and I were going immediately, and we agreed to take the children. We were told that we must leave in two days. We were to meet and pick up the children early in the morning at the Federation building on Parizska Street in the old Jewish quarter. At that time, I was told, we would also be given further instructions. By telephone, I informed my two uncles of my decision. They tried to dissuade me. They told me not to give credence to the rumors, and they promised that they would help me legally immigrate with them. I could not take that chance. I countered their argument by pointing out that because I was of military age, I could not secure exit permits until I fulfilled my two-year obligation. In two years, who knew what might happen. In fact, by late 1948, the borders of Czechoslovakia, like those of the U.S.S.R., were totally shut, and no one was permitted to exit. Thus, my family and I parted, hoping to be reunited later in St. Louis, Missouri.

By early 1946, communication with my father had become very difficult. These were Stalin's last days, and my father's letters became very sparse and were addressed to "My dear nephew." It seems that all letters, even those going to Czechoslovakia, were censored, and my father did not want to indicate in his writing that he had a son in another country. In fact, in his last letter, he informed me that he could no longer write and he would start communicating again at an appropriate time. Not wishing to harm him, I wrote him a note as a stranger, delivering a message, informing him that his nephew had left Czechoslovakia without leaving any forwarding address. Any hope that my father would join me in Prague had now been lost, and there was nothing to keep me there. The push forces to leave had now by far outweighed any reason for staying. It was time to say goodbye to that city and leave for Germany.

In spite of the reason and logic for the return to Germany,

to assure a good future for myself, I was nonetheless very apprehensive about returning to the country where I had been enslaved.
After all, it is difficult to return to a country whose population
had sought our destruction. Germany was responsible for all the
tragedies that had resulted from the war it had started against
civilization. Germans were also directly responsible for all my
present problems: the loss of family, my dislocation from the
town of my birth, my poverty, and my emotional distress. But
like the heroes of Greek tragedies, I found my destiny to dictate
my return to Germany. I had no other choice.

Chapter Ten
**Returning to
Germany**

The day of my proposed departure had arrived. The cardboard suitcase that I had received from the Jewish agency was packed. It was light for I had hardly anything to put into it. Chaim and I arrived at the Federation Building, across from the Old-New Synagogue in the Josefov section in the Old City, in the early morning. There, in front of the building, were about 15 children waiting for us.

Our instructions were simple enough. We were to take the children to a small border town, the name of which I cannot now recall, and wait in a particular restaurant there for someone who would lead us across the Czech border into Germany. Once in Germany, I would take the children by train to Munich to a displaced persons' camp, Funk Kaserne.

We took the children on the streetcar to the train station. Conditions at the stations already foreshadowed the restrictive policies of the impending authoritarian regime. Security agents and police guarded the platforms. They questioned every passenger waiting to embark on any train that was to leave toward the German border. The Iron Curtain was now descending on Czechoslovakia. No one was allowed to go to the border unless he or she lived there or had legitimate business in that area.

After having purchased our tickets, we proceeded to board the train. The police, however, stopped us. "Why are you going to that city?" a plain-clothed detective asked me.

No one had told me to anticipate these problems. Indeed, why was I going to the border? What legitimate- sounding reason could I give the authorities? On the spur of the moment, I thought of a response. I took out my Bulovka Hospital identity card, which was still valid, and showed it to the policeman. "These are children who have survived German concentration camps. They have been orphaned, and on top of all that they have TB. I am instructed to take them to the TB hospital nearby the village on the border."

Given my own foreign accent, my ID, and the malnourished look of the children, he accepted my explanation, and we were permitted to board.

We arrived late in the afternoon at the border town and proceeded to the pub where we waited for our guide. It was late evening when he appeared. He informed us that he had bribed the border guards with a number of bottles of Slivovitz, their favorite plum brandy. By midnight, we would be ready to cross the border. Nonetheless, we had to instruct the children to abstain from talking or making any noise, which would compel the guards to act. It was a moonlit night, and we all climbed to the ridge of the hill that marked the border between Czechoslovakia and the American sector of West Germany. Having arrived at the border, I was instructed to take the children down hill to the train station in the German village from which we should take the morning train to Munich to

Funk Kaserne. I was not given money for tickets or food for the journey.

We descended the hill to the village and found the train station, which was open. There, the children lay down on the hard wooden benches to wait for morning. In the morning, I was faced with two problems. First, how would I provide transportation for all of us to Munich, and second, how would I feed the children, who by now were very hungry. Food in Germany, aside from the cost, was still rationed, and we had neither money nor ration cards.

I had an idea. I consulted Chaim. We decided that one of us would act as an American official. My English was better than his and since I had worked with the American military, I spoke with an American accent. I would present myself as a CIC agent, that is, as an agent of the U.S. Army's Counter Intelligence Corps, for they quite often wore civilian clothes. Chaim would be my interpreter.

With my new identity, I appeared before the stationmaster and flashed my supposed identity card. The card with my photo and many official-looking stamps on it was in fact my student streetcar pass. It seemed to me that this German official was well-trained in accepting authority figures without challenge. Just the mention of my being a CIC agent and behaving as an official with the aura of authority was sufficient evidence to him of my legitimacy. Most likely, his submission to my authority without challenge was the consequence of his being a member of a defeated nation now facing a person who, in his mind, corresponded to the German Gestapo. Be that as it may, he complied with my request (or was it a command?) that an additional carriage be added to the train in order to accommodate gratis these new passengers.

But the problem of food was perhaps even more acute and imminent than getting adequate transportation. The children were hungry. Again, I conferred with Chaim and decided that if my impersonation of a CIC officer had worked in the first instance, why not try it again. We went into the village and found what we considered to be the best sources for food, a bakery and a butcher shop.

We entered the bakery and confronted the proprietor. Again I produced and flashed my tram ID. Through Chaim, as my interpreter, I told the owner that I was en route to Munich with a number of children and therefore was requisitioning a half dozen loaves of bread. I made my request in English. My hope was that no one in the bakery could speak English and challenge my claimed authority. Still, just in case there was anyone who understood English, I spoke with exaggerated American idioms and pronunciation. Fortunately, I was not challenged, and the loaves of bread were handed over. We gave a similar performance in the butcher shop, where we received a few kilos of ready-to-eat German sausages. We brought the food to the children, and we all sat down to eat, knowing well that this would have to suffice till we reached Munich.

Whenever I relate these events to others, I always experience a great sense of pleasure. The fact that I was able, in spite of my youth, for at that time I was about 20 years old, to take care of children entrusted to me gave me a great sense of satisfaction. Still, I think that what pleased me most was that for the first time I, a young Jew facing my former destroyers, was able to take some degree of revenge on them. I was able to command and make them comply with my will.

When I reentered Germany, I was quite apprehensive. Subconsciously I was fearful from being back in the land that was directly responsible for the Holocaust, the great conflagration suffered by European Jewry. Had I returned to experience again the destructive forces of a country that sought to make the world *Juden rein* (clean of Jews)? In a sense, I felt angry at the fates that had compelled me to return to this hateful country. This little bit of deception, my claim to being an American, which in a sense was an anticipatory fulfillment of my dream, helped me redefine my present. I did not return to Germany, I told myself; I was merely en route to the United States. I was in the process of fulfilling my dream.

The train arrived, and an additional coach was added for us only. There were few trains to Munich. Right after the war, the German railroads were in shambles. Bridges were out; engines were scarce; and all that meant that all trains were crowded. Seeing a fairly empty coach, Germans sought to enter it. I stood at the only door, which I unlocked, wielding a document as though it were an official order. With the document written in English on official U.S. letterhead, and with U.S. seals prominently displayed I claimed that this coach was reserved for U.S. military business. Chaim, dutifully, in his best German, translated my English. In reality, the paper I waved was the affidavit of support sent to me by my uncle that I hoped to use in my request for a visa to immigrate. The ploy worked, and we were left alone.

The train ride took many hours. The bombed and destroyed rails necessitated many stops and detours. It was evening when we finally arrived at Munich's main station. What now? Where do I go from here? How do I take the children and myself to Funk Kaserne?

I saw a sign, which read RTO, where many Americans in uniform were entering what lay beyond. In my view, where there were Americans I would find help. I entered the office, and a G.I., who sat at the front desk and who today would be called a receptionist, asked what I wanted.

"I want to see the commander," I replied.

He referred me to a lieutenant sitting at a desk in the back of the room. I approached him. "Lieutenant, I have just arrived in Munich. In fact, I am here with a number of children, all of us escaped from Czechoslovakia. I do not know what to do. Can you help us?"

He could and did help us. He ordered a truck, and we were transported to Funk Kaserne, which was located in a former military barracks in the outskirts of Munich. Although I now was in a different camp, nonetheless, I was back in a camp in Germany.

It was late evening when we arrived at the barracks, but the kitchen was opened and so we were fed. I turned the children over to the care of camp's UNRRA personnel. When we finally entered the dormitory, we were met by other displaced persons, who were the old residents in the camp. After relating our tales, how and why we came, I inquired about life in camp, especially about the food, not only of its quality but also the quantity. I was not especially concerned about the living quarters. There were rows of army cots set up in a very large room with a common shower and toilet. This I could accept, at least as a temporary condition. But what I wanted to know most was what I had asked: how often we were fed and how much food would be given.

At this moment in my life, the presence of food was my greatest concern and its absence, my greatest fear. It was not that at the moment I was hungry. I was quite satiated by the food we had had that evening. I asked these questions because of an innate fear of being hungry. In Prague, I had been hungry most of the time, never knowing whether I would eat the next day. When I did, very often I had to sustain myself with fried blood and potatoes. I was fearful of hunger, which is quite different from being hungry. There were many days, before the Holocaust and afterwards, that I fasted, as on Yom Kippur, or at other times when I was preoccupied with a task and I had not had a chance to eat. On such occasions, I was hungry. But being hungry is merely a temporary condition. Being hungry is a physiological response to the need of food. (Of course I am not talking about addiction to food.) Hunger is different from the temporary condition of being hungry. Hunger is a state of fear that one cannot control one's future needs for food. In the concentration camp, I was constantly hungry; I was always just one step ahead of death by starvation. In the year of my internment, I always dreamed about being liberated and being well fed. I was experiencing hunger. But, my dreams were not realized. I was freed; I was no longer imprisoned; but my fear of not having food persisted; I was still suffering from hunger. In Prague, where I was alone, hungry, and not knowing what the future held, my fear of hunger had not abated. My immediate concern when I came to a displaced persons camp was not for my ultimate future but to insure that I had an assured supply of food, enough food to feel filled. Hence, one can, I hope, understand how now, having arrived in this new environment, my first concern was food.

A young man who had been a resident in this DP camp answered my inquiry about food. "The food is almost adequate. Those who do not work are given two meals a day, totaling 1400 calories. But those who work are fed three meals with a total of 2400 calories." Two meals and 1400 calories will of course sustain any non-working person. But, of course, the quantity is not great, and one cannot get filled on that amount.

I decided I must find a way to work. To work not only ensured me a greater amount of food, it also gave meaning to my life. Work to me was not the Biblical curse that God inflicted on mankind as punishment for Adam and Eve's sin. To the contrary, work always enhanced my ego. I could achieve importance and status only through work. In the hospital in Prague, work enhanced my status, at least in my self-conception. Working in the hospital entitled me to wear a white coat, which made me appear as though I was a physician. I enjoyed my anticipatory status, my perception that I was but a step away (albeit a giant step) from being a physician. To work and be productive, and in this instance to work and help people in need, was more than just a way to insure an adequate supply of food. I saw work as a necessary activity that made me feel alive. Work was and still is the act by which and through which I acquire both meaning to life and social honor. After all, as a worker I had greater control over my environment. Rather than being passive and letting both the natural and human environment act on him, a worker acts, forms, and influences the environment. As a worker I believed I had some power over others, rather than being suppliant to others' power. Work, I knew, was power. With all this on my mind, it was inevitable that I should seek work. "How does one get work?" I inquired of the older DP.

"Go to the office to ask. Perhaps they can use you."

Next morning after breakfast, I entered the administration office. It was a large room with people working in close proximity to one another. There were a few partitioned private offices in the back area.

"What do you want?" asked a woman in civilian clothes.

"I want to work," I replied.

Soon a young woman came to see me. She was in her late twenties, wearing a British Army uniform with a badge on her shoulder to indicate that she was a UNRRA official.

"I hear you want to work?" She spoke to me in German with an unmistakable French accent.

"Yes, I do." I informed her that I had arrived the night before, bringing with me children. "Look, I was a medical student in Prague; I am a gymnasium graduate and speak a number of languages." I also informed her that I had experience in office work, having been not only an interpreter but also a sort of trouble-shooter (what today one might call a customer service consultant) in a U.S. hospital right after liberation. "You see, I have had experience working with people, and more important, I understand the people who live here since I have had similar, if not the same, life experiences."

No trouble at all. I was given a job working in the office. I easily made friends with all three official personnel, all Frenchwomen. In fact, I became a close friend with the youngest, a dark-haired young woman. She encouraged me to take up my discontinued studies of French that I began before the Holocaust engulfed me.

Work gave me privileges. I was moved into a smaller bedroom that I shared only with Chaim, ate three meals that were filling, and even received a ration of American cigarettes. Soon, my other two classmates, Hershi and Dudi, who had remained in Prague, escaped and joined us in the Funk Kaserne. The four of us were now reunited.

"Eugen, can you see me in my office?" (Being back in Germany I had changed my first name from *Evzen* to its German equivalent *Eugen*.) This request came from the middle-aged Frenchwoman who was in charge of the refugee camp. I entered her office where two uniformed persons were already present. I was not quite sure what occasion warranted my being called before the chief. I almost felt like a high school student called to the principal's office.

"What have I done?" was the only thought that came to my mind. But it was not censure but praise that was being directed at me. For my good work, I was now being rewarded.

"Eugen, you have done well, and I have a new job for you." She informed me that the headquarters of one of the army units was vacating its offices and turning them over to the UNRRA. The facilities consisted of a number of large houses that had previously constituted a mental hospital and its farm. It was now to be used to house the ever increasing number of refugees. Funk Kaserne would remain as a processing camp from which people would be sent to more permanent locations. I was given the task of preparing the houses for habitation. I was told to find about 25 craftsmen, plumbers, electricians, and carpenters; take them to the new camp; and divide the larger buildings into smaller, independent rooms to serve as private family dorms.

I was quite elated. After all, being only 20 years old and given such a responsible job was just what I needed, not only for my self-esteem, but even more importantly to overcome my fear for the future, of being alone without my father, and to develop an optimistic worldview. I took my three friends to help me with the task and set about in search of the craftsmen. All of them, they told me, had previous experience in construction. I assured them that their wives could, as soon as the place became habitable, join them. Thus, the 30 of us all climbed into a U.S. Army truck, off to the foothills of the Alps and Wasserburg, Bavaria.

Wasserburg, on the river Inn, was very near the city of Muhldorf and the last concentration camp in which I had been interned. So here I was, back in Germany, back in the place from which only a year earlier I had been liberated from the concentration camps.

Not only was the mental hospital vacated by the U.S. Army, it was also empty of patients. Hitler had not only waged genocide against Jews, he had similarly eradicated mental patients in German hospitals.

The hospital was located in a beautiful spot. The houses were all shaded by beautiful trees and surrounded by farmland. Our task was to divide the buildings into smaller, independent bedroom units with a common bathroom to serve as apartments. We were given about a month to complete the task, at which time, the refugees – stateless and homeless Jews – would be given temporary lodging. It was assumed that in time, all the refugees would immigrate to a country where they might settle to normalize their disturbed and displaced lives. Meanwhile, they would live in these displaced persons camps.

At the entrance to the camp there was a stately building, the home of the former director of the hospital, which we four claimed for our own lodging. We each selected a bedroom, but in addition we also had living and dining rooms, a kitchen, and a bathroom. In the truck with us, we also bought provisions. We entrusted those to a cook whose domain became the large institutional kitchen in which he cooked for all of us.

A few weeks later, the officials from Funk Kaserne came to inspect our work. Satisfied with our progress, they decided to advance the time of occupancy of the premises. As the camp would become a large and a complex enterprise, professional social workers and other UNRRA personnel were brought to take over its administration. We would, of course, remain to assist the professionals in running the camp. All four of us became unhappy. Till that moment we had been the persons in authority. We had enjoyed a great many privileges, and now we would lose our status and power and our lodging as well.

Before the full-time, mostly American personnel came, some refugees were already on their way to the camp. To my surprise, one person arriving with the first transport was Piroska, whom I had dated back in Munkacs. She was a few years younger than I and arrived at camp with her mother and a husband. Most unmarried survivors who lived in displaced persons camps generally married at an early age. Through marriage, they hoped to alleviate their loneliness, to develop some emotional relationships in a world in which they had experienced nothing but tragedy. The man whom Piroska had married had but a sixth grade education. Yet, in spite of his lack of education, later in the United States where they both settled, he was able to amass a fortune and become a multimillionaire living in Bel Aire. But in 1946, they were homeless and penniless. In my capacity, as pro tempore director of the camp, I was able to allocate them a small, but private, house. Forty years later, when I visited Los Angeles, Piroska called to insist that my wife, daughter, and I visit them. I all but forgot the earlier event but she had not, and both she and her husband insisted that we be their guests for a day. It was about 1984, and she and her husband lived in a large house among the movie stars.

Among the professionals who arrived to take over the camp's administration was Joe Fink, representing the American Jewish Joint Distribution Committee (JDC). The Joint, as it was called, was an American Jewish welfare agency working in displaced persons camps under the auspices of the United Nations. Since most displaced persons in camps in Germany were Jewish, the Joint offered services in addition to those provided by UNRRA. It supplemented the food rations supplied by UNRRA and also provided the foods used in celebrating the Jewish holidays. It dealt with immigration and the resettlement of Jews into various countries. Having seen our abilities on display in making the camp ready, Joe Fink inquired whether we would like to work for the Joint.

Of course, I was interested. All four of us were. Being a part of the UNRRA provided great many benefits. To me, first and foremost was that I would become one of the uniformed personnel, a member of the Allied Forces, a part of the victorious army, the defeaters of the Nazis. It was bad enough that political conditions had forced me to leave Czechoslovakia and that I was not able to immigrate to the U.S. And having to return to the hated German soil had been, perhaps, the worst possible scenario that I could have anticipated. However, being in Germany, in the uniform of the victorious army, gave me a sense of revenge. To walk freely on the streets and have the Germans show me deference or even some degree of fear fulfilled in me a need for revenge. Wearing a uniform, I could tell myself, that though I was back in Germany, I was now stronger and better than the Germans. I was now the conqueror, and they, the vanquished.

There were also practical reasons for joining UNRRA. The United Nations provided its employees with excellent living conditions. After we joined, we were transferred from the camp and sent to work in a warehouse in Munich. The four of us shared a large apartment, and each of us had our own bedroom. We ate in a military dining room, which in my view served very good food. We also were provided uniforms, including shirts, underwear, socks, shoes, and overcoats. To my great consternation, however, the uniforms we were given were British. They were sturdy woolen outfits; they were the uniforms of a conquering army; but, they were not the American uniforms that I hoped to receive. This slight discrepancy between my wishful thinking and reality I was able to rectify later.

Perhaps the greatest of all the privileges to which we as uniformed personnel were now entitled, was to shop in the army-run store known as the PX (Post Exchange). The PX was like a department store combined with a grocery. To enable us to shop there, half of our pay was given us in script dollars, the currency used by the military, and the other half of our pay was in German marks. Of course, compared with Americans doing the same or similar jobs, European members of the organization received far lower remuneration. But, my ability to purchase scarce food and tobacco more than compensated for this inequality.

Next to dollars, tobacco items, especially cigarettes, were the common and preferred currency in Germany. One could get almost anything for cigarettes. The population's tobacco addiction served my interests well. We were able to purchase only a limited supply of these scarce items, for tobacco and alcohol products were rationed for all military personnel. We were given a carton and a half of cigarettes, a number of cigars, and pipe tobacco. This was more than enough to support my habit and left a great surplus for me to use as currency.

Our initial assignment was supervisory work in the warehouse, which stored food and clothing for distribution to people in DP camps. Food was brought there from all over Europe. I still remember an incident that showed us our small-town naïveté. A shipment of cheese arrived from Norway. The workers started to unload rounds of cheeses, each weighing about 50 pounds. Unfamiliar with cheese products (in fact I had very limited experience and knowledge about most, if not all, of the items stored there), I thought that these cheeses were spoiled and hence unacceptable. Many had green mold. I showed the Norwegian officer in charge of delivery why I considered the cheeses spoiled and hence unacceptable. He laughed, took out his jackknife, cut into the round, and proceeded to eat, giving me some to taste. It was very good.

Our first job was clerical, and our rank reflected our assignment. Not wearing any visible military rank, our status was reflected by our uniforms and by our identity cards. My card showed that I held a Civil Service rank three, that is, a clerk similar in military rank to a sergeant. This rank entitled us to wear the uniform of English enlisted soldiers. I held this rank for a brief duration. I was soon given a new assignment and with it a new rank.

Life in the ABC apartments in Munich was very pleasant. We lived in what for us was great luxury, far surpassing the lifestyle which I had had at my parents' home. The four of us shared a modern apartment. I had a very large bedroom all to myself.

Once a week we visited the PX to buy our cigarettes and alcohol as well as a cornucopia of luxuries and food products that were new and strange to me. Fruits, like oranges and bananas, were now common in my diet. These were fruits that in my father's house were limited to one day a year as a part of the *lag-baomer*, the traditional celebration of the Jewish Arbor Day. In the PX, we also could redeem our liquor rations for beer, wine, and hard alcohol. In spite of our independence, we rarely indulged in alcohol. However, once I could not resist a PX special, namely, Italian pink champagne for the great sum of $1.20 a case. Although in my father's house we always had wine on the Sabbath, we rarely had hard liquor and never champagne. The wine at home had to be kosher, that is not *nesach*; it is certified that it was never offered to or poured over the altars of other religions.

Here, in Germany, my life was quite different from that of my childhood. After my liberation, I ceased to be concerned with *kashruth*. I strayed from Orthodoxy and violated the food taboos. I decided that it was time to shed my earlier *shtetl* lifestyle. My first foray into non-kosher food occurred while still home. After liberation, both of necessity and because of cultural diffusion and experiences in the concentration camp, I changed my philosophy of life and my lifestyle also changed. I ate the foods that were served in the dining hall and generally discarded the old taboo system. I may say that perhaps what I experienced were evolutionary changes. They also reflected a change in my identity and my worldview from my previous small-town, Orthodox self image, to a cosmopolitan one.

In Munkacs, my interpersonal association was strictly intra-Jewish. My high school was Hebrew and Zionist; the language of instruction was Hebrew; and all the students were Jewish. Outside of the classroom, my associations were also limited to Jews. I dated only Jewish girls and socialized only with other Jewish boys, and the clubs to which I belonged were Zionist organizations. Although we did not live in an officially segregated and fenced in ghetto, at least not till the Germans occupied it in 1944, there were enclaves with a high density of Jewish residents. The area around the Jewish street, I could say, was over 99% Jewish. We lived in self-imposed Ghettos. Now, in Germany, my earlier reluctance and fear of association with non-Jews had broken down. The freedom to change my way of life began in Prague where I dated someone non-Jewish. Now, in Germany, my life went one step further; I became friendly with the Strausses and their three daughters. While Mr. Strauss was nominally Jewish, his wife was a German Catholic, and their daughters had all been baptized in the Catholic faith. Above each daughter's bed, in true Catholic fashion, hung a cross. Mr. Strauss was a member of the German parliament and in addition had a thriving export-import business. They lived on Inn Street, number 9, in a very fashionable and exclusive neighborhood in Munich. I cannot remember why I went to their home, but most likely I was asked by some of my colleagues in the warehouse to join in a visit for social reasons. My three roommates never went there. It seems to me now that most of the young people I met at the Strausses' were Jewish. I wondered whether their desire to entertain young Jewish men was an attempt to seek redemption for being German. Whatever the reason, I was made welcome in their home, especially by Muti (as the girls called their mother). I spent many occasions there, and on one occasion I even stayed overnight.

In the Talmud, the rabbis warn Jews not to break bread with Gentiles. They warn that, once a Jew shared his meals with non-Jews, the following chain of events would occur. To make the bread palatable, the Jew would ask the Gentile for olive oil in which to dip the bread. Next, the Jew would ask to have a drink of wine with the Gentile. The drink would bring about familiarity between the two that would surely lead to intermarriage. Thus, to avoid the sin of intermarriage, the rabbis urge the avoidance of close relationships, beginning with activities such as breaking bread with Gentiles.

My association with the Strausses indeed brought on complications. The youngest daughter was barely in her teens; the middle daughter, 16 years of age, was extremely beautiful; and Erna, the oldest, about 19 years old, was an excellent cook with a tendency toward chubbiness; but because of the closeness in our ages and my need for friendship, I had a closer relationship with her than with the others. I frequently dropped in unannounced for a visit. I observed Christmas Eve with this family for the first time, and the next day I joined them at their holiday lunch. When I was invited to the Christmas celebration, I clearly indicated to them that I was coming as a friend and a visitor. I made them aware that this was not my holiday. They knew that I was Jewish, that I was strongly committed to my people, and that I worked for a Jewish agency helping Jewish displaced persons. Yet, in Munkacs, I would not have dared to take part in a Christmas celebration, even as a visitor. My being there on Christmas was first a matter of my curiosity about this holiday, new to me, and, second, I came out of friendship.

But I soon learned that their desire for my presence was from something other than friendship. Around May of 1947, I returned to Munich from a lengthy assignment in another town. One evening after work, I came to visit the Strauss family. As I entered the house, I met Mr. Strauss, and after an exchange of greetings, he asked me into his office. He shut the door and told me that he wished to have a private conversation with me. There was polite discussion about my work, after which he inquired about my future plans. I told him that I no longer saw myself as a resident of Europe. I informed him of my desire to immigrate to the United States where I hoped to continue my medical studies, to complete my education, and to fulfill my childhood dream of becoming a physician.

From his demeanor, I knew that he had another agenda on his mind. I sensed that the polite inquiries about my future dreams were merely a ploy to put me at ease, and he was about to bring up the subject of his genuine interest. Mr. Strauss went to his desk and took out a slim book, which turned out to be a Swiss bankbook.

"Let me tell you," he began in earnest, "Since you left Munich, even if it was for a short while, Erna became very unhappy. It was evident that she was disturbed about something. I had a long talk with her, and she told me that she had fallen in love with you and would like to marry you."

This was news to me. I was not aware of her feelings, perhaps because I did not reciprocate them. I had come to the Strauss family simply because I was lonely and needed some place where I could find pleasant social relationships. I never thought of Erna as a potential sexual partner, let alone a wife. Erna was a pleasant and plump young woman whose physiognomy reflected her character. She, as I saw her, was destined to become a typical German Hausfrau. She was shy and hardly ever carried on an extended conversation. She was not the beauty of her sixteen-year-old sister, who resembled Hedy Lamarr. To say the least, the sister was quite stunning. If Erna had looked like her sister, I know I would have had a difficult time saying "No." But, in this instance, Erna's appearance made my rejection of her as a wife easy. Moreover, just as in Prague, marriage was, at least for the moment, far from my desires.

I told Mr. Strauss that I was only 22 years old and not ready for marriage. In my view, first, I must have a future. I must also overcome the memories of the past and expend all my efforts on leaving Germany for the United States.

Undaunted by my refusal, he called me to his desk and opened the bankbook, which showed a balance of one and half million Swiss francs. "If you marry Erna, I'll give you this as your dowry. There is, however, one provision. I want both of you to go to the States. But instead of going to medical school, I want you to use this money to open an export-import business, and we will work together and have offices on both sides of the ocean." Again, someone was trying to buy me, to offer me money as an inducement to marry someone. Since I knew nothing about the export-import business, this also meant that I would have to stay in Germany, and like Jacob who worked for Laban, I too would have to work for the hand of Erna.

I thanked Mr. Strauss sincerely for the offer, but my mind was made up. I did not wish to get married to anyone. I proceeded to explain, "I know Erna would make a wonderful wife; she is already a skilled homemaker; but my goal is not business but medicine."

Of course, I did not tell him that marrying a Christian woman, and particularly one of German extraction, even if she had some Jewish ancestry, would be an abhorrent idea to me, let alone to my surviving family. I had to discount her Jewish descent. When I first came to the Strausses, I had had an opportunity to visit Erna's bedroom. There, above her bed, hung a large black cross. I remember my disturbance as I gazed at the cross. I wondered whether her commitment to Christianity was so deep that she needed to display the symbol. While the cross may not matter to many Christians, to me it was a negative stimulus. It reminded me of a millennium of Catholic atrocities, of pogroms, of iniquities during the Crusades, of Spanish Inquisition. No matter how much I could love a woman, her commitment to the cross would never let me become close or develop trust in her. Needless to say, my refusal to marry Erna put a strain on my relationship with the family. Although I remained friendly with them, my visits became far less frequent.

**Chapter Eleven**
**Promotion**

A few months after I began to work in the warehouse, the director of personnel called to ask me to see him the next day. I wondered why. My first thought was that I might not have performed my job well and now might lose it. I was quite apprehensive all that night. Next day, I went to JDC headquarters. After a short wait, he came out and escorted me to his office. I do not remember any details of the conversation except that he informed me that I would be taken out of the warehouse and would henceforth be employed as a caseworker at the Munich headquarters. This promotion also came with a change in my rank. I was promoted from a rank three to six. In military terms, my promotion was equivalent to being raised from a sergeant to a first lieutenant. Being now an officer, I received a new uniform, the one I coveted most, the uniform of an American officer. I was also given a jeep. Needless to say, all this made me feel as though I were on top of the world. Yet, I was still alone. By this time my uncles in Prague had immigrated to the U.S., my father was in Munkacs, and his fate was unknown to me.

One morning while driving to work, I noticed a uniformed person standing and waiting for the bus. I pulled over to the curb to offer him a ride. The shoulder patch on his uniform indicated that he was a member of a small organization, The Jewish Agency for Palestine. Late in 1946, that region in the Middle East was still Palestine; Israel had yet to be established. "Shalom," I greeted him and continued my conversation in Hebrew. "Do you wish a ride to the city?" I inquired.

"Yes."

As we were riding, I continued. "Where are you from?"

"I am from Haifa," he responded.

"I wonder, do you perhaps know my mother's uncle [her grandmother's brother] who lives in Haifa?"

"What is his name?" he asked.

"I forgot his name. He made *aliyah* long before World War I. I do remember, however, that he had a store selling wood and coal, and it was located on the Rehov Hanamal [on the quay]."

"Is his name by any chance Berman?"

That name jogged my memory because it was my grandmother's maiden name.

"Yes that is his name. Do you know him?"

"Of course," he responded. "I had a printing shop right next to his store."

I had met my grandmother's brother and his son around 1934 when they came to visit the family. "Are they well?" I inquired.

He informed me that my great uncle had died and that his son had drowned while swimming in the Mediterranean Sea. "His three daughters are well and they still operate the business."

As soon as I arrived at my office, I wrote a letter to these cousins, telling them that to my knowledge, I was the sole survivor of my grandmother's family in Europe. My grandmother had other sisters and a brother, who lived in Lwow, Poland, but none had survived the Holocaust. I posted the letter, hoping that someone would answer and I would be reunited with members of my mother's family even if they were in fact strangers to me. My hopes were not fulfilled. I never received a response to my letter.

Late fall 1946, Russia permitted the residents of pre-Second World War Poland, who had fled their country before the German onslaught, to return to their country of origin. Among those who sought to be repatriated were many Jews. For the most part, the returning Jews came back with their families, at least their nuclear families, intact. But when they returned to various towns and cities in Poland, they found their homes, as we had, destroyed or occupied by strangers. Most of these returnees later told me that they had not found any family member, nuclear or extended, who had not fled the Germans. They all were killed in the Holocaust.

The returnees, like me, found nothing but devastation, nothing that would keep them in the cities of their birth. Poland had always been antisemitic. Jews lived there, not as a part of that society, not as a member of an ethnic group that claimed a natural right to their places. They were strangers who very often were singled out for unequal and harsh treatments. For instance, long before Hitler, Poland had instituted anti-Jewish laws. One such law forbade Jews to slaughter animals in a kosher manner. That made it almost impossible for an observant Jew to live in Poland. The returnees, like the survivors of concentration camps, no longer had any compelling reason to stay in Poland. With their livelihood, family, and friends gone, there was nothing left for them but painful memories. Most of them thus  decided to leave Poland, to emigrate. Unlike Russia, Poland permitted them to leave only if they did not go directly to Germany. So the transports of Jewish emigrants left Poland via Czechoslovakia and Austria to Germany. There they became a part of the throngs of displaced persons, of people seeking new homelands.

I was sent to Bad Reichenhall, a city on the border between Germany and Austria. My task was to help the emigrating Polish Jews with their needs. To accomplish my task, I was to inquire of their needs and to inform them about the various camps where they could stay. I was considered a welfare officer, one who tries to alleviate problems of both new immigrants and those already living in camps. Since Bad Reichenhall did not have army facilities, I had to be billeted in a private hotel where I also took my meals. I frequently had to go to Austria, where I met trains which I accompanied to Germany. I was given blank travel orders, which, as needed, I issued to myself. These documents authorized me to travel. With such orders, I could go to cities within the occupied territories that I cared to visit. I visited Salzburg quite frequently and enjoyed the sites of that quaint city.

Bad Reichenhall was only a scant 20 or so kilometers from Bertchesgarten, the city in the German Alps where Hitler had his famous hill-top home. I went to visit the place. I drove there and checked into the officer's quarters, a former hotel for Nazi officers and now reserved for Allied officers. I do not remember much about the visit. I do know that I felt a great amount of apprehension going there. After all, the thought of Hitler has always filled me with anger. Though the visit itself was traumatic, to say the least, I nonetheless decided to visit his home. I remember taking the cable car that lifted me to Hitler's place; I remember looking around the Alpine vistas; but I do not remember anything else. It seems that I have blocked out most of my memory of that visit.

While residing in Bad Reichenhall, I had a visitor, an acquaintance from my hometown. The Spiegels lived in the city across the river Latorca that separated Munkacs from its suburb Oroszveg. I knew Spiegel well, as his family and mine had neighboring seats in the synagogue. Somehow he had learned that I was in uniform and that I could travel to many parts of Europe. Spiegel was in the truest sense an entrepreneur, although most of his wheeling and dealing was in the black market. In the days after the war, those who dared to operate in the gray or even black market made fortunes.

Spiegel came to me with an offer, which, because of the possibility of making a great amount of money, was very tempting. At the same time, however, had I been caught in black-market activities, I would lose my job with the United Nations. Moreover, my chances to immigrate to the United States would have been greatly diminished, if not downright eliminated. He sold watches, specifically Swiss-made Tissot watches. They were high-quality watches, just one step below the famous Omega watches, hence highly desired and definitely a status symbol. These watches were far cheaper in Italy than they were in Switzerland, the country of their manufacture.

Spiegel's proposition was as follows: he would provide the cash for the purchase of the watches; he would also market them; and my task would simply be to acquire them. I was to travel to Italy, purchase the watches, and bring them back to Germany where we would split the profits. I could have issued travel orders for myself and thus have gone legally to Italy. As tempting as the offer was, I declined it. For reasons that are unknown to me, even in my youth I refrained from taking chances, as I do now. Even to this day, I do not enjoy gambling in casinos or on the stock market. I am fearful of losing money. It is not only that opposition to gambling and gamblers had been inculcated into me. (Early in my teens studying the Talmud,

I learned that gamblers are not to be trusted and cannot be used as witnesses in court.) Gambling, I was taught, is totally antithetical to Jewish values. Hence, to take a chance of losing my opportunity to immigrate to the States, even though I could have made a great fortune in the black market, went against the very fiber of my being. The fear of losing my chance to immigrate to the States far exceeded my desire to make a small fortune. Perhaps, this fear was also a residue of the trauma that I had suffered when I lost the money that my father had sent me while I was in Prague.

I suggested that Spiegel see Joe Fink, the person who was instrumental in my getting a job with the United Nations. He was an American. No matter what he did, he could not lose his right to return to the United States. I later heard rumors that Joe Fink had accepted the proposition and returned to the United States with almost half a million dollars.

In postwar Germany with a depressed economy, a daring person could make a fortune. I am sure that there were many who did. Former wealthy Germans, now in dire need of cash, were forced to sell their valuables for prices that were far below their value. These were truly distress sales. One such item for sale, offered to me by the Strauss family as a favor to one of their friends, was a diamond necklace. The diamonds were, I am sure, of excellent quality, totaling 25 carats. The largest of the diamonds was three carats and graduated downward with the smallest size being 0.75 carat. The diamonds were set in platinum. The asking price was 2,500 American dollars, a very small fraction of its true value. Unfortunately, I did not have the money.

I did, however, make one purchase, but, alas, I was fleeced in the transaction. A Jewish wheeler dealer had an old Leica C1 for sale. It was an early model with a retractable 50-mm lens. Since my childhood, I had had two fetishes: cameras and fountain pens. As a young boy coming home from grade school, I would take a detour so that I could pass by a store that sold cameras. There, in the display window, was a Contax camera, an early model range-finder camera with f=2.00-mm lens. The lens appeared to me as big as the single eye of a Cyclops. I used to stand there to ogle that marvelous equipment, dreaming of possessing it.

While I lacked skills for painting and drawing, and in fact drawing was the only class in which I made an undesirable grade in the gymnasium, I still felt the need then, as I do now, to express my vision. The camera was the logical means to it. With a camera I could capture and depict my vision of life. Now, I had an opportunity to possess a camera. Then, as it is now, the Leica was considered the finest in craftsmanship of both camera body lens. Before leaving Prague, I had sewn my worldly possessions, consisting of four 20.00-dollar gold pieces, into the shoulder of my coat. Sewing the money into the cotton shoulder padding served both to hide the coins from possible searches by authorities and to provide for general safekeeping. I did not know the value of these rare gold coins; to me, at that time, I considered them to be just 80.00 dollars, which I gladly gave for having the object of my dreams. Unfortunately, someone stole the Leica, and so eventually I lost both my money and the camera. Now, with the exception of a ring and a brooch, which belonged to my mother, my material ties with the past were completely severed.

I had not heard from my father for about a year. Life for Jews in the Soviet Union was becoming, as in Czarist times, difficult. Russian paranoia, as in the United States during the McCarthy period, was becoming difficult, especially for Jews. It was particularly difficult for those who had relations in the West, especially in the United States. It is for this reason my father had ceased writing to me. My communication with my relatives, who by this time had left Czechoslovakia and settled in St. Louis, was at best, sporadic.

The letters that I received from my Uncle Nathan, who immigrated to the United States early in 1946 and now worked in the grocery store that he had received as a dowry in his recent marriage, were very depressing. His letters began to erode my idealistic view of life in America. I had inherited my idealism about the United States from my father. His view of the country corresponded to that shown in Israel Zangwill's *The Melting Pot,* a play that portrayed the United States as a country where European immigrants, purified from their ancient feuds and hostilities, could fulfill their age-old yearnings to be free persons.

In our early months in the concentration camp, before we were completely beaten both physically and spiritually, my father and I had dreamt about life in the United States. He also had an idealistic view of American immigrants, who he believed to be educated persons who were loyal to their heritages. He firmly believed that immigrants to the United States brought along their cultures, their languages, and a desire to maintain their ties with their ethnic heritages. The immigrants' ties to their heritages, my father often told me, perhaps to reassure his hopes, would create a demand for books in their native languages and by authors from their native lands. He hoped to help them maintain their cultural heritages by opening a multilingual bookstore. America was to him not only the land of opportunity but also a land where both literature and the arts flourished. I inherited this idealistic view of America. Of course, there were also my own experiences after liberation working with the GIs and those ideas that I developed from the movies that I saw. It is this idealism about the country, coupled with my wish to join the remnants of the family, which propelled me to seek entrance to the U.S. instead of to Israel.

My Uncle Nathan's letters, however, began to erode my

idealism. Life in the United States, he wrote me, was a constant state of drudgery. One must rise early in the morning and work till late at night. After work, he was too tired for anything but sleep. But Nathan's pessimism was affected perhaps more by the many tragedies that he had experienced than by his life in the U.S. His views reflected his anger at the cruelty of fate and the constant disappointments that fate had allocated him. He had lost two wives and three children. His first wife had died in childbirth and his first son was the victim of an infant disease and had died within two weeks of his birth. His second wife and two daughters were killed in the Holocaust. Perhaps he was equally angry at himself for submitting to the dictates of his brothers and not fulfilling his own wishes, desires, and dreams.

In my father's family, my grandmother and her physician son were the most ambitious members. They were most obsessed with upward social mobility. Status mobility is achieved through marriage, bringing an increased income that would provide a particular lifestyle permitting the bearer to become a member of a higher status group. We, the Schönfelds, came from a low social position. My grandfather Eliezer was an unsuccessful merchant who at the turn of the century had left for the United States to make his fortune. Without any particular skills and, of course, unable to speak the language, the best he could become was a cigar roller. But even from his meager income he would, as so many immigrants have, send money home. This money was set aside to be used to escape life in the Jewish street, a ghetto in a city where the majority of the population consisted of the poorest of Jews, people from the lowest social rung of the community. All effort was to be expanded to leave the ghetto and establish the Schönfelds as a respectable middle-class family. The money that my grandfather sent was used to leave the Jewish street and settle in a more acceptable area of the city. St. Martin Street, to which the family moved, was a more respectable area, but still far from the true middle-class neighborhood in which the family desired to dwell. With some of the money that Grandfather Eliezer sent from the United States, but primarily with the money that my father received as a dowry, the family bought a small bookstore which permitted the family to extricate itself from its low social position.

The name on the store's marquee was Schönfeld Henryk, which represented my father's work ethic and his frugality, instilled in him by his mother, and which made the store a financial success. The earnings of the store made it possible for Alexander, my father's younger brother, to attend medical school. To have a doctor in the family further increased its social status. The income from the store enabled the family to display the symbols of a respectable middle-class family: buy homes outside of the Jewish street and seats at the Eastern Wall in the synagogue, the place where all the elite members of the community sat.

Nathan, the youngest of my father's brothers, had the most tragic experiences. Nathan grew up under more affluent conditions than did his older brothers. He was pampered and indulged. He, and he alone, vacationed in the resorts at the Black Sea, and he, unlike his brothers who married through the use of a marriage broker, was allowed to date. Yet, when it came for marriage, the family, headed by the matriarch, insisted that his marriage should also be used for the further enhancement of its status. He was not permitted to marry the girl whom he dated and whom he loved. None of the sons had been allowed to seek their own wives. My grandmother insisted that each child owed a duty to the family and insisted that their interests must be second to her perception of what were the family's interests.

Life in an Eastern European small-town shtetl was not as idyllic as depicted by many writers. Unlike the romanticized accounts of authors such as Mendele, Peretz, and Isaac B. Singer, life in the shtetl was difficult.   In the shtetl, each person knew everyone else's affairs. This stifled individualism and independence of thought and behavior. The individual in the shtetl was subject to a communal dictatorship. Life was governed by tradition defined by the family and the community. So my Uncle Nathan, if he wished to continue to live in Munkacs, had to submit to his mother's demands and marry the daughter of a wealthy owner of a candle factory, who brought a large dowry to the marriage and the family. More important, this union increased the Schönfeld family's prestige in the community.

You must understand that wealth alone did not endow either a person or his family with social honor. *Yichus*, that is a person's social status, is distinctively different from social class. Earning money or increasing wealth, while desirable in its own accord, does not endow a person with yichus. Generally, yichus is bestowed by the community to families that have a long history of scholarship. Of course, some wealth is required to maintain a certain standard of life. But, above all else, the number of noted rabbis and professional people who were members of that family was the prime factor that influenced the family's status. Wealthy persons who could afford to provide their daughters with large dowries sought *shiduchim*, that is, matches with young men who, in addition to being scholars, were also from socially prominent families.

In this instance, the reverse prevailed. The bookstore that my father started provided the means to liberate the Schönfeld family from the Yiddische Gass, from the depth of the ghetto, the Jewish street, and set them into middle-class respectability. It was now time to provide the Schönfelds with social prominence; the boys, my grandmother insisted, had to marry well.

A year after the marriage Nathan's wife died while giving birth to a son. A week later so did his son. This tragedy, and his mother's sense of guilt associated with it, freed Nathan to marry the girl he loved in a quiet ceremony. Unfortunately, soon after his second marriage, the Hungarian government took over my city, in accordance with the Vienna conference and treaty, and brought with it anti-Jewish laws. Nathan lost his store license, had to shut the store, and proceeded to liquidate his stock. By the time we were taken to the concentration camp, Nathan had two children. Neither the children nor his wife returned from the camp. Coming to the states, Nathan went to work in a bookstore where he met a young woman with whom he fell in love. It was Nathan's hope to try to reestablish a family and live a quiet life. But again Nathan lost out. His brothers found him an appropriate wife who brought a dowry of cash and a grocery store. It is not only that the family wanted what it thought would be best for Nathan, but, above all, the family hoped that by this marriage, the brothers would be freed from their obligation to help him. As a salesman in a bookstore, Nathan, who was 40 years old, could not have earned enough to establish a secure future. Hence, he would have always required financial help, which the brothers in spite of their wealth were reluctant to give. Nathan again acquiesced to his brothers' demands and married an older spinster who was past childbearing. The store, which he received as a dowry, was in a changing neighborhood, and by the 1960s could not compete with the new supermarkets. And so, Nathan, in the end, had neither the store nor a family.

Nathan became bitter. His life in many ways was similar to that of the hero in a classic Greek tragedy. It seems, at least to me, that Nathan was subject to a conspiracy between the cruel fates and his brothers who, perhaps in their view of what was best for him, pressed him to sacrifice his own thoughts on how he might achieve a modicum of happiness. His letters to me showed that he was very unhappy, existing in a state of depression, which, perhaps, emanated from his sense of hopelessness. His letters depicted that life in America was nothing but time spent at work, a life without joy and the enjoyment of culture. "You rise in the morning and work late into the night," he wrote me. "I come home tired, and all I want is to sleep. I work six days a week and on Sunday I am too tired to enjoy life." The image that his letters conveyed to me was the land of Sheol where, like in Greek literature, the dead continue to exist but in a state of continual sadness. For the first time, I started to question the validity of my image of America and whether America was indeed the land of my dreams. If, as Nathan tried to show me, life in the United States was nothing but an existence character-ized by a permeating sadness arising out of constant struggle, then was it worth going there?

The working conditions for employees of the United Nations Relief and Rehabilitation Administration (UNRRA) were extraordinarily good. I came to enjoy the life of leisure and pleasure that working for UNRRA afforded me. I worked four and a half days and had enough money to enjoy the theater and music and to travel. There were times, like after reading my uncle's letters in which he bemoaned his life in the States, when I wondered whether it would not be better for me to stay in Europe and enjoy the lifestyle to which I had become accus-tomed and liked? But remaining in Germany was out of the question and so was going to other East European countries. But neither could I see myself as a Jewish immigrant in England nor France. The history of Jews in both of these countries was repeatedly marked by persecution. These countries had noth-ing to draw me. No matter what life in the United States might be, no matter the difficulties that, at least according to Nathan, one must endure, there wasn't any place for me but the United States. From the description of life in the U.S.A. that I gained from its citizens working in Europe, I became sure that Nathan's view must be stilted by the unfortunate circumstances of his life. I was ready to leave for the U.S. in 1947, but, alas, I encountered the heavy hand of red tape of bureaucracies and their laws.

I had an affidavit given to me by my Uncle Saul that assured the federal and state governments that I would not be a burden to the country. I had an open-ended ticket on TWA, also sent to me by my uncle, and I thought that these documents would assure me a rapid departure for the U.S.A. But these hopes were shattered, for I found that I had to wait at least three years for my turn to emigrate. This delay was due to an instituted quota system. The immigration quota introduced in 1924 specified the number of people each year who could immigrate to the States from various countries. East European countries, in contrast to Western ones, not only had far lower immigration quotas but unfortunately also had a far greater number of people seeking entrance to the United States. German, French, or British Jews did not have to wait if they wished to immigrate. But those of us from Eastern and Central Europe, from Russia, Poland, Czechoslovakia, and Hungary, had to wait our turn, which often meant three years.

When I returned to Munich from my task in Bad Reichenhall, I was informed that the Hillel Foundation, a subsidiary of B'nai Brith, a Jewish fraternal organization, was offering scholarships to qualified students who had survived the Holocaust. The scholarships were all inclusive, providing for tuition and the cost of living. Of course, I applied. A few months later I was informed that I was a recipient of one of the scholarships and that, based on my education and experience, I was accepted as a student by Columbia University in New York. I was unaware of the status and prestige levels among universities. All that I was concerned with was that Columbia was in New York and the remnant of my family was in St. Louis. I wanted to be in St. Louis, because being a part of my family was tantamount to stability. Ever since my liberation from camp, I had never experienced a sense of belonging. I had become the proverbial wandering Jew.

When I was in Prague, I knew that even were I to have an opportunity to complete my education in that city, I would not stay there. Even the mere idea of settling and living in Germany was abhorrent to me. The United States, were I to have the chance to go there, would not provide me with emotional stability if my location kept me apart from my family. It was not that I agreed with my uncles' way of life. In fact I sought a life that was quite different from theirs. I could, for instance, no longer accept religious orthodoxy, nor could I be submissive, as Nathan was, to their will. I knew that I wanted to live my life as a Jew, but not be subjugated by the ancient religious primitivism to which they were committed. Still, I wanted to maintain my relationship with them. Perhaps, because of not having parents, I thought that being near my uncles would give me a sense of security. So, regardless of the status of the university, I wanted to be in St. Louis. Luckily, Washington University, a noted and respected university, admitted me.

The effect of pure chance is often disregarded as having a significant impact on one's future. People still ask me, "What have you done to make it possible to survive life in the concentrations camp?" Surely, there were certain decisions I made which may have contributed to my survival. For instance, at one point in my camp life I decided not to work. Each day when I arrived to the work area, whenever I could, I would insulate myself against the cold Bavarian fall air by putting old paper cement bags under my thin, cotton, blue-striped uniform. After having padded myself, I hid among the bushes that were in the center of the work area. Were I to have been discovered, the least punishment I might have received would have been a severe beating. In the extreme case, I would have been shot. But unceasing work, carrying 50-kilogram sacks of cement to the mixing machine, would have surely resulted in my demise, just as it did for many others. Most people abide by rules not because they perceive them rationally as necessary for society to exist. People obey laws because they fear punishment. The same held especially true in the camp. We obeyed rules because we were afraid of the consequences; that is, nonconformity to the rules would result in being killed. But, by the time that I decided to hide and not work, my fear of death had abated. I had at that point already lived for a long time with the idea of dying in the camp. Because of the immanency of death, I lost the fear of dying. As I saw it, I had nothing to lose, so I dared. Let me point out immediately, I dared to hide not because I had courage. One needs courage to overcome fear, but I no longer feared. In fact, now in my old age, I fear death more than I did in the camp. From this perspective, I was not a hero, one who courageously faced God-ordained fate. It was simply my extreme fatigue from working, bringing home the bodies of those who died at work and seeing the many people who died daily from the combination of work and starvation, that made hiding a better alternative than working. Aside from this one decision, my survival was mostly a matter of being young and above all else lucky.

Luck or chance had an equally, and perhaps an even greater, determining effect on my promotions than my occupational skills. My earlier promotion and the assignment to work with the newly arriving Polish Jews, just as my next assignment, were given to me because I was available; I was a veritable Johnny on the spot. Since I was between assignments, I spent my time at the American Jewish Joint Distribution Committee headquarters, and when a new and large DP camp at Ansbach was opened, I was available for employment. I was given my new assignment to join the staff of the camp in Ansbach as a welfare and immigration officer. The new position came with a promotion to rank P11, equivalent to being a major in the army.

Ansbach in 1947 was a small city located about 30 miles south of Nuremberg. Its fame today is from its annual Beethoven festival. During the Nazi regime, Ansbach had a large military contingent, and consequently it had numerous military barracks. By 1947, as the U.S. soldiers were mustered out, parts of the military barracks became available and were allocated to the United Nations as housing for the swelling ranks of stateless persons. When I arrived in Ansbach, there were two compounds. One housed the displaced persons, consisting mostly of Jews who were able to escape from Poland and some from Russia. The other, across the street, remained occupied by the U.S. military.

My assignment was twofold. First, as a welfare officer I concerned myself with the many personal problems and needs, especially those related to ethnic and religious needs.   My second task was to assist the Jewish displaced persons in their quests to resettle in various countries.

To give families some degree of privacy, the large barracks rooms were portioned into smaller units, each occupied by a family, often consisting of parents and children. Privacy is, of course, a relative term. Walls made from boards gave the inhabitants their own spatial territory but not the privacy of sound. The units were partitioned with boards which were not insulated and hence did not serve well as sound barriers between the partitioned rooms. Living in one room, often with children, did not afford the kind of privacy that we, middle-class Americans, take for granted; namely, the privacy of bath and toilet facilities, the privacy of speaking and not being heard by others, and most of all, the privacy of sexual life.

There was nothing that I could do to alleviate these conditions. Neither could I change the food rations that were assigned. Meals were eaten in dining halls because the partitioned rooms did not have kitchen facilities. I could, and did, supplement their rations with special foods required for the Jewish holidays, such as Passover, and for special events such as circumcisions and weddings.

High-density residence often creates its own problems. Extreme propinquity not only between family members, but also between various families, coupled with absence of privacy, often resulted in quarrels and bickering. In spite of my youth and lack of training as a social worker, I had to bring the feuding parties to my office and try to make peace. The best I could hope for was an agreement for accommodation.

My most important task was to assist the displaced persons to immigrate and settle in countries of their choice. Many sought to find a way to immigrate to Palestine in the hopes that it would become a Jewish state. If this was their aim, I could not help. However, there were individuals in camp who could aid in this plan, who were members of various Jewish agencies that functioned to find extralegal ways to help survivors in their immigration to the hoped-for Jewish state. My work was to assist with legal immigration. Of course, there were times when I also had to resort to various nonlegal (as opposed to illegal), but nonetheless moral, practices.

Frequently, I helped people acquire false documents to facilitate immigration. For instance, in order for Jews to immigrate to South American countries, they had to have baptismal certificates, preferably in Roman Catholicism. I always saw to it that I acquired such documents, even though they were false. The first time I encountered this requirement was when a Polish Jew, whose brother lived in a South American country, received permission to immigrate there. The entrance visa also included the proviso that the immigrant must be *non Semitas*, he could not be Jewish. To help this man to immigrate, I requested that local priests provide certificates of baptism. In this manner the immigrants could prove that they were non-Semites. My wearing the uniform of the conquering army exerted pressure on a Roman Catholic priest who thereby complied with my strong request and issued a baptismal certificate.

I never doubted that my actions were moral. Overcoming even the violation of laws that are antisemitic is neither illegitimate nor immoral. Of course, I would have not chosen to immigrate into a country that was officially antisemitic. For the same reason, later in the United States as a graduate student in sociology, I violated the laws of segregation because I considered them to be immoral, and hence by their very nature lacking in legality. Laws of segregation violate, as the U.S. constitution proposes, the inalienable rights vested in every individual by nature's God. Segregation in any form is merely the exercise of power by vested interests, and such laws are not based on universal moral principles. Justice is the application of morals that are rooted in equal rights, and hence any law that violates the tenets of justice is not to my mind legitimate. This is similar to Durkheim's declaration that any contract which by its very nature is unjust, regardless of the agreement of the contracting parties, is not legitimate.

The use of subterfuge among Jews to overcome threats to their lives has a long history. It began with the anti-Jewish laws instituted by Constantine in 350 C.E. It continued in most Christian countries during the dark centuries of the Crusades. The rise of Catholic religious courts in Spain and in their colonies was instrumental to the development of the Inquisition. This institution forced many Jews to use subterfuge as a response to the church's threats of death by an *auto-da-fé* if they would not convert to Catholicism. Many Jews complied on the surface by feigning conversion. While outside their homes they appeared as Catholics, inside their homes in stealth they surreptitiously practiced their ancient faith. These were the hidden Jews, the *Conversos*, the *Marranos*, the pork eaters, as the Catholic population derogatorily called them. I considered the requirements by the South American countries that immigrants must be non Semitas as unjust, and hence I did not consider such laws as legitimate. I felt no compunctions when I knowingly helped to violate the unjust provisions in such immigration.

In the course of my work as an immigration officer I encountered a variety of interesting events. One revolved around a group of mostly Hungarian Jews whom I assisted to immigrate to Norway.

I received a communication from JDC headquarters that Norway was seeking Jewish immigrants. It seemed that this country wished to replace the Jews lost during the German occupation. I informed the residents of the camp and asked those who were interested to come to see me. Among those who came was Mr. W., a baker from Budapest, Hungary. While Jews in other cities in Hungary were taken to camps, the Jews in Budapest had been spared. Mr. W. from Budapest, his wife, and three children survived the war years without having been interned. Still, Mr. W. did not want to stay in Hungary and had come to Germany to be a part of the homeless and displaced persons seeking a new start some place other than their countries of birth. Being a baker gave him a useful and marketable trade. When he heard about the opportunity to settle in Norway, he came to see me. Mr. W. turned out to be sly and dishonorable. Yes, he wished to go to Norway, he informed me. Yes, he was aware that he had a good trade and that because of his trade he stood a very good chance of immigrating and settling there. But, he lowered his voice as though he was speaking in confidence, imparting to me sotto voce a man-to-man secret. He seemed assured that I, a man, would understand his desire and would help him to attain it. With a wink and a half smile on his lips, speaking to me in Hungarian, he told me, "You understand I want to go there by myself. I want to start a new life without having to take along a family." He wanted to abandon his three children and his wife, who I knew was in her sixth month of pregnancy. He was a vile and cruel man, I thought to myself.

While I could not do anything about the personal relationship and state of happiness, I could try to threaten him with serious consequences if he persisted in leaving his family. Angrily I told him, "Mr. W., if you leave your wife and children, not only will you not go to Norway, but I'll spread the word, and I doubt that you will have an opportunity to go any place. No country," I continued in my anger, "would want anyone who has such low moral standards as you, sir. I'll see to it you will rot in Germany." Even though I was relatively young and inexperienced, I was angry and hostile toward this person, for in my perspective he had violated what I considered to be (and still do) the essence of morality, justice and fairness. I threatened him with what I considered to be the greatest fear that was harbored by all Jewish displaced persons, to have to remain in Germany, the most hated of all countries. Of course, I knew that my threats were empty. Most likely, I could have not done anything were he to have left his family. But standing before the man in the position of authority in the camp who was clad in the uniform of the ruling government, he believed that I did posses the power and hence the capability to fulfill my threats. I promised though, that if he  took his wife and children along, I would insure, to the extent that I could, a successful immigration to Norway. This promise was mostly my attempt to insure that he and his family would stay together. I hoped that once they were in Norway without other families for support, their need for each other would act as a prophylaxis against their breakup.

There were five single individuals and two families who immigrated to Norway. I received a few letters from the immigrants after their arrival there. Most countries that accepted displaced persons did so with reluctance. For instance, the U.S.

never offered any welfare services to its new immigrants. What help the immigrants received came from various Jewish agencies. The responsibility for adjusting to the new country rested solely with the immigrants. This was not so with those who went to Norway. Of course, it is wrong to compare Norway with the United States. After all, the former had invited but a scant seven hundred persons and the latter had accepted many hundreds of thousands. Still, Norwegian treatment of the soon-to-be new citizens was exemplary.

As the ship that brought the new immigrants to Norway approached Oslo, a delegation of Jews and officials arrived on the pilot boat. As the immigrants stood on the ship's deck where they expected to be informed about their new lives, they were greeted by the delegation's leader, a Norwegian official, with the traditional Hebrew greeting *shalom*. Disembarking from the ship, they were taken to barracks which served as temporary homes. There, in the ensuing two months, they were taught to speak Norwegian, the country's customs, and its history. There they also met with prospective employers and were given assurance of jobs and living quarters. It was during the immigrants' stay in the barracks that Mrs. W. gave birth to twin boys. Mr. W., not wasting what he thought was a golden opportunity, wrote to the King of Norway and asked him to be the twins' godfather. To everyone's surprise, the king accepted the honor. The adjutant who represented the King at the *bris* (circumcision ritual) brought the monarch's gift. Mr. W. and his family received a magnificent gift, a bakery and an adjoining house in Oslo. The story made its rounds in the camp. Such an act of generosity by a non-Jew, especially by a king, to a Jew lifted everyone's spirits. "Imagine," said a Hungarian DP to me, "a King giving a Jew such a present. Maybe there is still hope."

During my stay in Ansbach, I helped many displaced persons to immigrate to new countries. At the same time, I could not help my own cause. By this time I had returned both the affidavit and airplane ticket to my uncle, knowing full well that neither of these nor my scholarship would help to hasten my immigration to the United States. I had to be patient and wait my turn. So I requested a change in my immigration status. I no longer applied for permanent residency, but I sought a student visa, that is, the status of a visitor. I hoped that by seeking a student rather than an immigration visa I would have a better chance for earlier immigration. I also hoped that once I was in the United States, I would be able to convert my visitor status to permanent residence status. I knew that a student visa would limit my stay in the U.S. to the years necessary to complete my education. Yet, my first concern was to leave Germany and enter the United States. I collected all the necessary documents and submitted a new application. There was nothing else to do now but wait.

Life in Ansbach was good. I had a nice room, and most important, I received a new driver's license that permitted me to requisition cars, in size up to a three-quarter-ton truck, from the Army motor pool. With my promotion to P11 I often had opportunities to dine with the military. With my new rank, my pay also increased, and I was able to indulge in various food items available in the PX. I also indulged on learning to ride. For two packs of cigarettes, a farmer I knew allowed me to ride his two horses, and on weekends I frequently spent four to five hours riding.

There was one ritual that I performed, almost with religious zeal. In Prague I discovered and fell in love with Glenn Miller's music. Each day, late in the afternoon, AFN (American Forces Network) presented a half hour of his music, a program titled *In memory of Major Miller*. But Glenn Miller's music was not just for listening. It was not passive music. The full enjoyment of Glenn Miller's music, or, for that matter, the music of any of the big bands that were broadcast on AFN, could only be achieved through dancing the jitterbug. I had to learn this dance.

How could anyone be a real American, a part of the armed forces, even if only tangentially associated with them, without the ability to dance to this wonderful music? I had to learn it. And I did. I found a very pretty, young Polish woman who was a waitress in the officers' mess hall who was a very good dancer. She was willing to teach me, and I became an eager student of the jitterbug.

I met this young woman at Thanksgiving dinner. The traditional dinner of turkey and all the trimmings was served in the officers' mess hall. After the main course, all the waitresses arrived in a parade similar to those common on present-day cruise ships. Each waitress held a large serving platter on which there was a white oblong-shaped object all aflame. "May I set this down on the table, for the dish is very hot?" The waitress asked. "Of course," I responded. "But tell me what do you have there?" "Ice cream, called baked Alaska," she responded. The idea that ice cream could be served as a hot dish was beyond my immediate comprehension.

In Ansbach, I had my first opportunity to interact with Americans as equals. It was from them that I got my first glimpse of how Americans think of themselves and their country. I learned from another welfare officer, from New Orleans, what Cajun life and food are. She introduced me to the spirit of New Orleans and to the music of Louis Armstrong. Yet, no one even hinted at the American tragedy of legal discrimination.

Among the people who shared lodging with me in a large stately home were two young, quiet, and demure Dutch women. From them I learned that for a century Holland had been ruled (as a constitutional monarchy) by queens. For a few generations, the queens had given birth solely to daughters. But now in 1947, there was hope that the pattern might be broken. Queen Julianna of Holland was pregnant, and as the due date for the birth of the hoped-for prince came closer, the two Dutch women increased their purchases in the PX. They were going to give a party to celebrate the birth of a prince. Bottles of champagne were stocked in the refrigerator; hors d'oeuvres were prepared; and the countdown to the birth began. Finally, the news came over the radio; the Queen had another daughter. Their disappointment was expressed with angry curse words, *Chod Verdume*, which they kept repeating. Holland was destined to continue to have queens, and no king was in sight.

I settled into a pleasant and comfortable existence in Ansbach. Sunday afternoons were reserved for chess, a game my father had taught me. When I played chess, I always felt some part of my father next to me. My usual Sunday afternoon partner was a military officer who had immigrated to the U.S. from Poland. We always had music broadcast by the American Forces Network, cut and peeled apples and pears, and two bottles of chilled Rhine wine. These somewhat sweet wines went very well with the fruit, and all in all, provided for a very pleasant afternoon. In the end, no one cared who won. In a sense both of us won a very pleasant afternoon. In addition, Ansbach had a symphony that I attended, and there were always friends with whom to spend time.

I tried to keep in touch with my classmates, particularly with Chaim, who worked in Stuttgart. Since we only worked till Friday noon, I had time for long weekends. One summer weekend, I took the train and went to visit Chaim. I spent a wonderful weekend there. In addition to visiting a charming city almost as hilly as San Francisco, I was privileged to attend a performance of *The Three-Penny Opera*, performed in German with the lead role sung by Lotte Lenya, the composer Weill's wife. This was a memorable event. Because Weill was Jewish, his music had been forbidden by the Nazis. A year earlier, in Munich, I had become acquainted with a German family. I had met the family through one of the daughters in the household who worked in the officers' mess hall. She brought me to her home and introduced me to her father, a retired, one-eyed commercial pilot.

The cause of this physical deficiency was never mentioned, but I assume that it was early in the war, and it changed him from a military to a commercial pilot. He insisted that he was never a Nazi, and to prove his claim he showed me his records of *The Three-Penny Opera*. These contraband records, he related to me, had been bought in Switzerland and smuggled into Germany. After all, had he been a member of the party, he would have never violated the sacrosanct anti-Jewish laws, that is, to possess books written by a Jew or music composed by one.

One evening while in my room in Ansbach, there was a knock at my door. As I opened it, there stood Erna, whom I had not seen since I left Munich. "What are you doing here?" I inquired.

"I ran away from home," she replied. Since I had left, she had dated someone else, who was unacceptable to the family. As an act of rebellion against her father's control of her life, she packed up and left. She came to me, knowing that, as a friend, I would make her welcome. I did. Still, I wanted to inform her parents.

Next morning in my office, I called her father to tell him that Erna was with me, that she was well, and, of course, that I would not take advantage of the situation. I further informed him that when she calmed down I would see to it that she returned home.

After a few days' stay with me, Erna returned. I had not heard from Erna for some years till after I had been in the States and was married. One day, to my surprise, I received a letter from her telling me that she and her Jewish husband had immigrated to Canada. Although my wife encouraged me to respond and renew my friendship, I did not. It seems that I wanted to rid myself of my German memories and cut myself off from the past. It was a time when both the Holocaust and post-Holocaust memories still had a disturbing effect on me.

While in Ansbach I had another visitor. One day a young

person appeared at my residence and introduced himself. "I am Alexander Sonnenwirth, and I am related to you." It turned out that Alex's mother's niece was married to my father's brother; that is, Alex was my aunt's first cousin. We were related through marriage in many different ways. Alex, who was older than I, was in the Hungarian Army's labor camp during the war. Although he survived the war years, his immediate family did not. He was from Transylvania, a part of Romania not too far from my home town. Like me, he went to Budapest and had escaped from there to Germany. But, Alex decided to continue his studies and had enrolled in Heidelberg medical school where he had completed nearly four years of the five-and-half-year curriculum. He later came to the States to St. Louis where he hoped that he would be permitted to complete medical training. But, medical schools in the United States had a gentlemen's agreement not to admit more than seven-per-cent Jews. Both Alex and I had to give up our dreams of becoming physicians.

It seems that some events in our lives become the frame of reference, the paradigm, by which we judge and give meaning to other experiences. We see events not as they are but as they are colored by our previous experiences. We hardly look at events from a Sergeant Friday's perspective of "just the facts, please"; instead, we look at events with a given predisposition. It is this meaning system that serves as our frame of reference when we judge events. For instance, being ill can be interpreted in different ways and may have different meanings. While most often we consider illness as an undesirable reality, sometimes it can have a positive symbolic meaning and thus serendipitously latent and unintended positive consequences. One such illness that I perceived as downright enjoyable was when I was hospitalized due to tonsillitis and strep throat.

Of course, illness can be life threatening, and strep throat may lead to serious complications and even death. As a European, even though I was working for the UN and in the employ of the U.S. government, I was had second-class status. I was paid far less than Americans in the same position, and I had far fewer privileges. I could not, as U.S. personnel could, send money to the United States. I could not establish a bank account there. Moreover, only part of my pay was in U.S. script dollars, military dollars that I could spend in the PX. I had even fewer privileges than did Europeans working for UNRRA who were citizens of a country and bearers of that country's passport. A year earlier when I was sick in Munich, in spite of wearing a uniform, I was treated as just another Jewish displaced person. I was sent to the ad hoc Jewish hospital and not to an American military hospital. Even though I was in uniform, as were other Europeans, Frenchmen, Englishmen, Hollanders, Norwegians, and Poles, who in sickness and in pay received the same privileges as did American civilians. I was told, by this simple act of discrimination, that I did not have the same status as others who occupied the same position. Regardless of my job, regardless of being a uniformed person, I was just a displaced person. In Ansbach, when I contracted strep throat, I was sent to Nuremberg to the U.S. military hospital, and not to the local hospital where displaced persons were sent as a rule. As I presented my ID I was given officer's accommodations. In all respects I was treated as an officer; I had status. But what gave me great joy was that others now, even the American military physicians, reinforced my self-concept as a person of status, and thus symbolically I perceived myself to be almost an American.

In the spring of 1948, I received a new assignment and with it another promotion. I was elevated to P13, and considering that I was only 22 years old, this rank was indeed very high. P13 is equivalent to being a full colonel in the army. This promotion, however, had a price. I was made director of a children's camp near Wasserburg. I had made a full circle. In 1945, I was liberated from a concentration camp outside of Wasserburg, and now I returned to the same place, as a commander of a camp and also of the region. But the camp, unlike Ansbach, was isolated and far from any military installation. True, I received a house all to myself and was given enough money to hire a house-keeper/cook. But I lacked companionship of any kind. I made sure that the children were well taken care of and helped with their immigration. Most of them were orphans whose parents had died during the Holocaust, and now they were waiting to immigrate somewhere. In addition to having had to experience the Holocaust and the loss of parents, home, and security, some of these children were also survivors of the English camps when they were evacuated from the Exodus. From this camp, they immigrated and were allowed to enter the new Jewish state, Israel.

My stay in this camp was very short. At the end of May, I was notified that I had received a U.S. visa, and I would shortly be permitted to leave for the United States. In fact, I did not get a quota number for I was given a student visa that limited my stay in the U.S. to the duration of my studies at Washington University. I left the camp and returned to Munich, working at headquarters and waiting to leave for Bremenhaven, the port of embarkation. May 1948 was a tension-filled time for me. This was the month when the United Nations debated the fate of the Jewish state, whether indeed it would become a reality. I listened to the debate over the radio and then to the vote. The resolution passed, and the dream of a Jewish homeland had now become a reality.

**Chapter Twelve**

**Zionism**

Like most Jews in the spring of 1948, I sat by the radio, mesmerized by the vote in the United Nations. The 2000 year-old hope and dream seemed to have become a reality. The State of Israel had come to be; Jeremiah's vision had been fulfilled for the second time; and Rachel's children were again returning to dwell within their own borders.

The establishment of the State of Israel was the fulfillment of my personal dream, too. After all, throughout my life I had been a Zionist. For 12 years, I attended a Zionist parochial school where the language of instruction was Hebrew. In prominent places in the school, the pictures of Theodore Herzl and Eliezer Ben-Yehuda were hung with a relevant quote from each person. Under Herzl's picture appeared his statement, "If you wish it – a Jewish state is not a legend." Eliezer Ben-Yehuda, the father of Modern Hebrew, advocated that "There cannot be a revival of a nation without the prior revival of its language."

Of course, not all Jews supported the Zionist ideal. Most Chassidic Jews, especially the Munkacser rebbe, abhorred the idea of a Jewish homeland. For him, and for most of the ultra-Orthodox Jews, the establishment of a national homeland before the advent of the Messiah was unthinkable. The existence of Israel was to be a part of the Messianic event that would come when the anointed one whose advent was proclaimed by Elijah would reestablish both the Holy Temple and the new and sacred State of Israel. Thrice daily, traditional Jews prayed for the rebuilding of the holy temple, to bring back the sacrifices as it is commanded in the Torah. In their view both the land and the language are holy and can never be placed in the secular domain. Hebrew is to be used only when one studies the holy script and never as the means of everyday communication.

But we, the students of the Hebrew gymnasium, held a different view. It was clear to us that history had provided ample evidence that the future existence of the Jewish people was directly tied to the establishment of a Jewish homeland. The tragedy that we call the Holocaust is twofold. First, of course, is Hitler's destruction of Jews. But we must also include the world's attitude and response to the Nazi atrocities.

Few indeed were the countries that opened their border to Jews who sought to escape the German atrocities and save their lives. The United States, a country that took pride (at least ideally) on being a nation of immigrants, a country where people might find their freedom from the ancient feuds that were so common to life among Europeans, kept its doors shut to those who sought to flee Hitler's madness. The United States, which publicly declared its supposed ideals on the bronze plate attached to the Statue of Liberty that welcomes with open arms the wretched refuse yearning to be free, refused to open its gates to Jewish refugees from the *S.S. St. Louis*. This ship, filled with German refugees who were seeking a reprieve from the Nazi death sentence that was passed on them, was not allowed to dock and let its passengers, who were far from being the refuse of Europe, land in this country. This country, contrary to its ideals, refused to grant safe refuge to the innocent victims of the prophet of racism. Its passengers were forced to return to Germany. Yes, a Jewish state would have made a great difference during the dark ages of Nazi rule.

From my childhood on, my father had imbued me with the ideals of Zionism. His political beliefs were to the left of the middle and coincided with the political beliefs of early Zionist leaders. Our home was often a meeting place for Zionists. I remember the visit of my father's childhood friend Avigdor Hame'eyri, a noted author and poet who immigrated to Israel after World War I and stayed with us while he was visiting his family. My mother's uncle, who also immigrated very early in his life to Israel, also stayed with us and told us stories about the land. The books that I grew up with were the legends of David and Solomon, and the history that I studied was primarily the history of the Jews.

Even though my father was a middle-of-the-road Socialist, in the mid-1930s, when the revisionist leader Zeev Zhabotinsky came to my hometown, my father took me to meet the leader and introduced us. Zhabotinsky was the leader of the militant Zionist movement whose members believed that Israel would have to be freed only through the sacrifice of blood. Zhabotinsky, because of his anti-British and militant attitude, was ejected from Israel by the ruling British. In fact, in 1940, as a reaction to antisemitism, I joined Zhabotinsky's militant Zionist group, the Betar. Many of my friends who survived the Holocaust went to Israel, and some became members of the Irgun, the underground Jewish army. Two of my classmates, Yaakov Weiss and Houseman, lost their lives in the attack on the Acre prison. Houseman was shot, and Weiss was captured by the British and was executed in the Acre prison, the inmates of which he had sought to free. His picture as a martyr is still displayed in the execution room in the death chamber of the prison.

Why then, as a Zionist, did I not choose, like some of my friends, to find my way to Israel and be a part of the people who were fighting for the redemption of the land?

Idealism and reality often are the two opposite dimensions in a personal dialectic. Idealism demands, for instance, that a person defers his personal ends and gives primacy to collective ends. The demands of idealism are similar to the demands of charismatic leaders; both require total submission. The idealist and the charismatic disciple must reject self-interest such as economic and family interests or the seeking of personal goals. The key concept in idealism, of course, is sacrifice -- at most, altruistic self-sacrifice, that is, the willingness to give one's life for a nobler cause -- for transcendental ends. At the least, idealism requires economic commitment and sacrifice even to the point that the idealist feels obligated to give up, if the cause demands it, any economic, familial, or other kind of future ends. Idealism recognizes no other ends except those that it proclaims. In 1948, the fledgling State of Israel demanded this form of sacrifice.

When Israel became an independent Jewish country, I was in the arms of a dilemma. Are my personal aims and hopes more important to me than the needs of Israel? Am I willing to continue to suffer for a cause after I have lost everything but my life? I decided that at that time I should seek to maximize my self-interests. My prospects seemed to be far better in the U.S. than in Israel. I had a scholarship to a prestigious university. My long wait for immigration had ended. I was to leave for Bremenhaven to embark upon my journey to the United States. In contrast to Israel where I had no one, my family was already in the U.S. and in the city of my destination, and above all, I still had dim hopes that my father might join me in the United States.

Even to this day I do not know where I would have been happier. Would I have been happier to have followed the Zionist ideals and settled in Israel? Would I have felt more at home there, together with other Jews who shared my experiences, or in the United States, a fundamentally Christian country?

I opted to go where I could seek to achieve my childhood dream to become a physician. Hence, I opted to come to the United States. I never became a physician, but I did get a Ph.D. and become a professor. In this sense, I realized my father's dream for me, to become an intellectual. But, as much as I admired and loved the United States, I was never able to consider it my home. In spite of its seemingly secular orientation, the U.S. is a Christian country in which, even though given full citizenship and privileges appertaining thereto, I am just tolerated. I have never fully developed a sense of belonging. Whenever I speak of the founding fathers, I speak of people with whom I do not share kinship. It was quite different 30 years ago when I first visited Israel. There, I felt some sense of belonging; I felt my historical roots. I was treading the land my ancestors walked. This was the land of my history, the land of David and Solomon, of Hillel and Rabbi Akiba. This was the land drenched by the blood of my heroes, who had defended a country that since my childhood I had considered my own.

In 1972, I visited Israel for the first time. I was invited to visit the country by the government, as a member of an organization of Professors for Peace in the Middle East. My wife and I, together with other university professors from the United States and Canada, both Jews and Christians, were invited for an official visit. While in Jerusalem, we went to visit the Western Wall, known as the Wailing Wall. With a skullcap on my head, I slowly approached this remnant of the Temple that was destroyed almost 2000 years ago. There they were, these massive stones that once constituted the outer defenses of the Temple, the Western Wall with little pieces of paper inserted in every crack. The papers were prayers that people hoped would be answered by God. As I approached the wall, I felt as Moses must have as he approached the burning bush. A sense of awe and trepidation fell over me. I experienced a feeling that only one who perceived the wall as sacred could achieve. It was the wall that was the symbol of 2000 years of yearning, of hope for self-governing. To me, this wall was far more sacred than Mount Sinai. Slowly I laid my hands on the wall, and I felt a transcendental spirit enveloping me. It was an emotional and spiritual feeling that I have never experienced before. At that moment, I believed I was at the center of the universe surrounded by my ancestors. I was there together with the spirit of David and his son Solomon; in my vision I stood next to the prophets Jeremiah and Isaiah, and I heard the voice that spoke to Ezekiel asking me, "Son of man will these bones live?" I knew I was home, that I belonged there, that I was a part of this land and its people. For the first time in my life I felt rooted.

And yet, in retrospect, I would have had a difficult life in Israel. I would have always been angry because I would have constantly been reminded of the world's failure to that country and because of Israel's politics. Long before Martin Luther King, I too had a dream. It was a dream that arose from my reading of Theodore Hertzl's treatise *Alt Neu Land* (Old New Land). I saw Israel as a second Switzerland, the neutrality of which would have been underwritten by the world, at least by the United Nations. Instead, I find that it has become a country with a holy soul torn apart by the necessity of self-defense. The people who contributed to the moral foundation of religion have again been rejected by the world.

While I, as an immigrant, never fully developed an historical kinship with the United States, my children are Americans in the truest sense. I guess my feelings are not unique, but they are feelings that all immigrants share. It is difficult to leave one's birthplace and the emotions that the homeland has inculcated and transfer these feeling to another country. This is true even when the home country has enslaved its people and they achieve a freedom that they have never experienced previously. I am an American by choice, but my children are Americans because they belong here. Their emotions are tied to this place.

Chapter Thirteen
**Immigration:**
**On the way to**
**America**

I was officially notified by mail that my turn had come to leave for the United States. I needed a passport. One must have a passport even when one is stateless. I was coming to the U.S. not as an immigrant but as a student. This meant that at the completion of my studies I would have to leave the country, but to where? I never thought beyond coming to America where I hoped to enter medical school. Under the European system, one enters medical school directly after graduating from the gymnasium. This is what I did in Prague, and I had hoped that I would be able to resume my interrupted medical training. I reflected that, under the European system, medical education takes five and half years. Five years is a long time. Who knows what can happen in five years? Most likely there would be a way for me to stay. But meanwhile I would be in America. I took comfort in my grandmother's teaching. "Remember, Tuli," she used to tell me, "When you find a gate that is locked, and it seems that you are barred from entering the premises, look for the little door. Next to a locked gate there always is an open little door." I knew in my heart that I would find the door even if the gates to America were to be locked to me. But in the worst case, even if I had to leave the United States, there was always Israel, and it would not be all that bad if I were to go there as a physician.

The letter I received told me to come to the offices of the HIAS (Hebrew Immigrant Aid Society) where I would complete the official forms necessary for immigration. I filled the forms and sent them off. Soon I received my passport, a document issued by the State Department. As a passport, its official title was "A Passport in Lieu of a Passport." I also received train tickets to Bremenhaven, the embarkation port.

However, prior to my departure, there were a number of tasks I had to complete. First, I had to turn in my ID, my uniform, and my PX card. I felt sad to relinquish the items that had given me a quasi-American identity. My second task was to collect a bonus check of 500 dollars. The JDC awarded this bonus for the two years of service that I spent in Germany, which, thanks to my work and the resulting privileges and comfort, had not been difficult.

During my stay in Germany, I had not thought of the country as the enemy, the country of my tragic experiences, but as a necessary stop on my way to reclaim a normal life. My work was not only enjoyable; it also provided other benefits. First, I had an opportunity to enhance my language skills. The official language of both the JDC and the UNRRA was English, and the two years of speaking and writing in English prepared me, more than anything else, to perform well in college. Second, my task as welfare officer had taught me management skills that were useful in a variety of occupations that I would later have.

In Bremenhaven, we had a few days' wait till the ship arrived. We stayed in barracks, and for the first time in two years

I was treated, not as the uniformed personnel of the UNRRA, but as the displaced person that I really was. The friends I made during the few days there I have long forgotten. It was easy to make friends, for we all shared the same history, the same present, and similar hopes for the future.

Finally, the ship arrived. It was a World War II liberty ship, the *S.S. Marine Flasher*. The ship was one of the many thousands that were built in haste during World War II. The sailors, who were part of the Merchant Marine, informed me (since I was one of the very few who spoke English) that these ships were not very sturdy and were known to break in half during storms. Luckily, we departed in June at a time when the usually rough seas of the Northern Atlantic are relatively calm. It was a cargo ship converted to ferry displaced persons to their new home. Even on this ship we had to have tickets. I presented both my ticket and my stateless passport, and I was sent below deck to the cargo hold. My berth was the top of a double-decked bed, right next to the door that led to the showers and bathroom. We were right at the water line. Women and children were given smaller rooms with beds on the upper part of the superstructure. Meals were served in shifts in the dining room.

The first section of our trip was down the English Channel. This stage of the trip was easy in the relatively calm waters of that body of water. We passed Dover with its white cliffs on the way to the Atlantic. Most of my waking hours I spent in the recreation hall, which was on the upper deck, looking at the sea, talking to the steward, and, when possible, playing cards or chess.

The meals were good and sufficient and were served on long, picnic-like tables, each seating about 15 persons. Before meals, a mimeographed menu was placed before each passenger. The menu allowed for some choices, and since no one at my table or the neighboring tables spoke or read English, I had to translate the menu into Yiddish or German and often had to explain what the dishes were. There were many foods, mostly American, with which the passengers were unfamiliar. For instance, I did not know the Yiddish words for shrimp and oysters. These foods are not kosher; I never had them in our home nor had I ever learned the Yiddish name for them.

Being young, I took advantage of the older and less experienced people at my table. I once ordered oyster stew for everyone at the table. When I was asked what they were eating, I tried to explain. People say that oysters are an acquired taste. Like all foods, its appropriateness is culturally defined. Oysters, according to the mostly traditional Jews that were sitting at my table, were not only *treyfa*, i.e., not kosher and inappropriate to eat, but they were also considered abominable. It is not that the people on the ship kept the dietary laws and ate only foods that were kosher. After all, the ship was not equipped to provide and cater for special religious needs. But meats like chicken and beef were familiar foods that were accepted even though they were not prepared according to Jewish law. But some foods were considered to be more taboo than others. Oysters were perceived not only as inedible but as downright disgusting. From that time on, I did not order the meals, unless I, first, explained what the food was and how it was prepared.

Two days after our departure, we had crossed the longest stretch of the English Channel and entered the North Atlantic. The seas here were choppier than before with higher waves. The ship began to rock and roll, and people started to become seasick. The passenger in the bunk beneath mine began to moan and kept on crying, "Just let me die," while running to the bathroom. But being in the bathroom merely intensified one's seasickness. The bathroom was right in the ship's prow, and there one experienced the full force of the ship's movement, a simultaneous two-directional movement, both rocking and rolling.

Although I did not get sick, I had to limit my time in the shower to a period of five minutes or less. Any longer and I too would have experienced the disastrous effects of sea travel.

Throughout my sea voyage I looked forward to seeing one of America's most profound symbols, the Statue of Liberty. I had read its history and of its inscription. So I stood on the deck as we approached New York. Still out at sea, the ship stopped to let the pilot and a number of other people climb the stairs and board the vessel. Soon we continued our journey, and just as we were entering the harbor, a number of people, the same ones who had boarded the ship, approached me. They were reporters for various news agencies and asked me to serve as an interpreter. Among the passengers was one most often solitary, who never joined any conversations, who I had frequently noticed in the ship's day room. He seemed to be content with his solitary activity, exercising his fingers on a long piece of cardboard that resembled the keys of a piano. The reporters came to the ship explicitly to interview him. It seems that we had a noted concert pianist on board. I do not remember the specifics of the interview. My task was simple enough, to translate his comments from German to English and the English queries to German. By the time the interview was completed, we had passed the Statue of Liberty, and we were ready to disembark.

From the harbor, New York looked as I imagined it would. Skyscrapers were rising majestically into the air. I had read much about this city with its teeming nationalities. I was somewhat acquainted with the history of the immigrants who had entered through Ellis Island and into New York and their great accomplishments. I was eager to disembark and meet my host, a family who offered to provide me room and board while in the city.

I took my place in line, passport in hand, to pass before the Immigration and Naturalization inspector. Finally, my turn came. I handed him my passport, and after inspecting it he commented, "You know, your passport is only valid for three months."

"I am glad you informed me about it. I will immediately seek to extend it," I replied.

Satisfied with my answer, he proceeded to stamp the passport, admitted. But, immediately , he seemed to have another thought in his mind. Turning to me, he casually asked, "Mr. Schönfeld, how would you feel if the United States would permit you to stay in this country permanently? Would you like it?"

No one had cautioned me about the slyness of the officers serving in the Immigration and Naturalization Service. Would I like to stay in this country? Of course I would. Was this not my dream? Had I not thought about this for many months? Is the representative of the government making my permanent residency a possibility? In spite of all my experiences, I was naïve. I was overwhelmed by his questions, and of course I misinterpreted its meaning and intent. I could not deny my desire to stay. Doing so, I believed, would indicate that I had contempt for this country, which I did not have. So my response was, "It would be an honor."

Of course it was the wrong answer. Immediately with an ink-pen, he scratched out the admittance stamp in my passport and said, "Mr. Schönfeld, would you please move to the side. Someone will be with you shortly." The man standing behind me also had a transient visa. He had come to New York in transit to Canada. The inspector asked him the same question. But his response was quite different. "Me stay in this no good country? Not on your life. I am getting out of here as soon as I can. You won't find me dead in here." His abhorrence of this country was quite evident. I still remember his voice and his demeanor, indicating utter contempt and bitterness for this country. The inspector's stamp came down on his passport. Admitted, it read.

When all the passengers were processed, I was informed that I would not be permitted to disembark but would be taken to Ellis Island. I was given a few minutes to speak with the family who was going to be my host during my stay in New York. I cannot remember their names, but I do remember that they owned a number of movie theaters in Brooklyn and that they lived on a street near Third Avenue in the same borough. I was soon taken with my few possessions in a locked car to a ferry and then to Ellis Island. While coming into New York, I had been saddened that due to my preoccupations as a translator I had been unable to see the Statue of Liberty. Now, on the ferryboat, as I approached the island of my incarceration, I became aware that I was to live in the shadow of the symbol of liberty. I was so near to the country of my dreams and yet also so far away. I was still without a home, and my future continued to be in doubt.

I entered a large building and was taken to a storage place where I deposited my suitcase, taking with me only my toothbrush, shaving items, a few changes of underwear and shirts. These I stored in a cubbyhole in a dormitory that many of us shared.

While being processed, I was asked whether I preferred to eat kosher meals or in the regular mess hall. Given a choice, I chose kosher food, not for religious reasons, but as an act of defiance. Moreover, I was also thinking that the kosher meals would be prepared in smaller quantities than the food in the regular kitchen and therefore would be better. Above all, I chose to eat in the kosher dining room because I wished to be with other Jews and be a part of the Jewish collective. We were given two meals, breakfast and dinner. Breakfast was served as a common meal in a large dining hall. Only dinners were served in the kosher dining room. The kosher kitchen was supported by the New York Jewish community and was under rabbinical supervision.

On Friday, the day of my arrival to Ellis Island, dinner was served at three in the afternoon. Since the cook was an observant Jewess, she left early on Sabbath Eve to have time for her own Sabbath preparations. A little before three, I arrived in the kosher dining room. With the exception of one other person the place was empty. Although there were many Jews incarcerated in this pseudo prison, most had chosen to eat in the main dining hall.

A young woman in her early 20s was serving a Hungarian dish, chicken paprika. It was the dish that was most often served in my parents' home for Friday lunch. The aroma of this delicious dish created in me a sense of *déjà vu*. The waitress spoke Yiddish, and I learned that she was from a village close to my hometown and was herself a Holocaust survivor.

Taking my tray, I joined the only other person in the room, a young Black man wearing a skullcap. Of course, I was more than interested in him. I was overwhelmed with curiosity. The anomaly of the situation intrigued me. Why does a young Black man eat in the kosher dining hall? I asked permission to join him at his table, which he granted. I had spoken in English, and he had responded in the same language. My next question was, "Are you Jewish?"

"Yes," he responded, "I am a Falasha."

I had read about the Falasha, Black people who lived in Ethiopia and who claimed to be Jewish by virtue of descent from the Queen of Sheba. According to legends, the Queen had married King Solomon, adopted Judaism, and brought that religion to her people. He told me about his people, who call themselves members of *Beth Israel* (the house of Israel) and observe the laws of the Torah. Unlike European Jews, they do not recognize rabbinical edicts. He was a sailor who had jumped ship and entered this country illegally in New York and been caught. He, like so many others, was being detained to be put on a ship to be returned to the country of origin of the ship he had fled. I saw him just once more and had to assume that he was then deported.

At noon on the day of my arrival, I was brought to the Great Hall of Ellis Island. It was the same great hall through which millions of immigrants had passed at the end of the 19th and the beginning of the 20th centuries, until open admission to the U.S. had been discontinued. In 1948, this hall was the day room in which the detainees whiled their time away till the immigration courts decided their fates, that is, who would stay in this country and who would be deported. From the window of the hall, I could see the Statue of Liberty, the symbol of America's willingness to accept the "huddled masses yearning to be free." I was one of these huddled masses, being held captive in the shadow of liberty.

The Great Hall was filled with a conglomerate of nationalities. In addition to a variety of immigrants who had violated some aspect of immigration laws, there were also war brides from all over Europe who were waiting for their future husbands to deposit a 500-dollar bond as the assurance of marriage. There was, for instance, a young Belgian woman of extreme beauty. Because of her beauty, she disturbed me and the other young men, and we wished that she would leave, and the sooner the better. She was tall and slender with a well-proportioned body and a face that one would find only among movie stars. We were envious of her husband to be. She did not stay long. In less than two days, her fiancé redeemed her, and she left not only with good wishes but also with sighs of relief. All of us young inmates felt a sense of relief at being free from such a bothersome sexual stimulus.

In contrast to the Belgian beauty, there was another bride to be, a German woman who, as the saying goes, was ugly as sin. To want a beauty and bring her to this country I could understand, but I could not understand why any American would want to bring from Germany a woman who was as totally devoid of any beauty and charm as this woman. I could not help but raise the rhetorical question in my mind, is there such a lack of women in the United States that one had to import this ungainly female? Unlike the Belgian woman, this one stayed in Ellis Island for many days, and I had ample opportunity to talk with her. In addition to her total lack of physical beauty, she was not educated and lacked charm and any qualities I would consider desirable in a woman. The GI who brought her to the U.S. to be his bride failed to come to see her or to place a bond, so she awaited her return to Germany. After she told me about her fiancé, I understood the situation better. In our conversations, I found out that the GI drank too much, and even when he was in the Army, he never had any money. He had tried to borrow the 500 dollars for the bond, but no one that he knew either had the money or was willing to lend it to him. I could see that such an individual, an alcoholic without education and occupational skills, could never have found an American woman to marry. In turn, I assume, she was motivated by her lack of attractive physical attributes and by the chance to come to the United States, perhaps her only opportunity for her security and future. Even though she was German, I felt sorry for her, for having her hopes shattered.

There were many others in the Great Hall. There were a number of Estonian families who had fled the Soviet Union in a fishing boat. For over a year, they were interned in Ellis Island. They were waiting the Appellate Court's decision whether they would be permitted, as asylum seekers, to stay in this country. I had mixed emotions about them. On the one hand, like me, they too sought to escape the harsh Soviet totalitarian state. On the other hand, I still remember that people from the Baltic States (Latvia, Estonia, and Lithuania) came to Nazi Germany as volunteer workers. They, like many Ukrainians, supported the Nazi regime, perhaps not out of conviction and love for Germany, but as a reaction to the Soviet Union's annexation of their countries. And, to me, anyone who willingly supported Nazi Germany was my enemy. I accept the validity of the dictum "the friend of my enemy is my enemy." Even today, in spite of my moral commitment to justice and fairness, I cannot accept their claims that they were victims of the war in the same manner as I was.

The largest group interned there were members of the German American Bund. They were immigrants of German descent who had supported Hitler and his ideas. They formed the fifth column in America, similar to the followers of Quisling who helped Hitler occupy Norway. They were perceived to be the enemy of this country and were interned in Ellis Island to be deported to Germany after the war. While on the Island, they performed all types of tasks from janitorial work to the responsibilities of cooks and waiters. I stayed away from them and hoped that they would eventually be sent to Germany. It is one thing to disagree with official policy and dissent. But there should be neither room for nor tolerance of those who seek to help this country's enemies and seek to subvert the democratic process. I am not sure what the final outcome was; I hope that this country's enemies were given their just desserts.

It is said that prison inmates often make good lawyers. I am not sure whether this is true. However, the only good advice I received regarding my immediate future came from other inmates. When I entered the Great Hall, I was met by a number of individuals whose status as residents in the United States was still being examined by the Immigration and Naturalization courts. After preliminary questions about my country of origin and camp experiences, they asked me why I was brought to the detention center. I related to them my story. I told them how I answered the question about being given a legal opportunity to stay in this country. It seems that this was a standard trick question asked of those who came to the United States with temporary visas.

The other inmates outlined what would follow internment. "In a few days," I was told, "You will be taken to a federal immigration court. They will ask you many questions, but remember, be decisive in your answer. Under no circumstances must you inform the court of your wish to stay in the U.S. You see that guy," pointing to a young fellow sitting on a chair, "He was foolish and told the judges that he would like to stay in this country. He has been interned here for eight months." It was the collective opinion that he would lose his appeals and be deported to Germany. I started to imagine a plausible answer if I were asked whether I wished to stay to become an American.

On Tuesday, my name was called. There at the door was an immigration officer. He informed me that I was being taken to New York to appear in front of a panel of immigration judges. The judges would question me to determine whether I should be permitted to stay or be deported. My court day arrived after three days of internment. I was led to a car and placed in the back seat of a station wagon, the door handles of which had been removed to eliminate opportunities for me to escape. The car was driven to the ferry. Arriving in Manhattan, I was driven to the federal court. This was the first time I experienced the power of this city. The tall buildings enveloped me and made me feel insignificant. I was overwhelmed by the sheer size of the structures.

I was brought into the court chamber to face a panel of three judges. They asked me whether I needed an interpreter. I took pride in my English skills and declined their offer. I do not remember all that the judges asked me. I am sure they had many questions. I remember vividly, however, the questions that were central to the case. The judges wanted to know whether at any time in the future I wished to stay in the United States. Having been forewarned, I replied that while it would be an honor to stay in this great country, I had other plans.

"What are your plans?"

"Your honors," I had been told to address the court in this manner. "I came here to fulfill my life's ambition. I wish to study medicine and practice psychiatry. I hope at the end of my studies to live in my people's new homeland, Israel. I am sure your honors are aware of the problems that we have endured. All these experiences have left many emotional scars, and I would like to help in my people's healing process."

It seemed that my explanation satisfied the judges, and they told me that their decision would be communicated to me.

I was brought back to Ellis Island and began my vigil for what I hoped would be a positive decision by the judges. Meanwhile, I had to settle to live my prison life. Most of my days were spent in the historic Great Hall trying to find ways to alleviate an otherwise dull existence. There were Ping-Pong, cards, and a very few books. Of course, there was conversation. I made friends with a Romanian chess master and began to experience the humiliations of constant trouncing. I knew how the pieces moved. I may have even managed a previsualization of one or two steps. But I never have learned an overall strategy. The best I could do was to play a delaying tactic and prolong the inevitable checkmate. To make the game more interesting to him, he gave me a number of advantages such as his playing without a rook and a bishop, and once he even forfeited his queen; but the end result was always the same, I would lose.

Twice daily, at ten and at two, the names of those to be released were announced. Days passed, and my name was not called. My only communication with the outside world was with the HIAS social worker who tried to console me. Each time I asked her about my case, she would respond with the same sentence, "We are working on it." On Fridays, the ferries ceased operation an hour earlier than other days, and those to be released that afternoon would be notified by 2 PM.

I was interned for four weeks and still knew nothing about my future. On the Friday that was the 28th day of my internment, the two o'clock announcement did not contain my name. I settled down to spend another weekend in Ellis Island. I was very concerned. Why had it taken so long for me to be released? I thought that the courts had been satisfied with my answers. What could have happened?

At 10 minutes to three an official came into the room.

"Eugen Schönfeld," he called out.

I approached him, "Yes, I am Schönfeld."

"Hurry, we do not have much time. The last ferry is leaving in a few minutes. Come!"

I followed him to the office.

"We have received your release forms late. We do not have time to process you, so we will release you on your own recognizance. You must come back Monday to complete your release forms."

I was being released. Wonderful! But where would I go? Where would I find lodging? After 28 days of internment, my designated hosts were no longer available. I decided to take a chance and call my aunt's niece who lived in New York. While I did not know them, I did know her daughter, with whom I had corresponded when I was in Germany. They were glad to have me stay with them and gave me their address on 72nd Street on the corner of Fifth Avenue.

Now I was set to leave. I picked up an extra pair of shoes that I had next to my bed, stuck them in the pockets of my army raincoat, packed an extra pair of shorts and a shirt in a paper bag, and was ready to leave for the big city.

On the ferry to Manhattan, the social worker who accompanied me told me to tell the cab driver to get to my destination via the East Drive so that he would not take advantage of a greenhorn. He hailed a cab for me and gave the appropriate instructions, and soon I was let out in front of a tall apartment building.

My new hosts lived on the third floor. After ringing the bell, I was let into a spacious apartment. It was Friday, and the household was busy with Sabbath preparation. Meanwhile, I took a shower and changed into a fresh shirt. I was asked many questions about my experiences. After dinner, we went out for a walk. I put my suit jacket on, and my hostess noticed the great bulge in my breast pocket. "What do you have there?" pointing to the pocket.

"My identity cards," I replied.

"How many do you have?"

I took out my leather wallet and proceeded to show her the various cards.

"Why do you carry them?"

"I must have these cards just in case the police or other authorities stop me and demand that I identify myself."

"This is America," she informed me. "You don't need them here; besides no one will stop you here."

This was incomprehensible to me. Even though for the last two years I had been in uniform and most often been treated as a military officer, nonetheless, I still was unable to shed my fear of officials. For many years, I had always carried many different forms of identity cards. Frequently I had to identify myself to police and to secret police. Having just been released from Ellis Island and the encounters with the INS had added to my fears of being stopped by officials. But at my hostess's insis-

tence, I left my cards in the drawer. I felt naked and defense-
less.

New York amazed me. I could not keep myself from
gawking at the magnificent and elaborately decorated foyers in
the Fifth Avenue apartment buildings. The wealth in furnishings
in foyers alone astounded me. I had never seen such display
of wealth. However, just a block away on Fourth Avenue, the
city assumed a different atmosphere; small businesses open late
at night and people shopping as though it were noon during a
market day in my hometown. Indeed, this city was true to its
name of a "city that never sleeps." Next day, I was taken to
another sight that was most impressive to a newcomer, Radio
City Music Hall. The show began with newsreels showing Babe
Ruth giving his farewell speech to the Yankee team and fans.
This was my first encounter with the American pastime of baseball. A Bing Crosby film was shown, but the greatest thrill, to a
young man barely in his twenties, was the bevy of beautiful and
scantly dressed women kicking their legs way above their heads,
the Radio City chorus line, the Rockettes.

But even now, sitting in the theatre, I could not escape
my pre-Holocaust memories. In January 1944, my father and
I took a business trip to Budapest. Since I could not attend
the university, I began to learn the art of running a bookstore.
In Budapest, I was introduced to various publishers and visited other wholesale houses which supplied our bookstore with
paper and other office supplies. I was eighteen, and it was my
first visit to a metropolis.

Budapest prided itself on having more legitimate theaters than movie houses. Of course, we saw some plays, but
considering me now nominally an adult, my father decided he
would be the one to introduce me to "male entertainment" and
took me to a burlesque show. Most likely, I would have enjoyed
it had I attended either by myself or with other men my age.

But looking at the less-than-half-clad women on the stage with my father made me very anxious. After all, how could I sit here in this theatre and be sexually stimulated with my father sitting next to me? It was as though I had uncovered my father's own sexuality. I remember that I was also angry at my father; for at that age, I perceived my father as a flawless person, a person who was devoted to family and to the moral ideals that he had taught me. I could not accept him as a man who had, as all men had, his own fantasies and desires. I perceived his enjoyment of the sexual spectacle on the stage as evidence of his infidelity to my mother. A faithful person, in my very young perception, does not put himself into the path of temptation, even when it is nothing more than a fantasy.

Now four years after the above event and an eon's worth of experience, I was in New York watching the Rockettes. Although the performance was enjoyable, I nonetheless could not help but be reminded of the past, and because of it, I sat through the performance with a sense of apprehension and sadness. But perhaps my emotional state was not purely a consequence of the Budapest experience. Perhaps it also, to a great extent, reflected my response to the public display of sexuality for its own sake. Public display of sex in the Jewish world of the shtetl was not dissimilar to the Victorian perspective, and my moral perspective was, and to some extent still is, a product of the shtetl. Even at my advanced age, I am reluctant to attend strip performances of any kind. It is not that I seek to deny others the opportunity. I simply have difficulties attending such performances because the result is always a sense of guilt. My reluctance to give myself any sort of extreme pleasure of the body has an additional root in the traditional Jewish worldview. The introduction of sadness into the experience of joy, the opposition to permitting total and unbounded joy, is a form of Jewish asceticism.

One of the customs pertaining to a Jewish wedding ceremony exemplifies this perspective. In the Jewish tradition, when the wedding vows have been exchanged, the groom shatters a glass by stomping on it. The reason for this ritual is to remind all present of the destruction of the Temple in Jerusalem. No one, the rabbis have instructed us, should give himself to experience uncontrolled total pleasure and joy. So, we add the memory of the past, a past that includes an element of sadness, as an antidote to giving ourselves up to total pleasure and joy. The memory of my experience with father, together with the traditional shtetl value system that continued to be my emotional baggage, had indeed accomplished that task.

My host family took me out for a Sunday dinner that I still remember. We went to the Lower East Side to a kosher vegetarian restaurant where I ordered a vegetarian Wiener schnitzel. It was an amazing phenomenon, a vegetable dish that tasted like meat.

Monday, I returned to Ellis Island to complete the paperwork and be formally admitted to the United States. Although I knew that my release was approved, I was nonetheless apprehensive as I left the ferry and proceeded up the stairs to the main office. My papers were ready. All I had to do was to sign the documents, gather my suitcase, say goodbye to some people I had befriended during my stay there, and leave as a free man.

I was happy that I had finally gained my freedom. But why did I have to be locked up for 28 days on an island in the shadow of liberty? The answer was the nature of the bureaucratic mentality. From the information I received, the immigration court had ruled in my favor. I could have been released two days after my appearance before the judges. But, it seemed that the bureaucrats in the immigration department were still bothered that my passport was valid for only three months. They wished to help to extend my passport so that I could start my studies without concern for my stay. After all, how could I finish even one semester when legally I could reside only for a very short time in this country?  As a favor to me, the Immigration and Naturalization Service agent in charge of my case sent my passport to the appropriate office to have it extended. Meanwhile, I had to stay incarcerated. Bureaucrats do not think; they follow rules. Their motto is *sine ire et studio*, without anger or emotion but the application of rules.

There were two places where my passport could be extended. First, of course, was the office where it was issued and, second, the State Department in Washington. To the official mind in the immigration department, the logical place to send my passport for extension was the office where it was issued. So, without thought or concern, my passport was sent back to Frankfurt, Germany. The cost of this decision was an additional 24 unhappy days of forced restraint in Ellis Island.

Chapter Fourteen
**Beginning of My**
**Disillusionment**

**M**y unfortunate experience with the Department of Immigration notwithstanding, I continued to maintain an unshattered idealistic view of America. The 28 days that I spent in Ellis Island were, in my view, then, merely the consequence of an overambitious immigration inspector and a bureaucratic snafu. My hopes for the future continued to be high. I was still convinced that this was the country that held fast not only to its tenets that "all men are created equal" but also saw to it that justice would always prevail. It is unfortunate that one must learn that there always is a difference between the ideal world and the real world, between the culturally proposed values and those that are practiced. This I had yet to learn as I came to St. Louis and settled to pursue what I hoped would be my medical studies.

I stayed in New York for a few days, during which time I met with the officials of the Hillel Foundation, the agency that had granted my scholarship. They arranged for my transportation to St. Louis. I was to leave in the evening on board the train *Spirit of St. Louis* and arrive in St. Louis the next morning. My hosts took me to the train, and after having said my goodbyes, I settled into the seat.

One condition seems to be a constant in public transportation; regardless whether the means is train or airplane, most often it is late. So I sat and waited. What could I do during this long train ride? It was announced on the train's PA system that the championship fight between Joe Louis and a contender whose name I do not remember would be broadcast. I was not then, nor am I today, a boxing aficionado. But I knew of Joe Louis, and I knew of his victory over Max Schmeling, the Nazi's icon of German physical superiority. I was also aware of Jesse Owens and the four gold medals he had won in the 1936 Olympics, thereby denouncing German propaganda claims for the Aryan superiority of body and mind. Anything that humbled the Germans and perhaps caused shame to Hitler himself was welcomed and loved by me. I eagerly awaited the start of the Joe Louis fight. I hoped that by listening to the radio, the next 12 hours on the train would seem shorter. Unfortunately, at the last minute for unknown reasons, the fight between Louis and his antagonist was canceled.

The night ride was long and uncomfortable. Finally, dawn came, and I knew that soon I should arrive in St. Louis, my final destination.

"St. Louis," the conductor called. I gathered my belongings, neatly packed in one medium-sized cardboard suitcase, stepped onto the Tarmac, and saw my cousin Flora whom I had met before. In 1937, for a high school graduation present, Flora was sent to visit the family in Munkacs. On that trip she also met her future husband. Shortly afterwards, in September 1939, at the start of World War II, she returned to my hometown and married my aunt's brother Alex and returned to the United States with him.

I was glad to see her waiting for me and had a warm welcome from her. She drove me to her father's house, that of my Uncle Saul, where I was going to lodge. In the afternoon, we drove back to Flora's home, where I met other members of the family. There they were, Alex, his wife Illi and their son Gus, Nathan, Saul, and my cousin Sanford and his wife, the whole St. Louis family. I related to them my stories of life in Germany and elaborated on my internment in Ellis Island.

After dinner I drove back with Saul to his home. It was summer, and in St. Louis that means that it was extremely hot and humid. His wife Lotti had gone to visit her family, and the two of us were going to sleep on the screened front porch. I was cautioned by my cousin, "Beware; Dad snores terribly." Yet, I was unprepared for it. I dreamed that the world was at an end and that we were experiencing earthquakes and that volcanoes were erupting and spewing their lava and that all that was accompanied by earsplitting noises. I woke up, realizing that I must have incorporated into my dreams the horrible snoring sounds that my uncle was emitting.

Soon my aunt returned from her out-of-town visit, and we settled down to a routine. I had the room that previously was their son Sanford's room. As payment for room and board, I started my apprenticeship in my uncle's second-hand store, "Sanford: The store with a thousand and one items." I worked from nine to six, Mondays through Saturdays. In payment for my work, I received two meals a day, my room, and laundry, and five dollars a week from which I had to buy my own lunches. Lunch was always the same, four White Castle hamburgers and a soda, which came to 25 cents.

Although I was his nephew, the son of his brother, I was still a stranger to my uncle. I had been only two years old the last time he saw me. True, he did take me into his home, and some years earlier he had sent me a plane ticket without question when I thought that assured transportation would enhance my chances to immigrate to the U.S. Still, there was a part of his personality that alienated us, and that part was his distrust of others and the need to test people.

Saul was a cynical person. His cynicism and distrust of others were the result of his experiences with distant members of the family who, when he immigrated to the U.S., never befriended him and instead treated him as a stranger. Recounting his experiences in the U.S., he told me how his family continually tested him and took advantage of him. The result of his treatment was that he had developed and now bore the same attitude toward everyone else, including other members of the family. He constantly feared that, unless he was careful, family members would take advantage of him. His experiences had left deep scars, which were manifest in his relationship with his son. He had to control everything, which included his son's life.

When I started to work in his store, my uncle considered me a stranger whose honesty had to be tested, and test he did. One day in the little space in the store that served as his office and where the cash register was, I found a 20-dollar bill on the floor. Of course, I picked up the bill and handed it over to my uncle, who took it without comment. My cousin, his son, who also worked in the store, told me that this bill had been placed there by his father as a test to see whether I would keep the bill or return it to him. Of course I did the latter; I passed his test; but his distrust of me, the need to prove my honesty, violated my expectations. I wished to be a part of the family, to be accepted, and to have someone to care for me, but his actions violated my hopes and desires.

I understood that when he came to the country long before World War I, he had had poor experiences with some family members who mistreated him. These experiences made him a pessimist about human nature. He doubted that human beings could be selfless. He was cynical about the existence of altruism. To him, human motivation is rooted in egoism. Without having read Hobbes, he shared the view that human relationships are governed by self-interest. Without being aware of any economic or political theories, the world to him was indeed a place best depicted as *bellum omnia contra omnes*, a world in which each person was in a constant struggle with all other humans. Although I understood him, and hence could excuse his attitude, still I did not want to be dominated by him and become submissive to his demands. I wanted to be free.

School was about to start. It was time for me to see that the provisions of the scholarship were fulfilled. The scholarship stipulated that I receive food, shelter, tuition, and some pocket money. I was to be provided for in that way so that I could pursue my education.

I went to see the rabbi who was the local director of the Hillel Foundation. Rabbi Jacobs was a nice person with a constant smile on his face as though he wanted to assure everyone that he believed in and practiced the commandment "Thou shall love thy neighbor as thyself." He seemed to be unhappy that I did not wish to live with my uncle. His great concern was not for me and my welfare. Instead, he was concerned that if I left my uncle's home and care, the Hillel Foundation would have to assume this obligation. He hoped that my family would provide for me, give me shelter, pay my tuition, and thus reduce Hillel's burden. To help with the situation, he offered to take me into his home, feed me, and provide me with the couch in his living room as my bed. I accepted.

My stay there was an unhappy experience. I came with the hope that my stay at the university would be pleasant and that my expenses would be covered by my scholarship. I did not want to be treated as a charity case whom people help because of pity. I can attest that there is no joy in being the recipient of charity. Going to live with the rabbi made me lose my dignity, self-esteem, and self-worth. I felt as many financially poor young men in my hometown must have felt who came to study in the *Yeshivoth* and who had to rely on the community to arrange for their meals. The practice was called "eating days"; that is, for instance, if it was Tuesday the student had his meals in the home of Chayim Schönfeld, my father's house. To live with the rabbi was, in my own mind, no different from eating days. But I did not have a choice. I needed a place to stay while I attended school. Moreover, although my uncles were well aware of my situation, they did not want to share the cost of my education. So Hillel had to pay my tuition, which at that time was 150 dollars per semester.

"Charity," wrote the great French sociologist Emile Durkheim, "changes nothing; it merely maintains and supports the conditions which made charity necessary in the first instance." But charity accomplishes one thing: It shames the person who receives it. No wonder that the great physician and philosopher Maimonides taught us that the highest form of charity is one where the giver does not know the receiver, and, complementarily, the receiver does not know the giver. It is only in this manner that the receiver of the help can maintain his self-worth and dignity. Living with the rabbi did not accomplish any of the above. I knew, because the rabbi often told me, both subtly and directly, that he did what he did out the goodness of his heart. Of course, under these conditions, I could not continue to live with the rabbi. I decided that I had to find employment and regain my freedom and dignity.

But the need for charity was not the only disillusionment that I had. I had come to the States fully expecting to continue my medical education. I had completed almost a full year of study. I did not know that medical education in the United States differed appreciably from that in Europe. In Prague, the completion of gymnasium education qualified me to enter a school of medicine. In the United States, high-school education had to be followed by four years of premed, and only then could one hope for admission to medical school. When I presented myself to Washington University, I was given some credit for my previous education, but I had to start as a freshman in college, and I had no choice in the matter.

College was easy for me. Math, for instance, was a repetition of what I had had in the gymnasium. Even English came easily for me. My only problem in college was with chemistry, for it was taught once a week, at night, and by the time I was taking it, I had already left the rabbi's couch and had a job. By eight in the evening, after a full day of work, I had difficulty keeping my eyes open and concentrating on the subject.

I also experienced disillusionment as a result of a disagreement with my history professor. I took a course in European history, and on the first examination I failed to make the A that I anticipated. A student who sat next to me and who had blatantly copied my examination received an A, while I was given a B+. Returning the exams, the professor chided me on my answer to the question, "What modern-day countries were included in the Roman Empire at its zenith?" One of the countries that I had enumerated was Hungary, and the professor's response was an unqualified ha-ha!

During a recess, I approached him. "Professor, I am sure you were referring to my answer." "Yes," he replied.

"Explain to me the following," I asked. "Do you agree that the Danube was the northern border of the empire?"

"Well, yes."

"Having lived in Hungary, I know that the Danube River

flows in the center of Hungary; one may say that it divides the country into two halves. If that is true, how then can we exclude Hungary as one of the countries that was a part of the Roman Empire? In fact, I visited many Roman ruins in Hungary including the famous baths in the Gellert."

He reluctantly agreed that I was right and I ended up with an A in the course.

The knowledge acquired in the Hebrew gymnasium in Munkacs was an extraordinary foundation for my American college courses. Gymnasium education was far superior to high-school education in the U.S. Because of that and my intensive reading during my teens, I was eager to prove my understanding of history and philosophy. This often led to my questioning my professors. The truth is that these challenges were merely a display of bravura. For instance, I challenged my professor of English literature on his view of the relationship between culture and literature. I argued that any meaning that we attribute to behavior is *a priori* culturally determined, for it is in this sense that we can indicate the meaning of the character's behavior in novels and plays. We had a prolonged discussion that was stopped only by the bell. That afternoon in the student center, where at four I had a standing game of bridge, one of the players commented that his English lit professor (whom we shared) out of the blue started to lecture his class on the relationship of culture and literature.

"Did he say this and that?" I asked.

"Yes," my companions replied in astonishment. "How did you know?"

"Well, I had a heated discussion with him on the subject, and what he told you were the exact ideas that I presented in front of my class."

In my second year of college, I became disillusioned in

the U.S., and the associated hurt and pain began. I was called into the office of the dean of foreign students for advisement. "I see that your major is premed."

"Yes," I said, adding "You see from my transcript that I have already completed one year of medical school in Prague, Czechoslovakia."

His next comment was given in the form of advice, and its impact was similar to having been hit in the solar plexus by Joe Louis. "Mr. Schoenfeld (the Americanized spelling of my surname), you are a foreign-born Jew without visible means of support; you will never be admitted to medical school."

I had never expected such a comment, not here in this country, which I had held up as my ideal of freedom and equality. Similar words had been spoken to me back in 1943 when I applied to medical school in Debrecen, Hungary. Of course, I should not have applied there in the first place because Jews were legally *personae non grata* at universities. Hungarian universities had a quota for Jews, it was *numerus nullus*, simply no Jews were to be admitted to the university. I later became aware that a similar system existed in the United States. The quota system in medical schools was an unwritten gentlemen's agreement that specified that no more than seven percent of the admissions would be granted to Jews. This sub rosa agreement limited the admission of Jews to most medical and law schools and even to some of the elite undergraduate schools. Upon his advice, I changed my major from premed to psychology. My dream of becoming a physician was shattered. I became aware that antisemitism even in the post Holocaust era was still flourishing. Antisemitism, I became aware, is a Western attitude rooted in Christian theology. It is only now, in the 21st century, that we experience the awakening of a Christian sense of guilt and an acceptance of the idea that the Holocaust would not have occurred without the various accusations leveled by Christians against Jews from time immemorial, accusations that are exemplified in and form the basis of various passion plays.

Antisemitism in colleges and universities also affected my Cousin Alex's desire to complete his medical training. Alex came to St. Louis two years after I did. He too received a Hillel scholarship. By the time of his arrival, Alex had completed four of the five years of medical curriculum in Germany. Also like me, he was sent back to undergraduate school. Upon completion of his BS in microbiology, he applied to ten different medical schools. He was sure that once his *curriculum vitae*, his prior medical education was seen, he would be admitted. Ten different schools rejected his application. He did not accept this as a setback and decided to complete a master's degree in bacteriology. Two years later, advanced degree in hand, he again applied to ten medical schools and experienced the same rejection. He completed a Ph.D. in the subject, and with time he became noted in the field. While working at the Jewish Hospital in St. Louis, Washington University's school of medicine asked him to join its staff as professor. He did. It is ironic that a person who was judged inadequate to enter medical school was good enough to teach in one of the medical schools that rejected his application. Let the reader himself conclude the reason for the earlier rejections. Can it be anything other than antisemitism?

My father was a Zionist, a Socialist (clearly distinct from a Communist), and an idealist committed to human perfectibility. This idea he considered to be one of the fundamental tenets of Judaism. He loved the United States and perceived it as an ideal country. He felt that the ideals that prompted the French Revolution were fundamental to this country and that these ideals would cleanse the United States from prejudice, especially the antisemitism that has plagued Europe for two millennia. "The future is in the United States," he used to tell me. This was my heritage. I inherited his idealism. I knew, as he did, that the Holocaust was a manifestation of a fetid disease of ancient tribalism and European Christianity. He insisted that I have a broad education with a broad spectrum, both secular and religious studies. That inculcated in me the knowledge necessary so that at maturity I could develop my own beliefs. It is from him that I inherited my false consciousness of the United States. My idealism about this country gave me hope that here I would find true brotherhood and not merely a shallow form of tolerance. This, I believe, was at the core of Jefferson and Madison's ideals as incorporated into the Declaration of Independence and the Constitution. Unfortunately, these ideals never guided this country's political practice.

Israel Zangwill was wrong. We have not been cleansed by the holy fires of liberty. Instead, we have kept our European heritage of hostility towards other religions, races, and ethnicities. I had not expected to hear the words that the dean expressed which essentially stated that because I was a Jew I would be treated as a pariah and not given the same privileges and opportunities as others.

I have often asked myself why my father was an idealist and why, indeed, I kept his political and values and worldviews. My father's idealism was not unique; it was a reflection of Jewish *Weltanschauungen* (worldview). In time, I realized that a great many Jews, not only my father, were imbued with this utopian idealism. Why indeed is idealism a Jewish trait? I am not proposing here that Jews have cornered the market on idealism. I do contend, however, that, compared with other ethnic and religious groups, Jews have shown that they are more likely to support liberal ideologies and idealisms. For instance, compared with members of other religions and ethnic groups, having the same income and occupational levels, Jews more frequently vote for democratic candidates and support more liberal causes, including the gender and racial revolutions. Why?

An immediate and obvious answer, at least to me, is the Jews' commitment to Hebrew Scriptural values rooted in the ideal of justice. Justice, in the Jewish tradition, is perceived as all people's right to an equal life chance. In fact, the Hebrew word for charity has the same root as does justice. This implies to me that charity itself is an act of justice rather than an act of empathy. In the ancient tradition, the corners of the fields could not be harvested, for the grains in them must be left for the poor. In short, it was the right of the poor to harvest those bits of land. The owner of the land did not leave the corners unharvested because he empathized with the poor nor because he loved them. He left that part of the field because the law commanded him to do so, and the law sought to exercise justice. In this instance, justice is contained in the collective's duty to supply the poor with the means of survival. But the Jews' commitment to the ideal of justice and equality, or, as I prefer to call it, to utopian idealism, is also rooted in and arises out of their historical experiences. These instill a consciousness which makes individual Jews aware that the exercise of justice enhances self-interest.

Let me propose that Jewish utopian idealism was further enhanced by their minority status in Christian Europe. The history of the Jews for the last 2000 years, both in Christian Europe and the Muslim world, has for the most part been the history of a people's persecution. It is this collective experience that serves as the ideological infrastructure of Jewish political, moral, and social philosophy.

In essence, utopian idealism consists of values that minority classes believe will open the political and legal fences that have kept them a politically, economically, and socially subjugated group.

The Holocaust is but one of the most recent, although perhaps the most dramatic, of the Jewish collective experiences. Throughout time there were others such as a thousand years of ghetto life, pogroms, and all types and all forms of physical, emotional, and economic attack. During the two centuries of the Crusades, the martyrdom of Jews was common. There were many massacres like those in York and the expulsion of Jews from France by Louis IX. These events were followed by the Spanish Inquisition and the practice of the *auto-da-fé*. There were the pogroms in Russia and antisemitism in the West exemplified by the Dreyfus Affair. Hitler's solution to the Jewish question had many historical precedents. Jews have long been conscious that even in the best of times they are no more than strangers in a land not theirs. When one becomes conscious of his group's history as a persecuted minority, a people without rights, one cannot help but develop a commitment to utopian idealism based on justice, equality, and freedom.

No wonder, hence, that Jews hold the ideal of justice ahead of love. Our experiences have taught us that love cannot be legislated nor can it be commanded; it is a personal reaction to individuals to whom one, for various reasons, becomes attached. I love someone because I, for whatever reason, empathize with him, because I may be able to place myself in his place, not because the individual has an inherent right to my love. But justice, unlike love, can be legislated. The law can endow all persons with equal rights, and these rights then become the basis for equality. Equality is the right to pursue the same goals as others and not to have one's path to achievement blocked for any reason save inherent incapability and unwillingness to work.

What else can I be than a supporter of equality and justice when a great part of my life was destroyed by inequality and legal persecution? When I reflect on my own experiences, I cannot be committed to anything less than equal rights. This commitment is not only the result of my Holocaust experiences but also from experiences in the United States where equal opportunity to pursue my dream to study medicine was denied me simply because I was a Jew. Let me hasten to add that I accept the legitimacy of inequality, but only when differences in lifestyle and honor are the result of effort and achievement. The only honor that I am willing to grant other people is that which one achieves by his own labor and effort. This is the principle of republicanism -- not of the party but the principles on which this nation is to be built -- namely, the moral principle of meritocracy.

Perhaps the most profound belief that led Jews to idealism is the view of the "perfectibility of the world," the central Judaic tenet of *Tikun Olam*. Jewish belief holds that God never completed the act of creation, that He deliberately left the world imperfect and gave mankind the task to improve the world and with it become a partner with God in the creation process. We, humanity, have been charged by God with the task that each generation owes the next one, the duty of making the world better.

There is a wonderful Midrashic legend that illustrates this idea. The tale revolves around Alexander of Macedonia. In the process of conquering the world, Alexander and his army came to Africa where they decided to pitch their tents and rest next to a beautiful stream. Alexander, so the story tells us, took out some dried and salted fish which he proceeded to wash in the stream. The fish, when immersed in the stream, became alive and swam away. "This must be a magical river," thought Alexander. "I must find its source, and perhaps I too can acquire some of its magic." He proceeded to follow the river to its origin. After a three-day journey, Alexander found himself in front of a tall stone fence that he was unable to climb. The river's origin seemed to be behind the fence. Seeking an entrance, Alexander followed the fence, and soon came to an iron gate that guarded the entrance. Taking his sword, he knocked on the gate, which soon opened. There, guarding the entrance, stood an angel with a fiery sword in his hand.

"Who are you and what do you want?" asked the angel.

"I am Alexander and I want to enter this place," he responded.

"What is this place?"

The angel answered, "This is the Garden of Eden."

"Can I enter?" asked Alexander.

"Only those who improved the world for the next generation may enter this place. What have you contributed to this end?" said the angel.

"I conquered the world," responded Alexander.

"This is neither a fitting nor a rewardable accomplishment," concluded the angel.

We, Jews, believe in the coming of a Messianic world, a utopian world, a world of plenty and of peace. But this era will not come because of faith alone. It must be earned. In short, we must create it ourselves. In the face of 2000 years of suffering, Jews have maintained their belief in the assurance of the coming of the ideal world.

I cannot deny that in spite of or, perhaps, because of my deep commitment to utopian idealism I am also a cynic. Idealism and cynicism actually go hand in hand. Cynicism is my ego-defense mechanism for the anticipation that society most likely will never achieve utopian ideals. This is due to the predominance of the iron law of oligarchy, namely, that people in power are motivated by class interests and personal greed to maximize their power and control the world's scarce resources. My cynicism is best reflected in the saying, so, what's new? Utopian idealism is the wish and hope for a better world, an idealism that is central to people who have historically been subjugated. It is not accidental that the Israeli national anthem, representing the central perspective of the Jewish people, is titled *Hatikvah*, the hope. Idealism is essentially a statement of hope in human progression to a socially just and humane world. Although this is my desire, still my personal experiences in camps and the content of my ethnic memory negate a belief that human progression is possible. This is also the source of my cynicism. When evil comes down and persons or nations turn against each other I can remark, of course, I told you so.

I could no longer endure my life in the rabbi's house. I was very unhappy that the scholarship that I was promised, including a monthly stipend covering my living expenses, was not given to me. Such a stipend would have been the means to independence. Having to live with the rabbi and ask my uncles to contribute towards my tuition made me feel like a charity case. For the two years that I lived in Germany I was not only independent but I had also enjoyed a relatively comfortable lifestyle. Compared to others, I had status and privilege. Now, in the United States, I reverted to the status of being a financially poor, stateless person dependent upon the dole. I yearned to achieve again my independence, to be free from needing to account for the little money that someone gave me, or to account for every move that I made. The solution, of course, was employment. I sought work that not only would enable me to pay for my lodging but would not demand all my time and would provide an opportunity to study.

I found such a job. I acquired a position teaching Hebrew and serving as the weekend cottage father at a Jewish children's home. It was not an orphanage in the generally assumed sense, but a home where courts temporarily assigned children whose parent were unable to care for them for whatever reason. Of course, there were also orphans. My job was to conduct two hourly classes in instruction in Hebrew. These classes were held evenings, Monday through Thursday, after supper. The job suited me well. It wasn't difficult to teach Hebrew; after all, both my grade-school and high-school education was mostly in Hebrew, and thus I spoke Modern Hebrew well. My main mission was to teach the children to read the language so that they could recite Hebrew prayers and could perform their *Bar Mitzvah* rituals. Sunday afternoons I was to relieve the full-time cottage parents, and I took over the job of in *loco parentis*, the cottage parent to the boys. I was to supervise those children who could not leave to be with their parents. I was to serve both lunch and dinner, which usually consisted of sandwiches and canned food. The meal service was easy. The food was the same every Sunday. I opened cans of herring in tomato sauce, heated beans and a vegetable, and served the meal to the boys and to myself. The rest of the time, I was free to attend my classes and even to have an occasional date. For my services I was given a salary of 50 dollars per month, a room with a connected bathroom, three meals a day, and laundry service. Fifty dollars, in 1948, was a great deal of money, and having my food and shelter provided meant that I had money that I could spend on clothes and other personal needs.

Life in the St. Louis Children's Home was tranquil. My life there was pleasant and made it possible to pursue my education without much concern for an income. For the most part, the boys were well behaved, and I made friends with the couple who served as cottage parents in the boys' home. It was October, and the country was in the heat of the impending presidential election. I spent a great deal of time discussing political issues with John, the husband of the couple of cottage parents. Both of us were committed to Democratic causes and preferred the Democratic candidate, Mr. Truman, to the Republican, Mr. Dewey. John was an ex-GI attending graduate school in psychology at Washington University. He was taking a course in psychological testing and asked me to be his subject so he could administer the Wechsler-Binet IQ test. I did not know much about this field, but I consented. To my great surprise, as he added my score he became increasingly excited. Even with a linguistic handicap, I achieved a score of 180 on the test. That score did not mean much to me, but the tester considered it phenomenal.

I lived long enough in St. Louis to become aware of racial segregation. But, as long as I lived in the St. Louis suburbs and never went near Black neighborhoods, I did not become aware of racism. One, of course, does not become conscious of conditions until confronted with them. It was during my stay in the Children's Home in St. Louis itself that I came face to face with the meaning and nature of racism as it related to Blacks in the United States.

Paul was a light-skinned and tall Black man, an ex-GI, who lived and worked as the maintenance man in the children's home. He and I became friends, talked to each other, and often played ball with the kids. One Saturday afternoon, bored and not wishing to study or read, I went to Paul's room, just to talk and spend some time. "Hey Paul, lets go to a movie."

"OK," he replied. "But where do you want to go?"

There was a movie house just two blocks from our premises, and I suggested that we walk there to see the next show.

"You know, Gene, I cannot go there."

"Look," I told him, "If you are short of money I have a few dollars."

"It is not that," he responded. "I cannot go because I am Black, and that theater is for whites only."

It had never dawned on me that Paul was Black. Paul was simply Paul, a nice guy and fun to be with. This incident opened my eyes to the racial realities in the United States at that time. Contrary to what I believed the United States stood for, namely, that all men were created equal, the people of this country and their constituent government did not necessarily follow the ideals which I believed to be the moral infrastructure of the country. I soon learned European ancient prejudices had not been altered or cleansed by the sacred fires that were supposed to have created here a New Zion, a new chosen people.

"Well, Paul, can I go to a movie that admits Blacks?"

"Sure."

We took the bus downtown and went to see a film in a Black neighborhood.

In spite of friendship with some Jewish students whom I had met at the Hillel house, I was lonely. Now that I had my own lodgings, I was seldom invited to my family. In fact, I preferred it that way. For, in their eyes, I was straying from the Orthodox religious path. Moreover, my Uncle Alexander, who considered himself to be the head of the family, was angry at me because I did not defer to him and his status, nor did I seek his advice, nor did I follow his suggestions. He still felt here, as he had in Europe, that a good marriage is one that brings status to the family. In his view, I needed to marry the daughter of a wealthy Orthodox Jew, and because of my learning and family status, I should assume an important position in the Orthodox Jewish community. I did not follow his advice, and in so doing he considered me a rebel, which, of course, I was.

I soon learned that people considered me a curiosity; I was a Holocaust survivor. Because of that, I was asked to speak to various groups, and also had opportunities to interact with young Jewish women. Yet, I had difficulties in securing dates. It seemed to me that, when it came to dating, Jewish women considered me a *persona non grata*. It felt as though an invisible curtain excluded me from the list of appropriate and eligible young men whom the Jewish women at Washington University dated. The reasons for my exclusion were my poverty and lack of status, and hence I was not considered appropriate husband material. Jewish women from wealthy homes, and one had to be wealthy to attend this private university, desired assured futures. That meant marrying wealthy, young Jewish men. I, a recent immigrant, a displaced person, sans money and car, could not show them a good time. In short, I was poor and therefore unacceptable.

I spent a great amount of time, especially evenings, at the Hillel house. It was there that I became Americanized, where I learned to play bridge and chat with fellow students. It was also there that I met a very pretty young woman, slender and with big eyes, a pleasant smile, and wonderful attitude. Even more important to me was that she accepted me for who I was, an impoverished student. Notwithstanding my poverty, she consented to date me even though it was often merely a walk in the park. We soon started dating seriously, and in less than a year I asked her to marry me. She accepted my proposal. When I announced my intentions to my family, Uncle Alexander became angry. I had to admit that Jean's family lacked status and that they did not have any worldly goods, and like other poor families there were ten siblings, mother, and an absent father. What they had was a great heart, and they cared and were concerned for me. These qualities, however, were not considered important by my family. Although these attributes, the family agreed, were nice, they were no substitute for money, wealth, and status. I finally had to tell the family of my decision. I was going to marry Jean. That was my decision, and if they were to continue as a family, they would support my decision; otherwise it would be better to estrange ourselves. Reluctantly, they accepted my decision.

I was a sophomore in college, with no family to support me and of course no visible future. Why then did I want to get married, and even more importantly why did I want to marry Jean? First of all, she was beautiful, and I fell in love with her. But what is love? Is it desire? Of course, it is. It is the sensation that compels one to start a relationship with a woman. But such sensations are fleeting and without lasting qualities. Yet, at the time when one says that he is in love, I am sure there are many other conditions that draw a person to another, which at the time of falling in love are not completely evident to the person in love. I was in love with Jean, but it is only later, after years of marriage, that I became aware of the true reasons that drew me to her. I once told my students when lecturing on the sociology of marriage and family that the feelings one has at the beginning of courtship and marriage are merely desire but that true love comes from sharing common experiences, common struggles, in having a common history. "My love for my wife," I told the students, "is founded in my knowledge that she will never do anything that will be harmful to me and to my happiness."

While the primary reason I fell in love with Jean was her beauty, of course there were many more reasons I sought her, why I wished to marry her and establish a permanent relationship. With time, I realized what I must have already known subconsciously, that she would be a good person with whom to build a future. Jean was the embodiment of kindness, understanding, care, and concern. Jean came from a family which, because of parental illness, was financially deprived. Absence of money, however, led to great family cooperation, care, and love for one another. One sister's problem became the problem of all. Her family was more than a tightly-knit nuclear family. They had strong relationships with their extended family. Her home was the center of the extended family's activities. For instance, Friday nights, the Sabbath meal was entirely a family affair. After the traditional Friday meal, the table would be cleared and the jars of pennies brought out for a hot game of poker. At the head of the table sat her grandfather, surrounded by her uncle and aunt and many of her sisters. The wonderful part of this was that I became a part of this family and felt that I belonged.

Because of her family's financial condition, Jean understood the meaning of struggle for survival. Unlike my family that constantly judged my worth by my future social and economic status, hers took me in and accepted me for who I was. Most important, Jean saw in me a future; instinctively perhaps, she saw my ability to achieve a future for her and what was to be our family. Also, because of her experiences, she did not impose on me the expectation of immediate gratification and financial reward. With her, I felt I could build a future and remain true to my ideals and to myself. Jean was not like the other pampered, spoiled, and demanding young women I had met at Washington University. Indeed, now after 55 years of marriage, I realize her contribution to whatever success I have achieved.

We were married on Christmas Day. It was the week that she could get off from work. It was also a day that people were not working and could attend the wedding. Of course, I was off from school during the Christmas vacation. I left my job at the children's home, moved into a room rented from an elderly widow, and got a job as a Hebrew teacher in one of the major Conservative synagogues. Prior to our wedding, Jean came to my room and opened my closet and proceeded to weed out from my clothing those that I brought with me from Europe. She hoped to Americanize me and began this process with my wardrobe.

The wedding was small, and it was performed in her mother's three-bedroom apartment. We were married by Rabbi Jacobs, the Hillel rabbi. Her mother provided a feast, a beautifully cooked turkey and trimmings, a bottle of whiskey, a case of soda, and the *pièce de résistance*, her homemade strudel. We spent one night in a hotel prior to moving into our apartment, which was a few houses away from the hotel. We ordered dinner for two to be sent to our room, and with that our married life began.

For two years, life was tranquil and comfortable. We lived in an efficiency apartment rented to us as a gift by the fiancé of a friend of Jean's. Between her income as a secretary and mine as a Hebrew-school teacher in one of the local synagogues, we managed very well. In spite of the fact that we wished to postpone having children till I finished college and established myself somewhere, a year after our marriage, Jean became pregnant.

I finished college with a degree in psychology and went to look for jobs. 1951 was a difficult year; the postwar depression lingered, and there were very few jobs for someone with a BA in psychology, especially a stranger whose status in the United States was not certain. Technically, I was still a visitor. Now that I had completed my studies, I was expected to go either back to Germany or to another country. I could apply for change of status, from being a visitor to being an immigrant. Were I to have been granted this change, I would have needed to leave this country and then reenter as an immigrant. Luckily, under the auspices of President Truman, Congress passed a law that granted individuals whose homes were behind the Iron Curtain the right to apply for permanent residence in the United States. I applied.

But when I submitted my application, I was asked to show my military registration card.

"You haven't registered for the military?" the INS officer rebuked me in a stern voice.

"Of course I hadn't. After all, officially I am a visitor in the United States. As a visitor, I am not required to register for the draft."

The logic of my answer finally registered. "But now, as a prospective citizen you need to register."

So, I did.

"We'll notify you of your status, and if you think you

want to change it you can appeal our decision," said the member of the selection board.

I thanked him and left.

A couple of weeks later, I was notified that my military classification was 5A. I knew what 1A was, and I also knew what 4F was, but what was 5A? I called the draft board, which informed me that 5A meant that I was classified as a World War II veteran with dependents.

"In case of war, they will take the women and children before they will take you."

I guess that they considered my Holocaust experience equivalent to being a veteran. This classification suited me just fine.

It was late at night just before Christmas of 1951 and in spite of the cold, I was walking the streets. "Dear God, why are you punishing me again? Isn't it sufficient that I lost my family and that I had to endure the torments of the Nazis at camp? And now, when I thought I might have some joy, some *nachas*, of having a family, must I suffer again?"

On December 17th, Jean had given birth to twin daughters. Like most twins, they were premature and lacked adequate weight. The problem with the younger of the twins, we learned two days after her birth, was a disconnected esophagus. This became evident when the nurses tried to feed Stephanie. The formula she was suckling from the bottle went to her lungs, rather than down the esophagus into her stomach. She was born with an internal deformity called esophageal fistulae. Moreover, by the time of the diagnosis, the milk that had gone into her lungs had led to the development of pneumonia. What was there to do? There was but one answer, I was informed by the physician, she must have an operation.

Anthropologists have found a universal phenomenon: When rational solutions to a problem fail or are tenuous, we turn to nonrational ones. When we lack empirical knowledge to control the world around us, we turn to magic. There was a rational solution to my daughter's problem, an operation. But the technique for performing this necessary corrective procedure was, in 1951, still in its infancy. We were given less than a 50/50 chance for her survival. In fact, after the surgery, we were told that my daughter's heart had stopped and that the surgeon had had to massage it to bring her back to life. I was powerless in this situation. What could I do besides confront God with my complaints about what I considered this seeming injustice? Had I not been punished enough, if indeed my past deserved punishment? I never really could accept the Biblical dictum that the sins of a father should be visited unto his progenies, even to the third generation. Confronting God is an old Jewish tradition. It started with Abraham when he challenged God regarding His proposed destruction of the cities of Sodom and Gomorrah. In the same traditional vein Rabbi Levi Yitzchak, the famed Chassidic rabbi from Berditchev, frequently demanded that God justify His actions. Of course, most people are familiar with Tevye's confronting God in *Fiddler on the Roof.* But was this all that I could do to help my daughter? I went back in my memory to my early days in Munkacs.

My infant sister Esther had been dying of pneumonia. It was 1934, long before penicillin was available. I remembered her lying in her crib in a coma while we awaited the crisis. All was done that could be done. Although the doctor was there, he was powerless. There were no magic bullets in his case. Now we were told to accept God's will. Prayers for the sick had already been recited, and my grandfather, a Berditchever chassid, sat next to the crib reciting *T'hilim* (the book of Psalms). Candles had been lit and placed at the four posts of the crib, and strips of red cloth were also tied to the crib posts as protection against the evil eye which, according to my fraternal grandmother, might have been the cause of my sister's illness. All these acts had not produced any alleviation in my sister's condition. Her fever was still rising, and we waited and hoped for the passing of the crisis and her survival.

Yet, there was one last chance. There was one more magical act that could be performed on her behalf. My father and I went to the synagogue for morning prayers. There, before the open ark and before the congregation, my father recited the prayer for naming a girl. "May her name be known in Israel as Esther Elyke Naomi, the daughter of Chaim." She was six months old and had already been named as Esther Elyke. Why did my father rename her by adding the additional name Naomi? In changing her name my father hoped to circumvent God's written and sealed decree in the book of life and death. The logic of this act comes from the belief that on Rosh Hashanah (New Year) God decrees everyone's future for the coming year, and this decree is written into the book of life. On the Day of Atonement the decree is sealed and is final. Therefore, if on Rosh Hashanah it was decreed and later the decree is sealed that Esther Elyke *bat* (the daughter of) Chaim should die, then, this decree does not pertain to Esther Elyke Naomi. With a new name she had become a new person and not subject to the decree of death imposed on Esther Elyke. The magic worked. My sister lived, only to be killed in the Holocaust. While I did not change my daughter's name, I did have yet a chance to name her in the synagogue. Before the surgery I went to the synagogue, and there I named her Chaya Liebe, following the belief of my youth that her name Chaya, meaning life in Hebrew, would give her life. She lived.

Chapter Fifteen
**Economic**
**Struggles**

Igraduated with a BA in psychology. The inevitable question that I now faced was what can I do with a Bachelor of Arts degree in psychology?  My studies of psychology, as pleasant as they were, did not provide me with any form of training that could help me secure a job even in best of circumstances. But what could I, an immigrant and not, as yet, a citizen, do to secure a job, especially during a period of economic depression? I was not trained for a sales job, nor could I work in accounting or in any manner of business enterprise. Although I was a college graduate with more than acceptable grades, a major in psychology, and years of experience acquired in Germany, did not translate into any acceptable position. I thought that my experiences and training in Germany would, at least, qualify me for a job in personnel work. I found an advertised position in that field. The job description associated with the position seemed to require the exact qualifications that I had.

Indeed, I thought, this was precisely the job for me.

I put on my good suit, took the streetcar, and went to a large, nationally known factory. I completed the necessary forms and was ushered into an office to see an interviewer. We chatted for a while, and I thought that all was going well.

Then he gave me the bad news. "Mr. Schoenfeld, although you have all the qualifications for the job, I cannot offer you the position. I see that your father is living in the Soviet Union, and that fact alone makes you a security risk. As a defense contractor we cannot hire you."

How could I be a security risk? In the opinion of those who thought that, most likely reflecting the government's point of view, persons with close relatives behind the Iron Curtain were considered security risks. I was considered a security risk since I might be subject to blackmail. If I were threatened with harm to my father, I might be induced to spy for the Soviet Union. With this rejection, the opportunity to start a new life in the U.S., to earn a decent income, and especially to work in an area that I might have enjoyed, was denied to me simply because my father lived in the Soviet Union.

Without employment and with a desperate need for an income, I availed myself of the Jewish Employment Agency. It had a position for me. I was given an introductory note and was sent to the offices of the John Hancock Insurance Company, to be hired as a prospective insurance agent. I got the job and a draw on future earnings, which alleviated my immediate need for cash. I was given a brief lecture on selling by the head of the local office.

He gave me the book that he considered to be the salesman's Bible, Dale Carnegie's *How to Win Friends and Influence People*. "If you follow the teachings in this good book you will become successful," the sales manager advised me. The American salesman must be a "joiner," so he informed me. "Join a synagogue and other fraternal organizations, become active in them, and in so doing, people will trust you and buy from you."

Indeed, it was good advice, but I could never overcome my sense of guilt that I was trying to sell someone an item that he might not need or an insurance policy that was far in excess of what he needed. But above all else, I always dreaded social situations, mixing with people, and having to make friends not because I liked them but because I wanted to use them. But, should I have wished to join a synagogue, I could not because I lacked the means, as well as the means to join any fraternal organizations or any country clubs. My job with John Hancock did not last long, and soon I was in search of a new position.

I had held other jobs even before I graduated from college. My first job was as a salesclerk in a Jewish delicatessen. This was simply a summer job between semesters.

In the summer of my third year in the U.S., I took a position as a salesperson in the Broadway Army Store. The store was located in downtown St. Louis, across from the Old Courthouse at the edge a of rooming house district. The customers were occasional laborers, people who lived on welfare checks. These were the last days of small stores, an era when the downtown was the central business district of the city, before its decline. "Do you know anything about selling clothes?" inquired the owner in my interview for the job.

"Of course," I lied, "My father had a clothing store."

It soon became apparent that I knew very little about pants, shirts, and jackets. The owner was patient with me, and I learned enough that in the last month of the two-and-half month employment I sold far more than my quota and received a bonus in each subsequent paycheck.

After my unsuccessful attempt to sell insurance, I applied for a position as sales manager for a clothing store owned by the Resnikoff Brothers. The store that I would manage was a small men's and women's ready-to-wear clothing establishment located in Easton, another declining neighborhood in St. Louis. I began working there early fall and stayed through Christmas of 1951. The next spring the store folded, and I was offered a new location in Eldon, Missouri, a small town near the Lake of the Ozarks. I gave up my small apartment and let my wife and Leslie (Stephanie, after three months, was still in the hospital) move in with her mother while I moved to Eldon and lived in a hotel. I did not keep this position long. I could not be away from my family, especially when the younger of the twins was expected to come home from the hospital. Three months after her birth, Stephanie finally came home. I should confess that I did not visit her often while she was in the hospital. It was not because of my lack of caring or the lack of time. I did not visit her because I just could not look at that tiny infant attached to myriad of drainage and oxygen tubes. But now this helpless little infant was home. Her body, marked with scars, was far below the size and weight normal for a three-month-old baby.

Before we brought her home, we were instructed on her care and feeding. "Don't give her a bottle of formula," my wife and I were told. "First, you must feed her from an eyedropper, and if the milk goes down the esophagus, then proceed with the bottle." Imagine the scene. We would feed our daughter with an eyedropper, just as one might do with a wounded bird.

A few days after her release from the hospital, we came face to face with the severity of her problem. At one feeding, just three days after her release from the hospital, as we gave her the bottle, her face suddenly turned purple and blue, and she stopped breathing. The milk did not flow into her stomach. It encountered obstructions in her esophagus and consequently spilled into her trachea and into her lungs. Holding her upside down by her feet, we slapped her back, and the milk from her lungs trickled out and she began to breathe again. We called an ambulance and rushed her to the hospital. Here we were in the ambulance with its siren blasting and the lights flashing, and still there were many cars whose drivers, contrary to the law, did not move to the side of the road to make room for the ambulance. There were some who even tried to pass the ambulance.

Next day, the surgeon who performed the first operation informed us that we had two choices. We could repeat the operation that she had already endured with a 50/50 chance of survival, or he could insert a feeding tube directly into her stomach, which would provide a far better chance of survival. "If she were my own child," the surgeon informed us, "I would choose the surgery." In his view, it would be far better for her to die than have her grow up as a freak.

In accordance with his recommendation, Jean and I opted for the operation, rather than certain survival as a freak. Of course I wanted Stephanie alive, but in my mind there is a difference between living and merely existing. To exist includes those who are kept alive but who have no consciousness or ability to fulfill themselves as human beings. To be alive is to be active, to produce, and above all else to have the capability to enjoy and feel life. It was clear to us that growing up with a tube in one's stomach would not allow my daughter to develop and be alive in the fullest sense. We chose to return her to the operating room for a second round of surgery. Under these conditions, I could not stay away; I resigned my position in Eldon and returned to St. Louis.

I was faced again with the problem, what would I do? How would I earn a living? I was becoming downwardly mobile both socially and economically. It seemed that I was not suited for any endeavor that I tried. I was bitter, to say the least. What was I capable of? The stress of needing an immediate income continued to drive me downward. I accepted a position as a collector of debit insurance.

For those among you who do not know what debit insurance is, let me clarify, it is one step above legitimate fraud. It is, I believe, an outgrowth of the Black ghetto insurance enterprise known as burial insurance. The company I worked for, one among many such companies inundating Black ghettos, sold life and health insurance, mostly to lower-working-class Blacks. Usually, we sold what is known as whole life. Theoretically such insurance, as we were instructed to tell the client, serves as a method of saving. If I sold a policy, it was usually valued at 500 dollars with premiums to be collected either monthly or weekly. I was given a territory and a leather-bound book in which I had a leaf for each client, indicating the value of the policy, the amount to be collected, and the best time to collect it.

I received a certain percent of the monies I collected and half of the annual premium when I was able to enroll someone for a new policy. For the company, the maintenance of policies for the benefit of the client was unimportant. Instead, the company benefited to a far greater extent if after a while the insured stopped paying the premium. Then we lapsed a person's insurance, and all the money that a person had paid into the account was forfeited.

Afternoons were the collectors' doldrums, for none of the insured were home then. At such times, the debit-men, as we were known, met at a shoemaker's store where we socialized some, played gin, and all waited for the evening when we began our rounds again.

On the Jewish New Year, when we pray to God for a good life, we include the request that we ask God to provide us with honorable work and sustenance. How well I remember that in the synagogue in Munkacs when such prayers were recited, people looked to heaven and sighed, reciting *Ribono shel olam*, master of the universe, give us sustenance. We also prayed, not for mere life, but for a high-quality life in which shame and disgrace were absent. While no work is disgraceful, at the same time there is work that is fulfilling and uplifting and then there is work that is a dreaded drudge, work that deprives a person of self-satisfaction and alienates one from one's own self. Debit work, at least to me, was the latter type. For work to be fulfilling, one must find meaning in the activity. Selling debit insurance made me ashamed of myself because I sold a product that was not in the best interest of the client. These insurance companies, mostly small and local, sought to take advantage of poor, uneducated people. Moreover, in my own eyes, I was not a good husband and father because I could not provide adequately for my family's needs. Contrary to the prescribed role as a provider, I failed to provide my family with a decent living standard.

I lived with my wife and two daughters in a one-room basement apartment next to a garage. The place was infested with roaches. My wife and I slept on a sofa bed, and each morning the noise of starting cars and the stench of the exhaust fumes permeating the air of our living quarters awakened us.

Even more degrading was the fact that I, a college graduate, with a variety of experiences, could not find work in which I could use my capabilities. There was nothing open to me. Work satisfaction is a relative phenomenon. Most of the people working in debit insurance, as I did, were quite happy with their jobs. They had lower expectations of themselves than I did of myself. Most debit men did not even have a grade-school education. Because of their lack of education and other skills, collecting insurance premiums was the highest level of white-collar work they could achieve. Their satisfaction was also the result of their social lives. The gin games in the afternoons and their association in a relaxing atmosphere with others at the same level made them quite happy. As for me, I was very unhappy not only because the job was demeaning, but also because it did not require any of my education, intelligence, or skills. Perhaps what was most negative about the job is that it required that we lie to prospective customers. We were required to tell them the great benefits of insurance when, in fact, most of them would never enjoy the benefits. I would estimate that more than three fourths of the insured would have their policies lapsed. Debit insurance, at least as it was practiced in the 1950s, was unethical and immoral because it required that we take advantage of unsuspecting people.

I sought ways to improve my position to find an occupation with a greater income and that provided some greater dignity, but often to no avail. On one occasion, a prospective employer was honest with me. I applied for a sales position in a large hardware store. "You have too much education," the manager told me; "You would be utterly bored with the job." I dreamed of a job that would pay me 100 dollars a week. "Master of the universe," I would complain, "Why can't you give me decent work so that I may feed my family and be proud of myself?"

I took another position, and while it provided me with a greater income it was one that did not require education. It was in a commercial laundry. My job consisted of making up packages of linens that were delivered to hotels and of tablecloths and napkins, delivered to restaurants. The routine of the work was mindless and difficult to take. I left this position also, still searching for an activity that would make me happy and content.

I tried to become a salesperson of janitorial supplies. It was difficult but bore the possibility of a better income that would give my family a better and more secure life. Indeed, we moved from the basement into a two-bedroom apartment to accommodate our third child.

Next, I realized that I could start my own business and thus make a larger profit. I started the S&L Chemical Co., selling soaps, detergents, waxes, insecticides, all forms of cleaning agents and equipment needed in the maintenance of office buildings. To supplement my income, I returned to teaching Hebrew at various synagogues. I also supplemented my income in another way. Each year during the Jewish High Holidays, I took on the responsibilities of cantor and pseudorabbi in small communities in Illinois. For the services that I conducted for three days of the Holidays, I received 600 dollars. In 1957, that was a large sum of money. The whole family looked forward to this money. My wife had an opportunity to outfit our daughters with new clothes; thus, the girls never felt deprived in school. Our income had increased so that we could move into yet a larger apartment located in a nice middle-class neighborhood.

Our lifestyle was improving; our economic condition was better; and yet I knew that business was not what would make me happy and content. I still did not feel that I was fulfilling my life's desire. I kept asking myself the question, "What do I want?"

I did not have to dig into the deepest level of my consciousness to answer this question. Of course, I wanted to practice medicine, but I knew that my childhood dream could not be achieved. But I could teach, and through that career I could enter the world of intellectual pursuits.

Learning, knowing, and seeking answers were always an important part of my being. From childhood on, I always derived great satisfaction in intellectual and dialectical exercise. Very often, even in my youth with my father, I took an antithetical stand to his and other people's theses. I always took delight in challenging accepted meanings and ideas in Jewish theology. I always derived satisfaction when I could find a *chidush*, that is, a new meaning, a new interpretation for old and accepted ideas.

Indeed, perhaps my father recognized this trait in me, and that was why he hoped that I would become a Doctor Rabbiner, a modern rabbi with a Ph.D. in philosophy. I thought of becoming a rabbi, a modern and reformed one. Toward this end, I applied for admission to the Hebrew Union College, the Rabbinical College for liberal Judaism.

I had, at least to my mind, fulfilled all the requirements to become a rabbi. Having met some liberal rabbis, I believed that my training in Jewish studies far exceeded theirs. Indeed, I had more training in the Talmud, the Bible, Jewish history, and Jewish laws, customs, and rituals than they did. I read and spoke Hebrew fluently and had great familiarity with modern Jewish literature.

Not long after my application, I received a call that a rabbi and faculty member would be in St. Louis, and would I visit him at his hotel for an interview? I was excited at the prospect. The time arrived, and I put on my one and only suit and went for the interview. After the preliminary greetings he asked me, "What do you think of Rabbi Isserman?"

Rabbi Isserman was the senior rabbi at Temple Israel. This temple was an old and established institution started by Jewish immigrants from Germany. The rabbi's theology reflected an ultra-reformed approach to Judaism. For instance, Rabbi Isserman rejected the commemoration of the Purim holiday for he saw this holiday as a celebration of violence. He eliminated the *Bar Mitzvah* ceremony as an anachronism. Most of the services were conducted in English. Were it not for the few Hebrew sentences spoken when the Torah was taken out of the ark, the differences between his services and those in a liberal Presbyterian church would not have been very great.

Each year, in the temple's social hall, the Brandeis University Women's club held its book sale. For that occasion, a booth was erected in the hall serving sandwiches and drinks.

The first item advertised on the menu that hung above the booth was roast-pork sandwiches. In our home we did not follow the rules of *kashruth* (i.e., keeping kosher). We did, however, for symbolic and not religious reasons, abstain from eating pork. I fasted on Yom Kippur, and I abstained from eating leaven on Passover. I performed these rituals, not because I feared the wrath of heaven, but because I identified myself as a Jew. I felt that there were certain activities that I must do if I wished to maintain my identity as a Jew. I am a Jew because I choose to be a Jew and my observance of Passover, of all holidays, is the way by which I declare my identity. I observe the rituals of these holidays because I believe them to be the coin by which I pay for my identity. Because I am a Jew, I do those things that other Jews do, and in so doing I am a part of the Jewish collective.

I felt that by rejecting some of the fundamental Jewish rituals, especially the rights of passage, Rabbi Isserman had crossed a symbolic line which separates Jew from non-Jew. Much of being Jewish, that is the maintenance of Jewish identity, especially outside of Israel, is tied to some aspect of religious performance. Rabbi Isserman's rejection of Bar Mitzvah, of Purim, and of Chanukah was tantamount to rejecting his and the congregation's Jewish identity, and for this reason I questioned his right to be a rabbi, even a reformed rabbi. But above all, permitting the sale of pork sandwiches in the Temple itself I considered to be the betrayal of a fundamental tenet of Judaism. Of course, this was the judgment of a young person who in the arrogance of youth was sure that he was right.

"What do you think of Rabbi Isserman?"
I had the answer, and I was glib about it. "Do you mean the Reverend Isserman?" I immediately knew that I had given the wrong answer. I later learned that the interviewer and the rabbi had been classmates in rabbinical college and were good

friends. The interview was soon concluded, and I was notified that my application had been rejected.

There is an ancient Hebrew saying that one recites when experiencing undesirable conditions, "This too is for the best." I later became quite aware of the difficulties associated with being a rabbi. The burdens imposed on a rabbi by the congregation and the synagogue board are very demanding. Most of these obligations arise from what the congregation believes a rabbi should be. Its judgment of the rabbi is not related to matters of theology nor to intellectual prowess nor speaking abilities nor ethics and morals. Instead, the rabbi is judged by the extent to which he or she conforms first to the synagogue board's wishes and then to the wishes of the congregation. The rabbi is not free to follow the beat of his own drum. He must submit to the synagogue board and surrender his independence. Rabbis in the United States are not leaders; they do not have the intellectual freedom to pursue their own visions. Instead, rabbis must reflect the theological perspective of their congregations. Under such conditions, I could not be a rabbi, and in retrospect I am grateful that I was not accepted by the Hebrew Union College.

"What now?" "Have I burned my bridges?" As I was reflecting on my problem, particularly seeking to combine an activity for which I was suited with what would bring me the greatest happiness, I decided that my best option was to become a high-school teacher. I had some experience in teaching, not only in Hebrew schools but also in public schools. I frequently was asked to be a substitute teacher in high schools. I began to prepare by enrolling in a mail-order course in the University of Missouri's School of Education. I did this while trying to sell janitorial supplies from my home, teaching Hebrew school, and occasionally serving as substitute teacher.

But after a while, I thought that the best future for me would be to return to graduate school. But what should I pursue? During my undergraduate studies, I took a class from Professor Paul J. Campisi in social psychology. I must say that of all my professors he had the greatest effect on me, and from that, I knew I would seek an advanced degree in sociology. After 10 years, I returned to my alma mater, to Washington University, and I entered the Department of Sociology and asked to see the Graduate director. My meeting with him went very well. After a telephone call to Professor Campisi, who strongly recommended me, I was immediately accepted into the sociology graduate program. I was excited about my future, and that afternoon I came home earlier than usual.

"Guess what I did today?" I asked my wife.

"What?" she queried.

"I enrolled in graduate school at Washington University."

"Well, it's high time!" was her response.

I was back in the world of intellectualism, of dialogue, of debate, of discourse, and of dialectic. It felt good to be associated again with the world of ideas. Of course I was not a full-time student; I still had to support my family. I gave up my business. To ease our economic situation, my wife secured a full-time position while I taught Hebrew school, and occasionally I continued to substitute at University City High School, in the St. Louis suburb where we lived. I soon had to face an unpleasant reality; I could not continue my education without financial help. Tuition at a private university was too expensive for me alone to pay. I applied for a scholarship, only to be informed that to be eligible for such aid I needed to become a full-time student. I told the university official that with three children to support I could not fulfill that requirement. I was granted a one-semester tuition-free scholarship. What could I do beyond that? Was my dream again foiled? "Compromise," I told myself. Become a high-school teacher. So simultaneously with completing my MA degree, I continued my work at the

University of Missouri correspondence school, taking courses that would give me a teaching certificate.

Luck, chance, serendipity, these are quite often the conditions that lead to success. In life I soon learned success is not solely the consequence of hard work and perseverance. Quite often, in the words of the Andrews Sisters, "You got to have a little *mazel*," you have to have a little good fortune.

"Gene, can I see you in my office?" Professor Campisi asked me in the Sociology Department's coffee lounge. I had heard rumors that he was leaving Washington University, but I did not know where he was going and what position he would occupy. Campisi was not a famous professor. He had not published scholarly treatises or books, just a few articles. He had been hired right after World War II when there was a dire shortage of university faculty coupled with a great influx of students who, as a result of the GI Bill of Rights, were seeking university educations. Having received his Ph.D. from the University of Chicago and having been a student of G. H. Mead, a most noted social psychologist, he was a great candidate for employment at that time.

I followed him to his office, where he closed the door and sat down. Since I had visited him often, I was familiar with his office. The place was filled with books, manuscripts, and all manner of publications. It looked as one expects a professor's office to look.

"Gene, I do not know whether you have heard; I am leaving Washington University. I have been offered the chairmanship of the Department of Sociology at Southern Illinois University in Carbondale. They have a master's program, but they wish to expand and build a department that will offer the Ph.D. They asked me to recruit good students, and I would like you to follow me there. In fact, I can offer you a graduate fellowship with free tuition and a stipend of 280 dollars per month."

Just a half hour before this event, I had doubted that I could ever earn a doctorate and would have to settle for teaching high school. Campisi's offer changed everything. The offer was even more enticing as he hastened to outline the additional inducements. "You know, I've visited Carbondale a number of times, all the while thinking how good it would be to have you at SIU. I knew that you needed financial support so I took the liberty of approaching the Jewish community, and told its leaders about you and your abilities. There is a small synagogue that serves the area, and they are looking for someone to act as their rabbi and are interested in you. They are willing to pay you 300 dollars a month for serving as a rabbi." What an offer! What luck! What opportunity! I wanted to leave his office and run home to share this fantastic news with Jean.

"Could you hold this offer for a year?" I asked him. "I would like to finish my MA here."

"Yes I will," he replied.

In July 1961, Campisi moved to SIU (Southern Illinois University) where he assumed the chairmanship of the department. A few weeks later, I drove to Carbondale to visit the university and at the same time to meet with the synagogue board. The synagogue Beth Shalom was small and beautiful. I met with a committee, and we came to an agreement. I would begin my tasks there on a part-time basis that same year. I would come to Carbondale to conduct the High Holidays and also for a few other holidays. It was a very congenial group. I saw that it would be easy to please both the committee and the congregation.

That fall I received a scholarship from Washington University. Taking a few extra courses would assure the completion of my Master's degree before I left for Carbondale. I began to gather the data for my research paper as the final requirement for the degree. At the same time, I was also offered a temporary position at Harris Teachers College to teach two introductory courses, an introductory sociology course and a course in social problems. The income from this and from teaching Hebrew school was more than adequate to live on. Jean resigned her position and returned to taking care of our children and the house.

I felt that it would be a matter of courtesy to inform the director of the St. Louis Hebrew Schools that I would be leaving my position after having taught for him now a number of years. I was indeed quite surprised at the response of Dr. Fish, the director of the community Hebrew school. He tried to dissuade me from going.

"You are too old, and you'll never complete your degree." Behind his negative attitude towards my plan to finish my advanced degree, I believe that there was an element of jealousy in his remarks. After all, when I received my degree and would become a professor, academically I would have achieved more than he had, or could have, achieved.

"I appreciate your concern for me, but my mind is made up. I am sure that I'll do well there."

In July, Jean, the children, and I drove to Carbondale to locate living quarters. Carbondale is a very small town. It took not more than a five-minute drive to traverse the township. There were no apartments, but we located a spacious three-bedroom house with two baths for rent, and I put a down payment towards the first month.

Back in St. Louis, we began packing. I located an independent mover who agreed to relocate our possessions inexpensively. We were set for the change in our lives. I had enough money to pay the rent, the mover, and some left over to carry us till my first paycheck in October.

A week before I was to leave I received a phone call from the head of the Jewish Federation of Southern Illinois. I agreed to visit him at his offices in East St. Louis. Since I was going to Carbondale, he suggested that I also assume a part-time position as advisor to the Jewish students on the campus. I was to organize a small Jewish student union. I accepted the position. It added another 75 dollars each month to my income. The three part-time positions combined to a monthly income of over 650 dollars. I would, the congregation assured me, earn additional income from conducting various ceremonies and would teach both Bar and Bat Mitzvah students. I felt economically secure, and with this income, which, by the way, was greater than the income of most assistant professors, I knew that Jean and the children were secure. And, I could continue to do what I loved, to pursue a career in academia.

When the day for the move arrived, I helped to load the truck. We were on our way to a new city and, we hoped, to a new life. The hard days of the past, the torment of meaningless and underpaid work, was, I firmly believed, to be a condition of the past.

We settled in the new house which was less than a block away from the public school. My youngest daughter, Karen, made friends easily, and soon we had neighbor children running in and out of our house. One day, Karen and her friends rushed in the house and went directly to the china cabinet, pointing to the various Judaic objects displayed there, such as the Seder plate, the menorah, and other Jewish ritual objects and proudly declared, "I told you we are Jewish." I was very pleased because her statement indicated to me that she was proud of her people and heritage.

I began courses that were seemingly far less demanding when compared with those at Washington University. I also began to teach an introductory sociology course. I was prepared for the course. After all, I had spent a whole year at Harris Teachers College teaching that course, and I brought along all my notes and exam questions. Most important, my preparation to teach various sociology courses was perhaps the best exercise in enhancing my own knowledge of the field. Teaching served me well when I took my Ph.D. comprehensive examinations.

The most difficult part of my life in Carbondale was performing as a rabbi. This was not due to my lack of knowledge. I was well versed in the Talmud, and I did not have any problems with reading the Torah or with performing the services and rituals. In the three years as a rabbi, my problem was always trying to fulfill other people's expectations. The synagogue, on the one hand, prided itself on its motto of being a place for all Jews. At the same time, the members of the board expected that everyone would conform to its view of Judaism. It was rooted in traditionalism. For instance, we used prayer books published by the Conservative movement. Men only were honored by being called to the Torah, and of course all men had to cover their heads during services. These practices were observed in spite of the fact that the synagogue sought to serve all Jews in a 30-mile radius, regardless of theological perspective. In reality, this was not true, for the board wished to make the members and all who attended the services conform to traditional customs. Among the synagogue members, there was one family that also belonged to a Reform temple in St. Louis. Mr. F., who owned a factory nearby and who lived in Carbondale, was committed to a Reform theology. Reform temples in those days, unlike Traditional synagogues, insisted that during services men sit bare-headed. Mr. F., true to his belief, insisted that when he attended services he would do so bare-headed, which, of course, violated our synagogue board's sensibilities, and some considered it an outrage.

The treasurer of the synagogue came to see me at my home. "Gene, you must tell Mr. F . that he must cover his head when attending services; otherwise we will reject him and not allow him to be a part of our congregation."

Although I was brought up in an Orthodox home, I also felt that in a small town we must permit people to follow their own beliefs and traditions in practicing their religion. Judaism, I told the treasurer, emphasizes the idea of *Echod*, oneness and unity. Most problems in the history of the Jewish people, such as the destruction of the Temple and the dispersion of the Jews in the Diaspora, were due to strife and divisiveness. If Mr. F.'s refusal to cover his head is a sin in the sight of God then, I told the treasurer, I would ask God to charge me with it.

Of course this answer did not suit him. I know my answer was terse and flippant, but I felt angry that he should be so small-minded.

In turn, the treasurer, who incidentally was economically the most affluent in the congregation, responded by threatening my position. "Gene," he said, "You better be aware of on what side your bread is buttered."

"Isn't it funny," I replied. "Every time I drop my buttered bread it invariably lands on its buttered side." I did not know what my answer meant. All I wanted to do was to give him an enigmatic answer and let him search out its meaning.

One task that I liked to perform weekly, although it required a great amount of mental effort, was to deliver the sermon. Most often I took a passage or an idea contained in that week's Torah chapter and tried to show its significance in modern life. In so doing, I increased my skill in developing theoretical explanations. That also enhanced my skills in the field of sociology. Sermons, the kind that I delivered, were explanatory treatises. I was seeking meaning about the ideas that are central to Jewish moral development. I came to recognize the importance and even the superiority of justice as a moral infrastructure over other ideals such as love and care. My interest in the Jewish roots of morality has since become both a theological and sociological problem with which I have been preoccupied for the greatest part of my academic life. The stress of being rabbi, including my attempts to please the congregation and the three years I spent in searching for meaningful sermon topics, in addition to the stress of pursuing a degree, took a toll on my emotional state. By the end of the third year, I chose to leave Carbondale, even though I was offered, at least financially, a very lucrative position there.

As the community's rabbi and advisor to the Jewish students, I had gained great insight into Jewish/Christian relationships. Briefly, Christian ministers perceive America as a Christian country in which other religions are to be tolerated but not to be taken into account or be the occasion of concern. For the most part in my relationship with the local ministers, I never experienced overt hostility either to me or to the Jewish community. To the contrary, they were very courteous to me. But at the same time, they never took account of my presence when we were together for official activities, either as a Jew or as the community rabbi. My presence among them in my role as rabbi went unnoticed. I was the invisible person. Most often, I felt that I was merely tolerated because toleration of other religions is a part of the value system of the American democracy. Indeed, I was invited to be part of the association of university ministers, yet my views concerning whether any proposed program might be acceptable from a Jewish point of view were never solicited. I was tolerated as one tolerates an inconsequential person.

The following incident may perhaps illustrate what I mean. I received an invitation to attend a breakfast meeting where all the religious leaders involved with students on campus were to meet and discuss common issues. There were representatives from all Christian denominations. I was the only non-Christian. When I entered the room, I introduced myself to all, indicating that I represented both the local Jewish community as acting rabbi and as the director of the Hillel house, the Jewish student association. We chatted informally, and when it came time for breakfast to be served, one of the ministers, who organized the event, spoke to his friend, "Brother Mathew will you lead us in prayer." Of course, Brother Mathew did, and even though I, a Jew, was present and my beliefs differed appreciably from the others in the room, he either disregarded me or felt that I did not matter. Instead of offering a prayer in which he might have evoked the blessing of God, which would have been acceptable to all, he asked the blessing in the name of Christ. I am quite sure that he did not do this out of malice. I think it just never entered his mind that such a prayer might not be acceptable to all in the room. I said nothing. But when the plate of bacon and eggs was served to me, I loudly requested the waitress to remove the bacon, proclaiming for all to hear: "As a Jew, I do not eat bacon." No one paid any attention to my statement.

Much later in my career, I experienced another incident like that at a Georgia Sociological Association meeting. When the professor of sociology on whose campus the meeting was held and who was also a Christian minister concluded his grace before the banquet (that no one had asked him to offer) stating, "We ask these blessings in the name of Christ," I decided to give the minister a lesson in the importance of being aware of multiculturalism. I stood up and asked my colleague loudly, "Hey Bill! May I now have equal time for Moses?" I know that my response may have been rude, but I had had enough of being the invisible Jew and not being taken into account.

One of the frequent issues that I have had to face was the growth of intermarriage both among the children of the members of the congregation and among the students. I realized that the low rate of endogamy so characteristic in the 1930s and 40s was changing. There had been a steady increase in Jewish/

Christian intermarriages nationwide, but the problem (and it is perceived as a problem by Jews) was most acute in small towns and college campuses. The reason for this phenomenon is related to three factors. First and foremost is the nature of small towns where the low numbers of young Jewish women and men dos not permit wide selection of dates. When I was in Carbondale, there were only two Jewish young men between sixteen to eighteen years of age and four young women. The absence of Jews as potential dates necessitated inter-religious dating. I have talked to a number of parents about inter-religious dating and possible marriage. Their views reflected the changes of times and values.

One father summarized a perspective most common to all small-town Jews. "Of course, I would prefer that my son marries a Jewish girl, but I'll be happy if she is a good girl and comes from a good family."

There were a number of men who married Christian women who joined the synagogue, attended services, and were heavily involved in the Jewish community. On occasions, they even taught Sunday school, but they never officially converted. There were an additional two reasons for the relatively high rate for inter-religious dating among students, propinquity and secularism.

On campus, Jewish students came in frequent contact with non-Jews. Jewish students on the campus did not keep themselves separate from non-Jews. Most Jewish students put their identities as secular Americans first and then as Jews. The separatism that was characteristic among Jews when they lived in self-imposed ghettos began fading with their exits from the city to the suburbs. Most Jewish students on campus came from middle-class suburban families. They attended high schools where they were the numerical minorities and shed the need of keeping themselves apart from non-Jews. The campus provided additional freedom from parents, which added to a sense of freedom to associate widely.  There is a sociological law that proposes that the greater the association among individuals, the more likely it is that such associations will lead to sentiment. Indeed, relationships among Jewish students, mostly males, frequently led to sentiment and the desire to intermarry.

In my capacity as both the head of the Hillel group and the pseudorabbi for the community, I was often visited by many young Christian women regarding their hopes of marrying the young Jewish men they dated. It seems that many young Jewish men still made conversion to Judaism a prerequisite to marriage. They came to talk to me about conversion. While I did not have the authority to convert anyone, still I could explain the conversion process and the Jewish belief system. Of course, I was aware that, according to Halachaic law, conversion solely for purposes of marriage was not considered a genuine, adequate motive. Such a convert, for instance, would not be said to follow the path of becoming a *Ger Tzedek,* a righteous convert. Nonetheless, I felt that it was my duty to enlighten these women about what Judaism is and what it requires of converts.

"You know Jews do not believe in the divinity of Christ. Would you be able to reject this belief that you have held for a long time?"

All of them informed that this would not be any problem.

Then I continued, "If you convert, and become a Jew and no longer accept the divinity of Christ, you also would have to give up Christmas as a holiday."

I immediately saw the shock register on their faces. "You mean to tell me that if I convert I cannot have a Christmas tree?"

"Of course not," I replied.

The rejection of their childhood dreams and memories of good times and presents was more than they could accept.

I did not want to tell them that many Jews celebrate Chanukah as a quasi-Christmas. After all, if one is to covert, one should accept the true Jewish creeds and not some modified form. If there was anything that kept Christian women from converting, it was the fear of the loss of Christmas, greater than their fear of parental disapproval.

In the summer of 1964, I received a call from the chairman of the department of criminal justice. "Gene, my friend Alexander who is the head of the federal prison system has a problem, and I know you can help him." I had met Alexander when he chaired the department of criminal justice at SIU before he was selected to head the federal prison system.

What was the problem? About 15 miles from Carbondale, in Marion, Illinois, the federal government had built a maximum-security prison. Among the 460 inmates were seven Jewish prisoners who felt discriminated against because they were not accorded the opportunity to participate in Jewish religious services. The Baptist minister in charge of religious services had offered to conduct Jewish services.

"Thanks, but no thanks" was their reply. "We want our own services."

The idea that the federal government was discriminating against a Jewish minority felt threatening to Alexander. The call from the chairman of the department relayed Alexander's concern. So he asked me, "Would you go to Marion and conduct services?"

Since there were no services on the Sabbath in the synagogue in Carbondale, I felt free to offer my services to the prisoners. I did not do it for the money. The 20 dollars per service, three times a month, hardly paid for the gas and the effort that it took to drive there. Moreover, by spending the Sabbath morning in Marion, I was depriving my family of the little time I could give them.

I went to the prison because I felt a moral obligation to

do so. It was important to me that I provide these Jewish prisoners a relationship with their heritage. In my view, when I offered the inmates Jewish services and something to enhance their Jewish spirit, I was fulfilling the moral commandment of freeing the imprisoned. They were grateful that I came, especially one person, who outside had not practiced his faith but now, inside, wanted weekly to recite *Kaddish* for his mother who had recently died. Under the guise of ritual food, I would bring them Challah, gefilte fish, and even a bottle of Manischewitz's kosher wine. They were faithful congregants and came each Sabbath to service.

These few Jewish inmates represented various types of felons. There was one young person who was imprisoned for transporting stolen cars across a state line; another, for bogus checks; then there was one who had violated the Mann Act by transporting women across the state line for immoral purposes. The most violent felon, about whom the others cautioned me, was a member of the Jewish Mafia, Murder, Inc. The prisoners were grateful for my participation in their lives and gave me insight into prison life in a federal institution.

I also made friends with the Catholic priest who was employed by the federal government. The relationship between the priest and the Baptist minister, who was in charge of religious activities in the prison, was somewhat strained. The latter wanted to exercise his authority over the priest, who felt that, as a priest, he should be given complete autonomy in his relationship with his parishioners. I often had lunch with the priest, at which time I listened to his problems and offered some advice on how to overcome the attempts by others to exercise bureaucratic authority over him.

In the spring of 1964, I passed my comprehensive examination and submitted my proposal for my dissertation, which was then accepted by my committee. I now gained a new status -- I was an ABD -- that is, I had completed all the requirements for my Ph.D. except the dissertation. I began collecting the data for my research, a sociological study of Jews in small towns. By the spring of 1965, I had completed the first draft of the dissertation and was faced with the decision of whether to stay in Carbondale or to leave for a position at another school. In Carbondale, Southern Illinois University offered me a position as lecturer, to teach one course and supervise a dormitory. Were I to accept this position, I would receive an annual salary of 6,000 dollars for nine months, an apartment in the dorm, and cafeteria food for my whole family. I could also retain my position as community rabbi. Financially, this was a very lucrative offer. I had, however, had enough of the difficult task of being a rabbi. It was time, I felt, that I now turn my attention entirely to my chosen profession, that of being a sociologist. After visiting different schools, I accepted a position as assistant professor at Memphis State University. In retrospect, this decision served me well in the long run, and finally I felt that I knew where I was going. In August, we moved to Memphis, into a rented a house, and I started to ready myself for my reconstructed life. I became what my father had hoped for me, a professor whose interest was also Judaism.

It took me two years to complete my writing and to defend my dissertation. In 1966, I passed my defense, and soon I was officially awarded the Ph.D. With my degree in hand, I was promoted to Associate Professor. Three years later I was invited to become the chair of sociology at Georgia State University, and I was promoted to Professor.

# EPILOGUE

In 1966, 21 years after my separation from my father, we were again reunited, albeit for a very short time. My father, who at that time had reached his 68th birthday, and his second wife Charlotte were given permission by the U.S.S.R. government to visit the United States. At that time I resided in Memphis, Tennessee, and was an assistant professor of sociology at Memphis State University.

My wife and I waited for my father at the appointed gate at the airport. The airplane from Canada finally arrived, and in a short while my father and his wife entered the waiting area. For weeks prior to their arrival, I was concerned about our reunion. What would I say to my father after so many years of separation? Having been alone for almost a quarter of a century and having had to struggle for my existence without him, we shared little in common. Our histories and experiences had diversified. I still harbored some bitterness for having been abandoned at a time when I needed him most. I could not think of him with the kind of love that I thought a son should feel toward his father. He was, to me, a father in name and a stranger in fact.

As I approached him, I could see that he, too, felt a great deal of apprehension. Was he apprehensive of what I might feel for him? Or, was his apprehension a sign of guilt for our broken relationship? I never found out since I never wanted to discuss with him our past or my feelings of having been abandoned. We kissed and hugged and shed some tears. As I looked at him, I found him not to be the person that I remembered. He was not, at least for the few weeks that he lived with me, the committed idealist that he had been in his youth and early adulthood. I saw an old man, beaten by life in the Soviet Union. He was bent and physically haggard. He was almost totally blind. His left eye had always been almost useless, the consequence of an early childhood injury, and with very little vision in the other eye due to an overripe cataract, he could see very little. The few teeth that he still had in his mouth were loose, and the dental bridge to which they were attached was dangling in his mouth, a condition that made clear speech very difficult. Was this indeed my father who had exercised so great an influence on my life and thought?

I vacated one of the three bedrooms in our house by putting all four of our daughters in one bedroom and tried to make them comfortable in the small house that we were renting. Our older daughters tried to talk to him, but communication with him was difficult for he spoke no English, and my daughters spoke neither Hungarian nor Yiddish. Usually, I sat between my father and my children and wife, and as my father spoke to me in Hungarian I translated into English and, of course, also the reverse. After a while, the need for instant translation started to confuse me so that I did not know all the time which language I was speaking.

One day, my daughter Karen asked me a question, and I thought that she had spoken Hungarian to me, and I curtly blurted out, "Karen, for heaven's sake, speak English to me."

Confused, she responded, "But, dad, I am speaking English. I know no other languages."

My stepmother, who was a physician and chief pathologist in the Munkacs hospital, sought to act as a surrogate mother. Knowing, for instance, that I loved the Hungarian pastry, *Kremes*, the Hungarian version of the French Napoleon, she spent a day preparing it for me.

For two weeks, after his teeth and sight were restored, my father rose early each morning to take Robin, my youngest daughter, out in her stroller. A few times during that period he also joined me in my class at the university, where at that time I was lecturing on Karl Marx. I was hoping that I could talk to him about the topic. After all, he had read Marx during his youth, and, of course, he had just come from the U.S.S.R., but by this time I had lost my Hungarian linguistic skills so that a discussion of philosophy was difficult. Still, I could see that he was more than satisfied that I had become, what in his eyes was a great achievement, a professor.

The first two weeks of his visit were spent taking care of his ailments. The infections in his mouth had to be cleared first; then his teeth had to be extracted; and only then could he be fitted with dentures. With his teeth now cared for, we proceeded to hospitalize him for five days to remove his cataract and for him to be fitted with new glasses. After all this, I had fewer than two weeks with him.

Soon he went on to St. Louis to meet his three brothers. We all spent the Passover Seder together in St. Louis, enjoying the memories of the past. Yet, I knew that I could not attach myself to him. My father and his wife decided to return to Munkacs. It was primarily her decision. First, she was attached to her niece and her children who lived in our hometown. She considered them as her true family and wished to return to them. Next, she did not want to become dependent on me or on my father's brothers. In the U.S.S.R. she and my father had pensions and lived in the house that he had built and in which I was born. Their pension and house, she argued, gave them some degree of independence. I do not wish to speculate which of these reasons was the dominant one. If I were to guess, I believe it was her attachment to her niece which kept her, and therefore also my father, from remaining in the United States.

They left, and again, as it was some 20 years earlier, neither his granddaughters nor his son could provide strong enough motivation to remain. I felt again abandoned. I continued my correspondence with him for 10 years. In early winter of 1978, my father, his wife, and the remnant of her family received exit permits and planned to immigrate to Israel. In December of 1978, just a scant few months before they were to immigrate to Israel, at the age of 79 years, he died of a heart attack. He was buried near his parents in an old Jewish cemetery which, a few years later, was demolished. Centuries of Jews interred there were exhumed, and their bones relocated to a mass grave. This was done in the name of progress, that is, to build new apartments for the thousands of Russians from Central Russia who were transplanted to Munkacs.

A few years ago, I was in Prague and thought about returning to Munkacs for a visit, but I decided against it. Munkacs of the present is a mere ghost of my hometown. There is nothing there for me but my memories of the past, my pleasant memories of childhood. I did not go back because I wanted to remember Munkacs as it was, a city alive with Jewish people, a center for Jewish religion and culture. What I have in Munkacs are my memories of my friends and family. I do not wish to disturb these memories by revisiting my hometown now. I do not wish to confront the emptiness that I know I will feel which, I am sure, would kill the memories of my pleasant life that I once experienced. My life is now in the United States. It is here where my family lives and where I have rooted myself through my children and grandchildren.

I began this retrospective biography with my wish to seek those inner forces which were most important to help me to reestablish my life after the devastation, the Holocaust. To do so, I have had to lay bare my feelings and seek what I considered the truth of my life. Now, at the conclusion, I recognize the two forces that I consider paramount in my efforts, the forces that gave direction to my life, my identity as a Jew and my dreams.

I am a Jew not because I was born to a Jewish mother, nor because I believe in the ritual traditions of my people, nor because I have accepted and maintained my faith in an anthropomorphic God who is the core of all faiths. I am a Jew because I find the philosophy promulgated by our people to contain the most inspiring ideals for both personal and social existence. For, in the final analysis, I have become aware that the two-millennia-old emphasis on love has not worked. The Holocaust and many other world calamities have occurred in spite of the Christian teachings of love for individuals and humanity. There were occasions in my career as professor of sociology when I had developed a cynical view of love as a motivating force. But most important of all, Judaism, its history and its prophetic teachings, imbue in me a sense of universal optimism. It has taught me that we can achieve a Messianic period of universal peace. Judaism has taught me not to despair even in the face of great tragedies. Human wisdom will eventually prevail. For the development of these views I am grateful to both my father and my teacher Rabbi Yaakov's idealism.

The force that has helped me to accept the challenge of overcoming the horrendous problems I faced after liberation and to seek to achieve some success in life, especially in the intellectual field, was rooted in my parents' teaching and in the Jewish philosophy and worldview. As you by now are fully aware, I had hoped to become a physician. When this dream was blocked due to antisemitism, I turned to my father's dream of my becoming an intellectual. This is a dream which again arose out of Jewish values, founded in the ancient Jewish teaching that emphasized that the most important human mission is to study and to teach. This dream was not as manifest and clear to me as was the dream to enter the field of medicine. It was a latent dream that required greater maturity than the one I had sought earlier in life. I must say that my father's dream for me was more suitable. I was for many years and even though I am retired still am seeking to advance my understanding of life.

It is over a half a century since my liberation from the

concentration camp. Still, I cannot forget the Holocaust, nor do I wish to do so. I often hear people who lost family members due to a crime speak of closure. Perhaps, because of the enormity of the crime and the consequent dislocation of my life, it seems that I cannot have closure. In my dreams I still am searching for my brother and sister. I still maintain the illusion, at least when I dream, that somewhere in distant lands I will miraculously become reunited with them. But this hope and dream I know will not come true. I have tried to make a new life for myself in the United States, and I have partially succeeded. I say partially because my past still haunts me.

I know quite well that my survival was a matter of luck. Nonetheless, I feel an obligation to pay for my good fortune, not only for my survival but for the privilege of having had the good fortune to reestablish my life and for the comfort I now enjoy. I, moreover, owe an obligation to those who died "for the sanctification of His name," as the ancient Hebrew text puts it. I have an obligation to tell people that there is a purpose for their deaths, and it is my mission to give testimony to that and to caution the public that, in spite of our claim that we are civilized, evil both as an individual attitude and a social reality still exists. In spite of the Holocaust, genocide is and continues to be a fact of human existence. Although the new genocides are not as organized or as widespread as the one we refer to as the Holocaust, they still are an abominable fact of human existence.

We, the survivors, owe a debt to those who died in the Holocaust. We can repay it only when we give meaning to their deaths. We can accomplish this by fighting evil. My task in this battle, at least at this stage of my life, is to bear witness to the past and teach new generations that evil is not a figment of one's religious imagination but that it is a reality that exists in us. It is our *yetzer harah*, our evil inclination, and we must constantly be watchful lest we succumb to it. I must enlighten students how easy it is to give up our freedoms when we encounter social chaos. How easy it was for the Germans to shed their freedoms and submit themselves to the dictates of a tyrant. I must teach because social chaos occurs in every society, and unless we become aware of the temptations to submit ourselves to tyrannical leadership that promises to solve all of our problems, other holocausts will continue to be a reality in human existence. This is my mission and the reason for writing this book.

# GLOSSARY OF YIDDISH TERMS

**Adar**: the 6th month in the Jewish calendar (February-March) in which the holiday Purim occurs.

**Algemeiner Zionist**: a general Zionist, a follower of the ideals set forth by Theodore Herzel.

**Aliyah**: lit. = ascent: To be called up to the Torah, to immigrate to Israel.

**Bal Taam T'filin**: a specific type of phylactery (see glossary entry for phylactery).

**Bar Mitzvah**: a rite of passage performed when a Jewish boy reaches the age of 13 and is considered an adult. He not only becomes a man in the eyes of his religion, but also accepts responsibility for fulfilling the laws of Judaism.

**Bekeshe**: a long, usually black, silk caftan.

**Beschprecht**: lit. = to be spoken on: A cameo or other small object, frequently a coin, which a rebbe has blessed. The blessed object is then considered to have the power to ward off the evil eye and other calamities.

**Beth din**: a Jewish court of law in which the judges consist of three rabbis who were given the degree of hatarath haraim. When settling a tort case among themselves, European Jews preferred to use such a court in which judgments and decrees were based on Talmudic law. In the United States such courts are used to grant a religious order of divorce.

**Bikur Cholim**: a Jewish women's organization that would visit the sick at home or in the hospital during the Sabbath.

**Bilkeleh**: a challah roll.

**Bimah**: a podium usually located in the center of the synogogue where the Torah is read.

**Birchat hagomel**:  a blessing recited whenever a person survives a calamity or a very serious illness.

**Bris or brit**: a Jewish circumcision ritual.

**B'yeshivah shel maaloh**: a declaration pronounced on the eve of the Day of Atonement which gives sinners, usually Jews who had been forced by threat of death to convert to Christianity, the right to pray in the synagogue.

**Chagorah**: a silk sash that girds the waist and is worn by Chassidic Jews during Sabbath.

**Challah**: a braided, egg-yolk bread served during Sabbath and various Jewish holidays.

**Chanukah**:  a minor holiday, celebrated as a quasi-Christmas, which commemorates the Maccabee victory over Syrian Hellenists.

**Chanukah gelt**: a few coins received by children for Chanukah.

**Chassid**: a very Orthodox Jew who dresses in a particular kind of black suit and hat and is the follower of a charismatic rabbi.

**Chazzan**: the cantor of the synagogue.

**Cheder**: the series of one-room classes where young Jewish boys study prayer and the Choomosh, the Five Books of Moses.

**Chevra Kadisha**: lit. = Holy association: the burial society.

**Chidush**: the act of finding a new meaning to a Talmudic text.

**Ch'nyok**: an uncouth and close-minded person.

**Choomosh**: lit. = five: The Five Books of Moses.

**Corso**: a wide sidewalk, usually a main street where people strolled during summer evenings.

**Dayan**: a judge and member of the Jewish court.

**Dayanim**: judges who render judgments based on Talmudic laws.

**Diaspora**: those Jews not living in Israel.

**Dreidel**: a four-sided top used by children during Chanukah.

**D'roshoh**: an interpretation of a passage in the weekly chapter of the Torah.

**Echod**: the Jewish belief which states as God is one, so are the Jewish people. This emphasis on oneness and unity is the product of Judaism, ethnicity, and history.

**Eruv**:   ritually symbolic fence that made any city a private domain; thereby permitting Jews to carry objects on the Sabbath. This is necessary due to Talmudic law which prohibits moving objects on the Sabbath from private domains to public ones because it is considered work.

**Eruv-halachah**: an egg and a challah-roll placed under a stone which, through the magic of prayer, became a symbol of a Jewish home.

**Eychoh**: a recitation of Jeremiah's Lamentation.

**Falshe fish**: a false or substitute fish dish, made out of chicken, served during the Sabbath.

**Gefilte fish**: the meat of a carp that is ground and minced with other ingredients and made into fish cakes.

**Ger Tzedek**: a righteous convert, a person who accepts Judaism for intrinsic reasons.

**Glat-kosher**:  a home or restaurant that stringently observes the religious laws pertaining to kosher food preparation.

**Hatarath haraim**: a rabbinical diploma that indicates the possessor has the right to teach and hold judicial office.

**Hatikvah**: lit. = the hope: the title of the present Israeli National Anthem.

**Havdalah**: a service held to indicate the end of the Sabbath.

**Kaddish**: a recited ritual to commemorate the dead.
**Kaparoth**: the Atonement service which is designed to transfer the human sins onto a chicken.

**Kashruth**: laws pertaining to the appropriateness of kosher food.

**Kateygor**: the defending angel who always seeks to provide mitigating reasons for sins on Rosh Hashanah.

**Kittl**: a ceremonial white robe worn by all married males on the Day of Atonement.

**Klipotoh**: usually a reference to a woman who causes trouble. Also refers to the Cabalist perspective of the breaking of God's unity. In this view the Messiah will come when God and the Shechinah, His spirit, are reunited.

**Kol Nidre**: the service that starts the Day of Atonement and its fasting.

**Korim**: a prostrating prayer during services for the Day of Atonement.

**Kosher**: food that is acceptable to eat according to both the Torah and Talmudic law.

**Kugel**: a dish made from grated potatoes and meat that is eaten on the Sabbath.

**Lag-baomer**: the traditional celebration of the Jewish Arbor Day.

**L'shonoh tovah und beyt achos a gut yuhr**: the greeting, "May your prayers be successful and may you be granted a good year." It is used during the ten days of Atonement.

**Ma'ariv**: evening prayers.

**Matzoth**: an unleavened bread eaten during Passover.

**Mechitzoh**: a physical barrier which separates males and females in an Orthodox synagogue.

**Meechutz l'aretz**: Jews who lived outside of ancient Israel.

**Mee shenechnaz**: a decorated placard that was nailed above the door transom to announce the month of Adar, considered a lucky month.

**Mehadrin min hamhadrin**: the most observant and pious.

**Menorah**: an eight-branched candelabrum used during Chanukah.

**Mikvah**: a ritual bath, usually the size of a small swimming pool, which contains water that comes from natural sources, such as a river. Men use this bath to baptize themselves before the Sabbath, and women use this bath to ritually cleanse themselves after menstruation.

**Minchah**: daily afternoon services.

**Mishloach Manoth**: gifts of food given to friends and relatives during Purim.

**Mitzvoth**: lit. = commandments.  Usually refers to good deeds.
**Mohel**: the ritual circumciser.

**Mussar**: moral chastisement.

**Nachas**: joy and pride that parents receive from their children.

**Nesach**: non-Kosher wine; wine that has not been certified free from use in services of other religions.

**Nisan**: the 1st month in the Jewish calendar (March-April) in which Passover occurs.

**Parnosoh**: a mere subsistence.

**Passover**: an eight-day holiday just after Purim.

**Phylactery**: one of two small, square, leather boxes containing slips of parchment on which are inscribed scripture passages and are traditionally worn on the left arm and forehead by Jewish men during weekly morning prayers.

**Pikuach Nefesh**: a Talmudic reasoning which states that saving a life takes precedence over all ritual laws.

**Pogrom**: violent antisemitic attacks (often government-sanctioned) occurring in Czarist Russia.

**Purim**: a spring holiday commemorating the rescue of the Persian Jews and told through the Book of Esther.

**Rebbe**: a charismatic leader.

**Ribono shel olam**: master of the universe.
**Rosh Hashanah**: the Jewish New Year, a high holy day.

**Saneygor**: the accusing angel on the day of Rosh Hashanah.

**Schnorers**: beggars who would ask for donations so that they could purchase the groceries for their Sabbath.

**Seder**: a ceremony held during Passover where a child would ask "The Four Questions."

**Seudah**: a Purim feast.

**Shalom**: a traditional Hebrew greeting which wishes peace.

**Shalosh S'udoth**: the traditional third meal eaten during the late afternoon of the Sabbath.

**Shatnez**: forbidden cloth containing a mixture of wool and linen.

**Shehakol**: a blessing over food or drink.

**Shemini Atzereth**: a Jewish holiday.

**Sherayim**: the leftovers in the plate. It is a custom that the rebbe would invite his honored disciples to eat out of his plate.

**Shiduchim**: an arranged marriage.

**Shochet**: the ritual slaughterer of animals in a kosher manner.

**Sholent**: a bean, barley, and meat casserole which is eaten on the Sabbath.
**Shtetl**: a small Eastern European town with a large Jewish population and a particular form of religious culture.

**Sh'vuoth**: a holiday commemorating the giving of the Ten Commandments at Mount Sinai.

**Simchath Torah**: lit. = rejoicing with the Torah: An autumnal holiday in which the Jewish communities worldwide celebrate the completion and restart of the annual cycle of the reading of the Five Books of Moses.

**Slivovitz**: plum brandy.

**Straymel**: a fur-covered hat.

**Succah**: a nonpermanent hut constructed during Succoth to symbolize the temporary journey of life.

**Succoth**: an autumnal holiday which celebrates the fall harvest and commemorates life in the desert during the 40 years of wandering after the liberation from Egypt.

**Talith batel**: the container in which the talith shawl is carried.

**T'chum Shabbath**: the distance which is allowed to be walked on a Sabbath. It measures 2,000 feet from the last Jewish home.

**T'hilim**: The Book of Psalms.

**Tinkun Olam**: a central Judaic tenet of the repair or completion of the world.

**Tishah B'Av**: the fast of the 9th Day of Av, the day when the Jews commemorate the destruction of the Holy Temples.

**Titchadesh**: lit. = may you be renewed: A greeting extended to those wearing new clothing.

**Treyfa**: non-kosher food.

**Tzedek**: justice, charity.

**Tzedokoh**: charity, a derivative of the word tzedek.

**Tzerass it gesunter heit**: lit. = may you wear it out in good health: A wish extended to those wearing new clothing.

**Tzitzis**: a four-cornered garment with wool fringes which are worn by Orthodox Jews.

**Yeshiva**: a school where the Talmud is taught. Plural Yeshivoth.

**Yamim hanoraim:** The days of awe – Rosh Hashanah and Yom Kippur.

**Yetzer harah**: a human's innate evil nature.

**Yichus**: a social status honor, often attained through a good marriage in which a person's social status is distinctively different from his social class.

**Yiddische Mame**: a very understanding and kind Jewish mother.

**Yiddische Gass**: from the depth of the ghetto, the Jewish street.

**Yohrzeit**: a candle lit during Yom Kippur to remember those in the family who have died.

**Yom Kippur**: The Day of Atonement, a high holiday, celebrated in the autumn, meant for Jews to confess and repent of their sins.

**Yomim Hanoraim**: the 10-day holiday that begins with Rosh Hashanah and ends with Yom Kippur.

**Zionist**: a follower of Zionism.

**Zionism**: the belief in Theodore Herzl's teachings for the need of a Jewish homeland, Israel, as a haven against antisemitism.

Printed in the United States
33111LVS00002B/7-9